First published 2013 by Coptic Publishing Limited, London

A catalogue record for this book is available from the British Library.

Library of Congress Cataloging-in-Publication Data

Rosengard Peter, 1946-
Talking to Strangers: The Adventures of a Life Insurance Salesman

ISBN 978-0-9558771-6-2

1. Biography and true stories
2. Economics, finance, business and management.

Printed and bound in Great Britain by Lightning Source

TALKING TO STRANGERS

THE ADVENTURES OF A LIFE INSURANCE SALESMAN

PETER ROSENGARD

*For my remarkable loving parents, Sally and Jack,
married for 67 years, and my wonderful daughter Lily, who has
had the distinct pleasure of watching her own father grow up.*

ACKNOWLEDGEMENTS

I would like first and foremost to thank Bill Dale, my good friend and volunteer editor, who kept telling me to 'keep writing'... for five years! My publisher Paul Lewis, for believing that the adventures of a life insurance salesman were worth telling. Also Guy Marriott, my old school friend; he always helped me with my homework – and he still does. A big thank-you to Kate Gowrie in deepest Dorset and Roberto de Vicq de Cumptich in New York for their design skills and to Charlotte Smith for eliminating the most glaring errors (any that may remain are entirely my responsibility). And appropriately finally, the world's most tolerant indexer, David Atkinson.

I am very grateful to Methuen for permission to use material on the early days of the Comedy Store I had written for a previous publication, and to the *Independent* and the *Jewish Chronicle* for allowing me to revisit several stories that had previously featured in my columns for their respective papers.

More generally, Alexei Sayle, Ben Elton, Rik Mayall, Ade Edmondson, Dawn French, Jennifer Saunders, Arnold ('I'm a very good friend of Peter Rosengard's, to some extent') Brown and all the other comedians who came to the Comedy Store in 1979-81; Sid Sheinberg, Mig Drummond, Jerry Sadowitz, John 'Smeato' Smeaton, Bernard Shapero and especially, Shirley for being the best ex-wife and greatest mum in the world. Finally, thank you Gamblers Anonymous; without you I wouldn't have been around to write this book.

Thanks also must go to all my good friends over the last thirty years at Claridge's, the world's greatest hotel: including General Manager Thomas Kochs; Michael Bonsor; Glenn Piper, David and Roberto in the foyer; Tom Keatley and Martin Ballard (the world's greatest head porters), Bill, Michael and everyone on the porters desk; the wonderful head door-man Roman and all his team; the remarkable Pat More; and finally the legendary King of the Breakfast Restaurant, Nobby Clark.

I am of course very grateful to all the people who I've sold life insurance to across my breakfast table at Claridge's, who know there's no such thing as a free breakfast. And finally, to all the marvellous waiters, many now in mental hospitals, who over the years have put up with me – I wish you all a speedy recovery.

"Work is more fun than fun!"
Noel Coward

"Life is far too important a thing ever to talk seriously about it."
Oscar Wilde

"I'm writing an unauthorised autobiography."
Steven Wright (American comedian)

"When I die, I want to die running at full tilt and empty!
Totally burnt out! 100% used up!"
Peter Rosengard August 1997
(Speech to the 25th Life Underwriters of Japan conference)

CONTENTS

INTRODUCTION

I became a life insurance salesman in London in May 1969, for the glamour, the fast cars, the groupies... the beautiful women who'd stop at nothing to buy life insurance.

It's a very well-kept secret.

Reading this book you'll learn how to be successful, make lots of money, conquer your fears, pick up beautiful women, be happy, speak in public, make new friends... and have your Rolls Royce repossessed. And how to throw a celebratory party for 2,000 of your closest friends and have three people turn up (one a drunk who walked in off the street).

You'll get useful health tips, including how to take up smoking at 50, plus practical advice for everyday living, like how to sell life insurance to a Mafia hit man, how to start a Middle East war at breakfast, how kidnapping the one you love is a bad idea and how taking LSD on entering a casino is a very bad idea.

In passing, you will find out how to open the world's most famous comedy club, how to sell a $100m life insurance policy from a cold call in a phone box and get into the *Guinness Book of Records*, how to discover a No. 1 world best-selling pop group and how to manage a baggage-handler hero who socked al-Qaeda on the jaw.

I know what you're thinking... just another 'How to' book.

When my daughter Lily was six years old, I told her that she must never talk to strangers.

"Don't worry, Daddy," she said. "I don't know any strangers."

This is the story of how her father has spent his whole life talking to strangers.

CHAPTER 1

How to sell the world's largest life insurance policy
The Guinness Book of Records – July 1990, London

I woke up one morning and thought I'd sell the world's largest life insurance policy. For some people this might be an unusual first thought, but I was a life insurance salesman and after selling thousands of little policies for over 20 years, I felt ready to go for the big one. I'd read in the *Guinness Book of Records* that the largest policy on record was $34m, on the life of a Texan rancher. As my biggest policy to date had only been $1m, I knew I had to find a very rich guy.

Over breakfast I read the papers. That day's big financial story was the $500m takeover of Geffen Records in LA by MCA Universal. I'd read about David Geffen for years; the hugely successful music mogul with an incredible gift for spotting new talent, and also terrific deal-making flair. I had a gut feeling that most of the money MCA were paying was for Geffen the man, rather than any assets on the balance sheet. In the music business it's the people you're buying; there's not a lot of plant or machinery around, apart from a few guitars and drum sets.

I went into a call box at Oxford Circus and dialled up 153, for international directory enquiries: "MCA Universal in Los Angeles, please."

"What country do you want?" the operator asked.

"Los Angeles, America," I said. "California."

"What business?"

"MCA Universal, in Hollywood."

"How do you spell that?"

"Hollywood?!" I said. "It's the most famous town in the world! You know, where the films come from!?"

"Is that one word or two?"

"HOLLYWOOD... one word, two syllables."

"Can you spell it please?"

"H for Harry, O for Oliver, L for London, L for London, Y for Yes, W for Window, O for Oliver, O for Oliver, D for DUMB... Duck! I mean duck."

I wrote down the number on the front of that day's *Times* business section. The headline read: 'MCA buy Geffen Records for $500m in surprise deal'. I dialled the number.

"MCA Universal."

"Sid Sheinberg, please."

Later in the afternoon, when it was 9am in LA, I called again.

"Sid Sheinberg, please." The paper had said he was the president of MCA. I was put through to his office. "Good morning. It's Peter Rosengard in London calling Sid Sheinberg."

"Mr Sheinberg is not available right now, Mr Rosengard."

"When will he be back?" I asked the efficient-sounding woman.

"I cannot give you that information, sir."

"Who am I speaking to? Are you his personal assistant?"

"I cannot give you that information." I promised I would get back to Mr Sheinberg later. "Can I tell Mr Sheinberg what it's about, Mr Rosengard?"

"It's a surprise!" I said.

Twenty phone calls around the building later, I found out where he was. The president of MCA Universal was in Italy, attending a film festival in Florence. Now it doesn't matter how big a city is, there's only a few hotels where someone in his position would stay. In London, it would be Claridge's, the Connaught, the Dorchester, the Savoy – or the Halcyon, a small private hotel in Holland Park used by a lot of film and music industry people.

Half a dozen calls round the five-star hotels of Florence and I got lucky.

I asked for the concierge's desk. The concierges of the world's leading hotels have their own association internationally. It's called the Golden

Keys, or Les Clefs d'Or. These guys are seriously wealthy. One I'd met had homes in the UK, the South of France and the Swiss Alps. It's good to know the Aga Khan.

"Hello, concierge speaking. Giuseppe here."

"Good afternoon, Giuseppe, it's Peter Rosengard, calling from London. Are you by any chance a Clefs d'Or member?"

"Indeed I am," he replied with pride. It's an exclusive club, an almost freemason-like fraternal society, and not many outsiders know it exists. "How do you know of the Clefs d'Or, Mr Rosengard?"

"I am a good friend of John Spahr at Claridge's."

"Ah, Johnny Spahr! He was our international president, you know! How can I help you, Mr Rosengard?"

"I am trying to reach Sid Sheinberg. Do you happen to know where he is, Giuseppe?"

"Ah! Mr Sheinberg has been coming here for many years. He has gone to the Gritti Palace in Venice before returning to America."

I waited until it was 7pm in Venice. I figured even the most powerful businessmen have to go to the bathroom and get ready for dinner. 7pm seemed like the right time to catch Sid in his suite, and the odds were he would be alone, without the aides that accompany the Big Guys everywhere.

I rang the hotel and asked for him. It picked up after a couple of rings. A deep bass voice answered, "Sid Sheinberg."

I have a deep voice myself, but I went 50 feet deeper still; he wasn't going to out-deep me.

"Good evening, Sid." I figured it was okay to call him Sid: that's what the newspapers had called him. "I am Peter Rosengard. I'm a life insurance salesman in London."

I thought, 'If he's going to put the phone down, now's the time!' But this is what I always do: put it up front. "I am calling to congratulate you on the Geffen deal. It's the top story in all the UK papers. Congratulations! EMI and Colin Southgate have been left with egg on their face!"

Britain's EMI records had thought they had Geffen in the bag, and the MCA deal was announced just hours before EMI was due to buy it. Real cliff-hanger stuff. It turned out Geffen had been holding last minute, parallel secret discussions with MCA.

I once heard that the only time people congratulate you in Hollywood is if they've heard you've got a terminal illness. There was a silence, so I said again, "Congratulations, Sid." I also once heard that the sweetest sound a man can hear is the sound of his own name.

"Well, thank you very much," Sid said. "We're pretty pleased ourselves." Another pause. "How can I help you, Peter?"

"Actually, Sid, I have an idea that I think could be tremendously valuable to MCA. I will ask you just one question to see if you think so, too. If I am wrong, I'll say congratulations once more and let you get on with your evening."

"What's the question, Peter?"

"If David Geffen walked under a truck tonight on the Santa Monica Boulevard and was killed, am I right in assuming MCA would have just lost hundreds of millions of dollars?"

I shut up. Not an easy thing for me to do. The silence at the other end seemed to last 30 minutes. After a few seconds, Sid said, "You would be correct in your assumption. What do you propose?"

I could hardly believe it. If I had written a script, Sid was reading from a copy! But what did I propose? I couldn't suggest he bought a $1m policy on Geffen. That would sound ridiculous. But it was the biggest I had ever done. I took a deep breath. My heart was now beating so fast and loud I was sure he could hear it.

"I propose, Sid..." I deepened my voice and tried to control its shaking at the same time. "I propose that you insure David Geffen's life for $100m dollars!" I said, trying to sound as if I sold $100m policies every day.

There was a deafening silence. I knew the old rule: the first one to talk loses. I forgot it.

"So Sid, what do you think?" I'd lasted five seconds.

A pause. "Do you know what chutzpah is, Peter?" Sid said slowly.

"My name's Rosengard, Sid. I am a Scottish Jew. A Hebrew Highlander. I think it rings a bell."

"Well, Peter. We are not total schmoks here at MCA. It's obviously something we would have got round to... but your timing is excellent."

He asked me a couple of questions. How much would it cost? Small stuff like that. I just multiplied the price for a $1m policy by 100. He seemed unfazed. Later I realised, of course, that he was used to talking in hundreds of millions of dollars.

"So what do we do next, Sid?"

"I want you to talk to Dick Baker, my CFO... and take it from there."

"Okay, Sid. Can I say we've spoken and you think it's a good idea?"

"You certainly can, Peter."

"Goodbye, Sid. And once again, congratulations."

By an incredible stroke of luck, Dick Baker was in Manchester that night, visiting an MCA unit. The next day we were having breakfast in Claridge's.

A week later, the MCA board voted to insure Geffen for $100m.

And that's how I sold the world's first $100m life insurance policy and got into the *Guinness Book of Records*.

And you know something? It's 2013 and still the world record, and for 20 years it's been a great feeling, being in it for something I've spent my whole life doing, rather than for having the longest fingernails, or the biggest ball of string! My daughter has always been proud I am a world champion. "My daddy is in the *Guinness*, you know," she would tell her friends.

There must have been a million American life insurance salesmen who read the same story in the newspapers that morning, but I was the only one who made the call.

And if you don't make the call, you can't make the sale.

Postscript:

In August 1991, I threw a surprise party to celebrate getting into the *Guinness Book of Records*.

The invitations read, 'Peter Rosengard is delighted to invite 2,000 of his closest friends to celebrate his achievement of getting into the *Guinness Book of Records* for selling the world's largest life insurance policy... for $100m.'

Three people turned up.

One was a drunk who'd wandered in off the street.

"Peter, this is good for your humility," I told myself.

How to breakfast like a king
An introduction to Claridge's

"Pete, I have a staff of 35 people who assist me in my Dallas office. How many people do you employ in your office in London?" asked Marvin, the giant Texan in the Stetson and hand-tooled cowboy boots.

It was June 1991 and we were having breakfast in New Orleans, at the world's most famous sales meeting – the Million Dollar Round Table convention of 5,000 of the world's top life insurance salesmen.

"Six hundred and thirty-five, Marvin," I said.

"Six hundred and thirty-five!?" He dropped a huge slice of blueberry waffle into his lap and almost fell out of his chair.

"Well it might be 636, actually... I can never keep up with them."

"My gosh, Pete! That's sure some big operation you have there!"

"Of course, only half of them are in full uniform... you know, velvet breeches, waistcoats, buckled shoes. The clients like it and we Brits are sticklers for tradition. The rest are quite casually attired, just morning suits and bow ties; I like to keep it relaxed around the office. Anyway, please excuse me Marvin, but I have to go and give my speech now. Have a nice day."

And the thing is, I didn't even have an office... and I still don't! And I've never employed anybody! But it was all absolutely true... because for the last 30 years my 'office' has been Claridge's in London, the greatest hotel in the world. And every morning all those years, as soon as I've walked through the front entrance I really have been looked after by an army of 600 people in uniform. In fact, I've been greeted as if I am a member of the Royal family.

Every day at 7.25am, as I come through the revolving doors heading for my first breakfast meeting of the day, six immaculately-dressed young men and women welcome me enthusiastically with big warm smiles: "Good morning, Mr Rosengard!"

"How are you today, Mr Rosengard?"

"Everything is fine with you today, Mr Rosengard?"

And all this before I even sit down at my table in the foyer.

I only call them if I'm not coming. My plan is to drop dead aged 100, selling a life insurance policy over bacon and eggs at my breakfast table.

When I die, I don't want to go to heaven... I want to go to Claridge's.

I am a life insurance salesman.

Now, maybe there are some people who think selling life insurance isn't the most exciting or glamorous job in the world, but let me tell you something: every morning for 30 years I have breakfasted in the company of Audrey Hepburn, Winston Churchill, the Queen and many other of the world's most famous people – Henry Kissinger, Naomi Campbell, Madonna and the King of Spain, to name just a few. I have even regularly passed the Duke of Windsor on the way to the Gentlemen's cloakroom; and he always looks rather sheepishly at me, holding his bowler hat out in front of him.

All right, maybe some of them today are only framed photographs on the walls, but they were and are still just some of Claridge's regular clients. For over 100 years, it has been the home from home for kings and queens, presidents and prime ministers, film stars and millionaires.

And since December 1982, for a life insurance salesman called Peter Rosengard.

One morning, shortly after beginning my life as a breakfaster, Nobby, the legendary head waiter, then in his 38th year at the hotel, informed me that I had inherited the 'Greek millionaires' table in the alcove.

"Mr Onassis kept this table, for over 40 years until he died," he said. "He would sit here every morning for hours when he was in London. He kept a permanent suite in the hotel, and his friend Niarchos and he would sit here with Maria Callas, they would do their shipping deals at this table, and he would write all the figures in pen on the tablecloths! So every month, we would charge him for his breakfasts and 20 tablecloths."

I might not be an Onassis, and I don't have any supertankers... but when it comes to breakfast I'm definitely in a class of my own. I am a 'super-breakfaster'... you see, I've discovered people find it very difficult to say 'No' to you when they've got your food in their mouth.

In 1989, I had 859 breakfasts at Claridge's. Often I have three breakfasts a day, one after the other. I know what you're thinking... 'That's a lot of bacon and eggs for a good Jewish boy.'

My doctor, the wonderfully eccentric Donald Rau (when he gave me my annual ECG, I had to jump on and off an upturned wastepaper basket in his surgery, fifty times) once told me, "Peter, you don't have a blood stream, you have a cholesterol stream."

"Is that good?" I asked him. "Do you think having 859 bacon and eggs in one year could be a contributory factor?"

How to learn a big lesson from a children's party
1954, East Acton, London

Nanny is on the phone to my mother. "Hello, Mrs Rose. I think you had better come and collect us. Peter is standing in the corner and he won't talk to any of the other children. Mrs Collins has tried to get him to go over and talk to them, but he just won't!"

I was very shy as a child.

I always tell people I was very shy... until I was six months old. But the truth is it took me until I was about 13 to realise that if I wanted lots of friends and to meet pretty girls and be happy and successful I had to change. So one day I decided to act extroverted; and I became an extrovert. Some people would say I've overcompensated ("I'm exhausted! Slow down, Peter!" In New York they tell *me* to slow down!)

At my Barmitzvah on 11th December 1959, I was so nervous about standing up in the synagogue in front of my entire family and the rest of the congregation and reading the Torah portion, which I had learnt by heart over the previous year at special Hebrew lessons, with the rabbi leaning over me. Dripping with sweat, I managed to stumble to the end of it, with lots of anguished pauses and loudly whispered prompts in Hebrew, which I still didn't understand a single word of, from the rabbi.

But at the catered lunch party at home in East Acton afterwards, for a hundred family and friends packed into every inch of the lounge and dining room, I just couldn't stand up to give my Barmitzvah speech, and this was in English... which I could speak quite well.

So my younger brother Stuart, who was 11, volunteered and gave it for me, totally ad-libbing. Stuart's a natural extrovert who would have tap-danced naked on the table in front of everyone if anyone had asked him to, without giving it a second thought.

I read once that every year there is a poll to discover Americans' greatest fears. And every year, cancer is No. 2 on the list... and No. 1 is always 'fear of speaking in public'.

People would rather die than speak in public!

It's hard to believe that many dozens of times over the last 50 years, the same person who was so stricken with shyness that he stood facing the wall in a corner at parties, who was too frightened to give his own Barmitzvah speech, has stood alone on huge stages all over the world, from Delhi to Darling Harbour in Sydney, from Tokyo to Taipei, in front of 10,000 people at a time... and made them laugh!

In 1991, I was asked to address the annual meeting of the Million Dollar Round Table – 5,000 top life insurance salesman from over 70 countries – in New Orleans. Paraphrasing Groucho Marx (whose eyebrows I inherited, if nothing else), I told them that "East Acton is a small town on the outskirts of Wishful Thinking.

It's not the end of the world, but you can see it from there."

How to start a war with Henry Kissinger
Across the breakfast table – August 1991, Claridge's

Henry Kissinger was at the next table one morning, with the foreign secretary, Douglas Hurd.

Halfway through his scrambled eggs, he turned round, wiped his mouth with a white linen napkin, and asked me what I thought they should do about Saddam Hussein.

"Do you think we should go to war? What's your view?"

I told him... and two weeks later they started the first Gulf War.

How many life insurance salesmen get to start a war and have breakfast at Claridge's at the same time?

A year later, when he was next at Claridge's, I saw him standing by the lift.

He had his arm in a sling. I walked over. "An assassination attempt, Dr Kissinger?" I asked.

"No, I slipped on a rug in Sacramento," he said.

How to grow up in East Acton
1950s/1960s, West London

East Acton is a mile down the road from Shepherds Bush. For many years the BBC headquarters was just round the corner, but in the 1950s it was mainly known for one thing, the huge grim Victorian castle of Wormwood Scrubs prison.

I have a scar on my top lip, running diagonally from top to bottom. "I got it in a Berlin strip club, winter of 1965," I'd say, or at other times "a fight in Stockholm with six Swedish soldiers in 1968" or "my Israeli war wound in the Six-Day War".

The truth is, I fell onto a metal toy telephone in my nursery aged five in 1952, and my father's young Greek assistant, Dr Zilliacus, sewed up my lip in the surgery downstairs.

Over the years to come a lot of people have wished he'd done a better job.

Working in the warehouse: Brick Lane, July 1958

My mother's family business was a wholesale grocery warehouse, Silverstone and Sons in the East End.

It had been started in Hanbury Street in 1895 by my great-grandmother. Her husband was a scholarly rabbinical man who couldn't earn a living, and she was the driving force. Old family photos showed a thickset, steely faced woman in a long black dress.

It was now run by her eldest son, my Grandpa Mark and his brothers, my uncles Alf and Jack. My mother's brother Jack, then about 30, worked there as well.

The three brothers had worked in the warehouse all their lives. Grandpa, now 59 years old, was a kind, gentle man outside the warehouse, but once he was there it was like a war zone. All of them quarrelled loudly all of the time, and every day there would be at least two or three explosive arguments. Uncle Jack, who reminded me of Humphrey Bogart, was a tough looking man in his mid-forties, at five feet seven inches the tallest and youngest of the brothers. He was always outside in the warehouse, which he ran with an iron fist, barking out orders like a sergeant major to his squad of a dozen men; they were a great bunch, and when I worked there in my school holidays, I liked to be outside with them, getting the boxes and listening to Uncle Jack fire the orders out like a machine gun: "Five gross of Kellogg's... Three gross of Heinz beans... Three gross of John West Salmon... Get a move on!" (Those boxes of beans weighed a ton; I always tried to be the one to collect the cornflakes.)

Uncle Jack would stand in the loading bay, biro in hand, another pen behind his right ear, ticking off the orders on a clipboard for some of the thousands of products that lined the 250-foot-long warehouse from floor to ceiling. I had to climb up 20-foot ladders to get to the top shelves and throw the boxes down to the waiting men below. They were a mix of Cockneys and Irishmen; my two favourites were Big Vic, a former docker from the Isle of Dogs, a bald, barrel-chested man with a Woodbine always tucked behind his ear, and Mick, a happy-go-lucky stocky Irishman who drove the lorry that delivered the goods to their grocer customers.

Grandpa worked in the office with Uncle Jack, his son. Uncle Alf's role was to travel all over London, getting the orders from the grocery shops.

August 1958

I was 12 years old and I had gone to work in the warehouse for three weeks to earn some extra pocket money.

We left my grandparents' flat in Baker Street, where I was staying during the week, at 5.30am and walked down the empty street to the tube station. We caught the Metropolitan line tube to Aldgate East.

Grandpa was a kind and modest man, who loved knowledge and learning of all kinds. He had been born in the East End in 1899, not more than 200 yards from where the warehouse now stood. He had left home every morning at 5.30am, five days a week, since leaving school aged 14.

He loved his family and his work and that was his whole life. He was a wonderful grandfather. Grandpa and Grandma would come over to us every Saturday for lunch, and when I opened the front door he was always holding a huge box of groceries for Mum.

He loved to sit down in the lounge and talk to me about any subject in the world. I have always loved news and current events and so did he, so there was always a lot to talk about. All his life he was a generous giver to charities, particularly Jewish charities. The young State of Israel was very dear to his heart. There was only one 'no go' area; as for so many of his generation, Jewish and non-Jewish, the only good German was "a dead German".

He could draw beautifully and play the piano without ever having had a lesson in either art or music. He loved to travel and every summer, he and my grandmother Diana would go away for a two month holiday on a cargo boat to South America or the West Indies or South Africa. In London, every night after a 12-hour stint at his desk, he would sit alone at the kitchen table after dinner with his thick blue invoice books. With a pencil in hand, he would add up in his head page after page of long columns of figures for all the goods that had gone out to their customers' shops that day. This would take him two hours. Then at 10pm he would go to bed, leaving my grandma watching the television.

At Aldgate East, we walked out onto Whitechapel High Street, past Blooms the Kosher restaurant and the old lady with her tray of fresh bagels, and left into Brick Lane. Almost all the shops in the street had Jewish names: Goldberg's, Rubin's, Cohen's. This part of London had been home to successive waves of immigrant Jews since thousands of them had begun arriving from Russia, Poland, Latvia and Lithuania, from the late 1800s onwards.

Postscript:

My father was born in Durward Street in 1915, just off Vallance Road where the first victim of Jack the Ripper had been found. When he was only a couple of weeks old they went back up to Glasgow, where his mother Rebecca was from.

The night my ears melted: Greenford, 1960

Every Saturday night I caught the Number 12 bus up the Western Avenue and went to the youth club at Greenford synagogue.

I fancied a girl called Gillian, who I thought was the prettiest girl there. Unfortunately, her boyfriend Stuart Solomons also went there with her.

Now, Gillian, almost six feet tall with her beehive, stilettos and pencil-thin skirt, was a very good-looking girl and Stuart had a round head like a billiard ball and I couldn't see what she saw in him. But he was the club leader and was 17; Gillian was 15. It was the first time I had come across the older man syndrome.

As I was 14 and had sticking-out ears, I was clearly out of the picture – if she even knew I existed. But one Saturday evening, I had a last look in the mirror before getting the bus up to Greenford. And I ran my comb through my new hairstyle: I was the first boy at school to have one. My uncle Ernie had given it to me as a present a few weeks before. He was a hairdresser in a fashionable salon in Knightsbridge. He played the guitar and danced flamenco, took Spanish lessons and lived in Chelsea Cloisters in Sloane Avenue. And he had once styled the hair of the wife of the Shah of Persia. So I knew he definitely was a better hairdresser than Leonard Ludwin, the barber next door to the school where all my friends went.

He had swept it up from my forehead into a big wave-like quiff, like Tony Curtis or Elvis. I wasn't sure it would stay there but he had said, "Persist, Peter... train it. You won't be disappointed, I promise you."

I had always liked and trusted Uncle Ernie. My father's youngest brother, 14 years younger than him, he was only a kid when Dad went off to join the army in 1939. So when he said persist, I did. I trained it daily. And he was right, after a few weeks.

Amazingly, it's still perched up there 50-odd years later, and pretty much still intact.

Anyway, that evening, as I looked in the mirror I decided that if only my ears didn't stick out, I would be a good-looking guy; the Hollywood heartthrob Tab Hunter leapt to mind, instead of the skinny-faced kid with the big ears staring moodily back at me. The thick-rimmed Buddy Holly glasses didn't help, either. But the problem was that when I took them off, I couldn't see a thing. A few years later, at the Whisky A Go-Go in the West End, I had to ask Robert Steinberg to point me in the direction of a pretty girl I had seen across the dance floor, before I took my glasses off. I went up and with a very deep put-on voice that I thought would make me sound sexy (but probably made me sound like a 17-year-old Henry Kissinger on steroids) said, "Would you like to dance?"

"No, thanks," she said. I then had to make that hundred-mile walk back across the now empty floor, with everyone watching my shame, to my own lines where all the boys were.

I pressed my ears flat against my head. "There you are Peter... perfect," I said to myself.

I had an idea.

I found a tube of Bostik model aircraft glue and squeezed a few drops behind each ear. Then I held them tight against my head for about five minutes. I let go... the ears were stuck flat. Amazing! With my new ears there was no question... I was going to be a lady killer.

My only worry was, would everyone notice that my ears had disappeared? I had to take that chance. If I kept moving, I thought it unlikely.

I left the house, the tube of Bostik in my pocket in case of emergencies.

When I arrived the club was already crowded and Buddy Holly's 'Every Day' was playing. I talked to my friends Stephen and Philip... nobody noticed anything. I could see Gillian with her friends, dancing around their handbags. This was going to be the night, I had decided; with my new ears, I would ask her to dance. How could she refuse?

'The Twist' by Chubby Checker came on. It was the top record that month. And everyone was doing the dance, it was a huge craze all over the world; I had spent hours in front of the mirror mastering it.

I went into the Gents and had a final check of my ears – they were holding up well. I ran the comb a few last times through my hair. I was ready.

I walked over to her. "Like to dance, Gillian?" I said nonchalantly in a mid-Atlantic accent, like I imagined Kookie Byrnes would, in the TV series *77 Sunset Strip*.

"Okay," she said.

We were busy twisting away when I felt my right ear pop out. I'd had a meltdown...

I have always been a very sweaty person, and the lights and heat had melted the glue. I put my right hand to the side of my head, smiling crazily. A new variant of the twist, I hoped she would think, maybe something I'd picked up in a West End jazz club. She put her hand to the side of her head, too. Then I felt the left ear pop out. I clasped my left hand to my head too. She did the same; everyone was watching us and they started doing the same thing. David Gelernter said, "Nice moves, Peter, where did you pick this up?"

"Oh, you know... here and there," I said as I grooved away like a lunatic, both hands clasped to my melting ears.

As soon as the record ended I ran to the toilets, locked myself in a cubicle and got out my little tube of glue.

Postscript:

I had my ears finally put back when I was 18. I couldn't keep up with the sky-rocketing price of glue and so one night, coming back from the youth club in my parents' car, I had blurted out, "Can I have my ears put back please? I have been gluing them back, it's crazy."

"Your father's ears stick out and he doesn't worry about them, do you Jack?"

"No, to tell you the truth son," he said as he drove back down the Western Avenue. "I've never given my ears so much as a second's thought."

"Well Dad, you don't have to go up and ask a girl to dance or go out on a date, do you!? You've got Mum!"

"Okay, son, I'll have a word with my friend Professor Calnan at Hammersmith Hospital. He is very good with ears, I've heard."

A week later, after a 45-minute visit to outpatients, I had two new flat ears.

I went home and threw out my supply of Bostik tubes.

White City, West London, 1961

My bedroom had iron bars on the windows and at night I used to gaze through them across the half mile to the jail blocks of the Scrubs, where the inmates were probably doing the same thing; looking out towards me.

But I definitely used to escape over the wall more often than they did.

I'd bought a pair of winkle picker shoes and an Italian box jacket suit at Smart Weston's in January 1959, just after I was Barmitzvahed. But my mother wouldn't let me wear them in case I was mistaken for a Teddy boy and beaten up, so I had to put them in a bag and throw them out of the lavatory window at night, then climb down the drainpipe, changing in the garden before heading off to the local Jewish Youth Club dance in Ealing.

My father would do his surgery every evening and if I managed to climb up the mulberry tree and sit very still, I could sometimes just about see into the room; and once in a blue moon, if I was very, very lucky, I would see a young lady get undressed to be examined.

Unfortunately, one day I fell out of the tree and cut my big toe on a large, rusty garden fork lying on the ground. Dad's assistant, Dr Zilliacus, took a huge syringe and gave me a tetanus injection in my bottom. It hurt a lot. That was the last time I ever climbed the tree.

My father, Jack, was a Glaswegian, and a great character – "I'm a Hebrew Highlander... our family motto is 'Och aye, my life!'" He was always immaculately dressed by Mr Kruger, his patient who was a Savile Row cutter. Another patient was the world champion oyster shucker at Scott's in Mount Street, Mayfair; but he left it to Mr Kruger to make his suits.

Being from Glasgow, Dad also loved a drink, which is not something

Jewish people are usually known for. By the early 1960s he had somehow managed to have nearly all the pub landlords in Acton, Shepherds Bush and Hammersmith amongst his patients; and he always had a new joke to tell them. A "large Bell's, with a half a lager chaser" was his drink.

He was a very popular man; a true Glaswegian, always with a twinkle in his eye, he had the gift of the gab and was the life and soul of any group. If I close my eyes, I can always see him standing in the lounge at home by the cocktail cabinet, in the centre of a group of patients with glasses in their hands, smoking cigarettes and laughing.

He had come down from Glasgow after the war ended and married my mother, still in his captain's uniform, on 22nd November 1945 at the beautiful synagogue in St Petersburg Place in Bayswater. Fifty years later my mother told me that when the rabbi saw her smiling at my father as they were about to be pronounced man and wife, he said, "Wipe that smile of your face young lady, this is a serious matter."

My mother's father, Grandpa Mark, had bought them the national health medical practice for their wedding present. It was in Old Oak Road, East Acton, and it came with a five-bedroom detached house. I was born in Queen Charlotte's Hospital in Hammersmith on 11th December 1946.

It was a big corner house on a main road connecting the Western Avenue with Uxbridge Road and which really ran all the way to Marble Arch, changing names to Bayswater Road and then becoming Oxford Street. Being the local doctor's children and living in this large house, I suppose we were 'posh kids'... at least compared to nearly everyone else in East Acton.

When I was five, I went to prep school, Norland Place in Holland Park. My brother Stuart, 18 months younger than me, followed me there, and finally Esme, who was born in 1950.

Mum performed the multiple roles of practice receptionist, Dad's secretary and prescription giver-outer as well as looking after the five of us. Daisy Moll was our cheerful cockney 'daily', always with a smile and a heart of gold, a colourful handkerchief always around her head.

And then there was Nanny Piper. She had come to live with us three weeks after I was born. Kathleen Piper was from Lewes and straight out of the army, in her early thirties and single. She was to became a second mother to us over the next ten years. We all loved Nanny. She was always there, to hug us if we needed a hug and look after us if we hurt ourselves.

Chapter 1

She was also very strict and always told me that if I was naughty, Mr Kessler, who lived at the back of the dark cupboard in my bedroom, would come out when I was fast asleep and get me.

She stayed with us until I was 13... until Dad's great crisis of the summer of 1960.

One morning, I came down for my usual breakfast of cornflakes and ice-cold milk, but couldn't open the kitchen door; some great weight was keeping it shut. I finally managed to open it just wide enough to poke my head through, to see my father half-lying, half-sitting with his back against the door, fully dressed in his suit and tie. For a terrible moment, I thought he was dead. "Dad!" I shouted. "Wake up! Are you all right?" Then I heard him snoring.

He had been there all night, dead drunk. Fallen-down drunk.

I felt sick and angry and very upset... all at once.

I didn't want the others to see him like this. I managed to squeeze through the door. "Wake up Dad! You have to wake up. How can you do this to Mum? To us?"

Somehow, I got my arms round him and got him into a chair. He had to start work in an hour; the patients would soon be turning up for morning surgery. I made him a cup of black coffee and forced it down him.

His drinking was nothing new to me, but this was the first time he had not made it upstairs to their bedroom.

Dad was a gambler. But not a normal gambler; he was a gambler like a heroin addict is with drugs. Only I didn't know it at the time. All I knew was that he gambled, and kept losing all his money.

Ever since I was old enough to know what was going on, there had been crisis after crisis caused by his gambling. I used to fall asleep with the pillow over my head to drown out my mother's shouting. He never said anything back, but her pent-up frustration and worry and fear would come out, all at once.

I became an expert eavesdropper. Sitting in my favourite position halfway up the stairs, I would hear them arguing in the lounge or their bedroom upstairs. These rows went on for years while I was growing up. My mother would sit at the window in the lounge every night so she could see all the cars coming along the road, hoping each car was his. He would go out after supper and always say, "I'm just going on a few calls, I'll be back soon." He wouldn't come back until 10pm or much later; once the casinos opened around 1961, sometimes not until two or three in the morning.

It was a miracle how he kept the practice going, between the betting shops, White City dog track and then the casinos. I cannot count the number of times I would get on my bicycle and go round all the pubs, looking for his car outside. When I would finally spot it, I would go in, take him by the arm and somehow make him come with me.

He never got angry or violent when drunk. I don't know how he managed to drive home without crashing, but he always did. It wasn't until he was brought home by the police for the second or third time that they finally charged him with drunk driving and he was banned for a year.

Mum then had to take him on his visits, but at least he couldn't drive to the casino. Although sometimes I know he made her drive him there and she would just sit there by the tables, watching while he lost all our money once again. If she didn't she knew he would have called a taxi or walked there. He had to gamble. At least she knew where he was.

He would get in big trouble, with the bank, with the patients who had lent him money... everyone wanted their money and weren't prepared to wait any longer. My Grandpa Mark had to bail him out time and again to prevent him going bankrupt and losing the practice. Every time, he swore on all our lives he would never gamble again. And within days he was back at the dog track or the casino.

For years, when the phone rang it was fifty-fifty whether it was a patient who was ill or a patient he owed money to. You could immediately tell which by the tone of their voices. The latter were not so diffident, less respectful; in these post-war years the GP was still a pillar of the community, someone to be looked up to.

One Saturday morning, I was on the stairs, my usual listening post.

Mum, Dad and Grandpa were in the lounge. Even with the door shut I could hear my mother shout, "Why are doing this to us Jack!? I can't stand it anymore, you are destroying your family. The children hate you, can't you see this, Jack?" She broke down. As usual, my father didn't speak. It was always Mum, shouting and then crying. After a while, he came out of

Chapter 1

the room and left. Once again, I'd heard him promise he would never ever gamble again.

I ran downstairs, out the door, jumped on my bike and pedalled as fast as I could towards White City dog stadium. I just knew he was heading there in his car. I got there and threw my bike to the ground, just as he was about to go through the turnstile.

I grabbed him by the shoulder and as he turned, I punched him as hard as I could in his stomach.

I've never forgotten that look of self-loathing on his face. He went inside.

"You bastard!" I shouted.

In July 1964, he was at rock bottom, but still determined to carry on gambling.

My mother had locked him in the bedroom one evening to stop him going to the Olympic casino in Bayswater, and he'd smashed his fist against the door, so hard he made a hole in it. He was like an angry caged lion. "Let me out, Sally!" he shouted over and over. "Open this door!" And she'd had to let him out.

We all thought he was finished this time and would be hauled before the General Medical Council and struck off. He was in such financial trouble; he had bounced cheques and owed £20,000 to over 90 patients and friends. He would have ended up penniless and in prison. He could never have done anything else in life other than be a doctor. We had all begged Mum time and again to leave him. But she never had.

Then that month, a miracle happened.

Gamblers Anonymous came to England from America. My mother read about it in the newspaper and dragged him very reluctantly along to the third meeting.

His attitude that first night was: "I'd gambled myself into the mess I was in and I was going to gamble my way out of it." But in the room that night he found others just like him; a gambling policeman was in the 'chair' and others present were Eli the cab, Ron the print, Harry the milk, a Harley Street plastic surgeon and an accountant.

And he stopped gambling.

He never had a bet again after that day. It was 13th August 1964... a very lucky day for our family. I found out recently that he had stopped gambling on the GA programme longer than anybody in the world. I am very proud of him. But without my mother's loyalty and undying love and devotion he could never have done it. It is a remarkable story.

I have never met any couple who turned their whole life around like my parents did.

CHAPTER 2

How to show people what terrorism does (part 1)
11th September 2001, London

I had just walked into the Allied Dunbar offices in New Cavendish Street to drop off some policy applications I'd sold the previous week. The office was buzzing as usual, full of life insurance salesmen at their desks, making calls. "Peter! Look at this! A plane has just crashed into the World Trade Center!" shouted Will Adkin, one of the branch managers.

One of the towers was on fire high up. "What was it? A Cessna?" I asked. Before he could reply, a plane came into view and smashed straight into the second tower.

"It's a terrorist attack!" I said. "America's being attacked!"

I rushed downstairs, got in the car and sped off to meet Lily as she came out of prep school in Holland Park. She'd had her sixth birthday two weeks earlier. She was my only child: it was her first day back after the summer holidays and instinctively I just wanted to be with her, to protect her. She lived with my ex-wife, Shirley.

I had the radio on and all the stations were carrying live reports from New York. Nobody could believe what they were seeing. They had eyewitness accounts from people who had just run out of the buildings.

The World Trade Center?! You couldn't visit New York for the first time without taking a photo of them or sending a postcard of the Twin Towers home. If you hadn't seen them, you hadn't been to New York! They were the symbol of America's power and financial might; they had been the tallest buildings in the world when built in the early 1970s. Thousands of people worked in them.

As I raced west along the Westway flyover I remembered how in 1980 when I was there with a girlfriend, I'd been refused entry to the 'Windows on the World' restaurant on the 106th floor of the north tower. I didn't have a jacket, but when I said we'd come all the way from London just to have a drink there, the maître d' took me thirty floors down in the elevator to an enormous room full of waiters' uniforms! "What size jacket do you take, sir?" he'd said.

And so we'd had our drinks, with the greatest view in the world; New York City from a quarter of a mile up in the sky.

It didn't seem possible that the towers were now burning out of control and that thousands of people must be either dead or trapped above the floors where the planes had crashed.

I got to Norland Place school in record time to find a group of American mothers talking outside, looking very anxious. There were more parents there than usual, and a lot more dads. Shirley arrived minutes later; she'd heard the news. I sat in the car, listening to the news. Suddenly one reporter shouted, "Oh my God! It's collapsing! I don't believe it!!" Nobody did. Without warning, the south tower had just collapsed. It took just ten seconds.

The children came out and Shirley rushed over to hug Lily. "Why's Daddy here, Mummy?" she asked.

"Oh, I just was passing, darling," I said. After seeing them into Shirley's car, I went home and watched on TV as the second tower collapsed. I didn't stop watching for the next two days. I never left my flat except to buy the papers. It affected me far more than any other horrific event had ever done. I'd been old enough on 22nd November 1963 to remember exactly where I was when Kennedy was shot; but terrible as that day had been, 9/11 was of a completely different magnitude altogether. Terrorists had just murdered, before the eyes of the whole world on live TV, thousands of innocent people who had just gone to work that morning as usual.

Eight years later, I discovered, at the back of a shelf full of books in my bedroom, that I had kept the copies of the newspapers from that week.

Chapter 2

8th September 2009

I had just finished my last breakfast of the morning at Claridge's when I read in the *International Herald Tribune* a story that was to set me off on an incredible journey.

Jeff Cox, a 15-year-old going for his Eagle Scout badge in a small town called Windermere in Florida, had called his mayor and said, "If I can get you a piece of steel from the World Trade Center for our town for a memorial to 9/11, would you like it?" The mayor thought he was crazy: nobody had ever got steel from the WTC in the eight years since 9/11.

But Jeff knew something the mayor didn't.

The story, by Michael Wilson from the *New York Times*, went on to explain how the Port Authority of NY and NJ, owner of all New York's airports and the bridges and tunnels into Manhattan, also owned the World Trade Center.

Immediately recognising the historical significance of the attacks, and once it was realised that there were weren't thousands of critically injured people buried under the millions of tons of rubble – they'd only dug out 20 people on the first day and nobody was found alive after that – the Port Authority had put together a special team of museum curators, structural engineers and architects to go into what became known as the 'Pile' at Ground Zero and over the next three months they recovered 2,000 pieces of steel.

Wilson wrote that the steel had been quietly stored in a huge hangar, Hangar 17 at JFK, under heavy security in special temperature-controlled conditions, with a curator and conservation team. Millions drove by every year not knowing that inside this anonymous hangar, among the hundreds surrounding JFK, were some of the most historic artefacts in America.

What Jeff Cox knew that his mayor did not was that the Port Authority had just decided to release the steel for the first time, ahead of the tenth anniversary in September 2011, for memorials in towns and cities across America and abroad.

As soon as I read the word 'abroad', I put the paper down and called *my* mayor, Boris Johnson.

I didn't know Boris, but I'd literally bumped into him at Lords cricket ground two years before, leading out 11 little mop-haired blond boys for net practice. They all looked like him. "You're Boris!" I said unnecessarily. "Come and have breakfast with me at Claridge's." He'd given me his mobile phone number, but I had just got the answer phone on the twenty times I rang.

I didn't get through this time either, so I sent him a text message.

They were almost the same words that Jeff Cox had said to his Mayor. 'Boris, if I can get you a piece of steel from the World Trade Center for a memorial for London for the tenth anniversary of 9/11, do you want it?'

Five hours later, I got a one-word text back: 'YES!!'

One week later, I had breakfast at Claridge's with Dan Ritterband, Boris's right-hand man and former campaign manager.

"You do know where Boris was when he got your text?" he asked over the boiled eggs.

"No, where was he? City Hall?"

"In New York! We'd just arrived from JFK and were getting out of the limo at Ground Zero with Mayor Bloomberg!"

"Well, that's amazing! What are the odds of that!? That's certainly serendipity," I said. Clearly this was meant to be.

(It had been Boris's first official visit to NY as Mayor of London. He gave a speech there and revealed he was actually born in New York! He called it our 'sister city'.)

I thought it was all going to be so simple. I would ask New York for the steel, they would say yes, we would dig a hole and put it up.

How complicated could that be?

If you had told me that morning that over the next two years, over one hundred people and companies on both sides of the Atlantic would be working pro bono to achieve this and that I would become founder and chairman of a charity which would create an internationally-acclaimed 9/11 education programme for British schools, I'd have said you were crazy!

There were to be many more such serendipity moments over the two years leading up to the tenth anniversary.

Chapter 2

Instinctively, I knew we'd need a lot of money to get the steel over to London and put it up somewhere, but I had no idea at the time just how much.

When you sell life insurance, unlike a tractor salesman who spends his life talking only to farmers, or a drug company representative who just talks to pharmacists, everyone in the world is a potential client. You get to meet thousands of people from all walks of life.

Stanley Fink is one of the country's biggest philanthropists; I had cold-called him a couple of years earlier when he was running what had become the world's largest hedge fund, the Man Group. I called and told him what I planned to do. "Great idea, Peter!" he said. "I'm on board. It's important we do this." He told me he had been in the US on 9/11 and was due to fly to his office in downtown New York from LA that morning, but all the planes had been grounded.

Over the next couple of weeks, whenever I sold insurance to someone, I found myself telling them about my idea. Everyone I met said it was a great idea; then they would all tell me exactly where they were on 9/11.

I formed a committee with Stanley and me as the first two members, and then I invited the most enthusiastic people I'd told about it to join us. At our first working group meeting in November, we had ten people present. Of course, they were all my clients; Tom Betts, the commercial director at ITV who offered to host the meeting at their South Bank offices overlooking the Thames, Julian Soper, Bernard Shapero, Roland Cowan, Neil Blair, Toby Davey, Charlie Lexton, Ed Harding, Stan Fink and myself. Harry Hampson of JP Morgan was, as usual, flying somewhere and sat in by conference call.

At that first meeting I'd taken along a list of the top ten sites I'd come up with. Top of the list was a park between Tower Bridge and City Hall that ran alongside the Thames and gave an uninterrupted view of the opposite City skyline; it was called Potters Fields. Number two was More London, a new business development on the other side of City Hall, and then at number three was Canary Wharf. I knew I wanted our 9/11 memorial to be somewhere very central and prominent, where millions of people could see it.

I now had so many people who wanted to help that I ended up with not just a steering committee of Stanley Fink, an old client of mine called David Ross, Dan Ritterband and me, but also the ten-man project working committee and a few weeks later, an advisory panel as well!

An early member of the advisory panel who was to play a very important role over the next two years was Simon Schama, the world-famous historian, Columbia University professor and award-winning broadcaster and author. Like many others who were to get involved, I had never met him, but he'd written a great article about the threat that a nuclear Iran posed in the *FT* one weekend that September. I did something I'd never done before; I emailed him to say "great piece!" and five minutes later I got a reply from him thanking me from New York. So I replied, thanking him for his reply and said, "By the way, you might be interested to hear about my 9/11 project..."

"Count me in!" he replied.

I then sent an official letter of application to the PANYNJ requesting the WTC steel for London along with an accompanying letter of support from Boris. We were advised that in order to raise funds we should be a registered charity. We decided on the name 'The 9/11 London Project Foundation'. I became the chairman and Stanley was the other trustee; over the next six months we were joined by Maqsood Ahmed, Tom Betts, Keith Carby, Yvonne Burne and Professor Chris Husbands.

I began calling Peter Miller at the Port Authority in NY two or three times a week, to try to arrange to visit Hangar 17. He was in charge of distributing the WTC steel to the successful applicants. He said I could maybe get into the hangar by the end of 2010! There were thousands of applicants in the queue. "Sorry, Peter, but we're overwhelmed over here."

A couple of weeks after first getting the idea, someone asked me if I knew that there was already a memorial to 9/11 in London. No, I didn't.

It turned out to be a one-minute walk from my breakfast table, in Grosvenor Square, facing the US embassy. I passed it every day of the week but had never realised it was there. I soon found out that almost nobody else in London did either.

There were 67 British people among the 2,976 victims. It was the greatest single loss of life in a terrorist attack that we had ever suffered. We were the second-largest country by numbers of dead, after the US, which accounted for nearly 90% of all victims.

I contacted the September 11th UK Families Support Group. To my surprise, their chair wouldn't meet me but emailed back to say she didn't like our idea. "We already have a piece of the WTC steel buried under the ground at Grosvenor Square."

I didn't think it would do a lot of good under the ground.

I had thought they would come at the very top of the list of our supporters, as the PANYNJ had told me was the case with the September 11th Families Association in New York who were the driving force behind the release of the steel. It was my first introduction to the world of 9/11 politics; but it wasn't to be my last.

My committee's view was that if something's worth doing, it will have lots of obstacles in the way. If it was easy it probably wouldn't be worth doing in the first place.

We agreed that if the families didn't want what they clearly felt was a rival memorial, then we wouldn't do one. We didn't want to upset them, or anyone else, but we strongly felt that nobody 'owned' 9/11. The whole world had been changed by 9/11 and we were going to bring the steel over and put it up to show people, especially young people and future generations, what happened on that terrible day, in an effort to stop it happening again.

So we now decided that, instead of a memorial, we would find an artist to transform the steel into a public work of art. We also hoped that some of the UK families would support us at a later date, or at least, not publicly oppose it.

On 17th December, I went on holiday to visit my sister Tabetha in Bali (it's good to have a sister in Bali... it beats Balham.) She's been there 25 years and loves the place; we call her the Queen of Bali. I couldn't live there – if you live in paradise, where do you go for your holidays? While I sat by her pool in my Panama hat, I thought a lot about the project.

A couple of odd things had happened in the weeks before I left the country.

One afternoon, after I had only just read to the committee an email from a very well-known public figure, telling us how honoured he would be to be part of the project and to be on the steering committee, I'd got home to find another email from him, saying, 'Sorry, but I cannot now be part of this, please do not ask me why.'

The same thing happened with someone else in a very prominent job, who'd emailed me angrily to ask why was I telling the prime minister that he was on our committee and to say he wanted nothing further to do with us. I'd replied that sadly I didn't hang out with the PM much, in fact I had never even met or been in contact with him, and so hadn't told him, or anyone else for that matter, that he was on the committee. He wasn't, anyway; he had been a member of our advisory panel.

Someone somewhere was clearly making some calls.

Mid-January 2010

If you really want me to do something... just tell me that I can't do it.

When I got back from Bali, I was more enthusiastic and determined than ever, and started looking for an artist to work with the steel. Although I still didn't know what steel we'd get, or even if we would definitely get it!

In my calls to Peter Miller at the Port Authority, I kept saying we needed a huge piece, a really monumental piece. "This is London, Peter! You know? The 'Special Relationship'!? We're the guys side by side with you in Iraq and Afghanistan!?"

"I'm sorry but we've now got thousands and thousands of applications. You'll just have to wait until we can get you into the Hangar," he kept telling me.

I had read somewhere that there had never been a major artistic response to 9/11 and I couldn't understand why no leading artist had created, as Picasso had, a 'Guernica'.

One of the committee suggested a world-famous sculptor, so I invited his agent for breakfast. He told me the artist was very busy, but might be interested as he had already been asked to do another memorial in New York. Later he confirmed he *was* interested and might be able to do both the NY one and ours for approximately $1m. He also said, "Of course he might not want to use the steel at all, you can't tell an artist what to use!"

"But the whole point of the project is to use the WTC steel!" I said. I also realised he didn't quite understand I wasn't expecting to be charged anything. How could he even think of charging us to create a work for 9/11!?

Simon Schama emailed me one day to say he'd had a revelation. "We don't need a famous artist! The work will make the star, not the star make the work."

I immediately knew he was right! I asked him if he knew about a young artist called Miya Ando from NY, who had contacted us a few months before, offering to donate her services; she worked only with steel. Yes, he replied, he knew of her work and felt she could do something wonderful and memorable.

I rang Miya and she was very enthusiastic. A Russian Jewish Japanese American, her father was a mechanic who had taught her as a child how to weld metal, and she'd just "fallen in love with steel".

But I still hadn't got the steel. We now had a pro-bono team of project managers on board and even a structural engineer, Bill Baker of Skidmore Owings & Merrill (SOM). He'd worked on more skyscrapers than almost any man on the planet and had just built the world's tallest building, the Burj Khalifa tower in Dubai. They also were building the new 1,776-feet WTC Freedom Tower at Ground Zero.

On 7th April 2010, I was fed up! I called Peter Miller. "I'm flying into JFK late tonight... I'll be at Hangar 17 at 10am tomorrow."

There was a pause, then he said, "Okay, I'll meet you there." I'd taken a big risk; he could easily have told me to get lost. But I'd thought, 'Why not!?'

I arranged to meet Miya for breakfast at the airport Sheraton at 8am. Lily, who was now 14, was in NY for the Easter holidays, so I asked her to come along as well.

I liked Miya straight away. She brought photographs of her art; she worked exclusively with flat steel panels and had developed a way of grinding and polishing them to create extraordinary effects. We were driven out to Hangar 17. Luckily we had detailed directions or we'd never have found it; there are hundreds of identical, anonymous hangars surrounding the airport. It wasn't on the driver's GPS, but finally we found it.

There was only the number 17 on the side as identification and that was all.

A man in his fifties, wearing a linen jacket and panama hat, answered the doorbell. "Peter? We've been expecting you," he said. "I'm Peter Gat. Welcome to Hangar 17. I'm the curator. Peter Miller is in his office, we'll see him after your tour."

"You must have had lots of Brits here," I said as we stepped inside.

"No, you're the first," he said. I was amazed. "You have to understand, only a few hundred people have ever been allowed in here."

It was a vast 80,000-square-foot building; originally built for Pan Am in the 1950s, it had been one of the largest hangars in the world. Inside the entrance was a bike rack with six or seven bicycles in it. "Their owners never came back for them; they worked in the towers," he said. The wheels of some were bent and their frames twisted and rusted.

We started our tour in total silence. We were the only people in the building, apart from one maintenance engineer we saw working on a fire engine. The front was totally destroyed and the back untouched, like a giant hand had reached out and crushed it. All the guys in the front died, our guide told us, the men just inches behind all survived.

The hangar was dimly lit with fluorescent lighting that gave off an eerie glow. In one sense it felt like we were walking alone through a museum where nothing had been deliberately arranged. Hundreds of massive rusted beams, from as little as four or five feet to columns 30 feet or more long, were laid out in lines, some piled on top of each other six or seven feet high. Among them everywhere were strewn huge, unrecognizable pieces of mangled steel.

On steel supports was an enormous molten, misshapen lump, about four feet high. I thought it must be a meteorite.

"That's six storeys of the World Trade Center," Peter said. "If you look carefully you can still make out the words printed on this piece of carbonised paper," pointing to some blackened material lying on a part of it. I reached out to hold Lily's hand.

We walked for two hours round this enormous, terrible place.

"You know, Peter," I said, "if you really want to show children and future generations what terrorism is and what the human cost is, you should keep everything here, just as it is... and simply put a sign up outside, saying '9/11 Museum'."

In one section were subway train carriages, totally intact. We clambered up a plank into one and it was like stepping back in time. The US Open tennis had just been on at Flushing Meadows and bright yellow and blue adverts were on the carriage walls with the names of the star players: Sampras, Agassi, Hewitt, Safin. I sat down on a seat, Lily and Miya sat opposite me. We could have been at a station, waiting for the train to move. The PATH train ran under the WTC; this one was found stopped at the WTC station after the attack.

In another area were smashed police motorbikes, burnt-out ambulances, squashed police cars and several fire engines. A gigantic mound of twisted steel cables, that could have been created by a giant spider or a 1960s pop artist, was at least 15 feet tall and the same across. In another part was a huge section of the communication aerial that stood atop the north tower.

We came to an area where they'd taken all the walls with the thousands of 'missing' notices that had sprung up all over the city in the days and weeks that followed the attacks.

All the photos of their loved ones, who they would never see again – men, women, black, white, Hispanics, Muslims, Jews – they were all here with descriptions written in hand by the families searching for them. We stood and read the messages.

We moved on to a room full of toys from the Warner Bros store in the mall under the towers; a seven-foot Bugs Bunny stood incongruously in one corner. Then there was a display stand of glasses from an optician's in the mall, and a table of baby clothes, salvaged from another store.

Peter showed us some twisted bits of metal, all that was left of the massive Alexander Calder steel sculpture that had stood in the plaza.

I saw four or five pieces of glass in a wooden box. "That's the only glass; the rest was pulverised, melted in the heat."

"From the whole buildings?" I asked in disbelief. "This is all that was left!?"

"That's all we ever found," he said.

An hour later, we were at the far end of the hangar but I still hadn't seen the piece I wanted for London.

Then I saw it. It was the very last piece of steel we saw in the hangar.

It was huge; not one but actually three twisted, rusted columns – the longest almost 30 feet long – joined together by a giant, twisted central steel panel.

"I knew this would be the one you wanted, which is why I kept it to last," Peter said.

I looked at Miya. "Yes, this is perfect... this is it!" Lily agreed it was quite different from any of the thousand or more pieces we'd seen; nearly all had been single columns. This certainly was monumental and Miya could transform the central panel, polish it, make it shiny again whilst keeping the columns exactly as they were recovered, rusty and twisted.

Before we left, we spent ten minutes with Peter Miller, whom I had talked to so often across the Atlantic. On the way out, Peter Gat handed me a memento of our visit: a large rusty bolt from the towers.

It had been for all of us an unforgettable morning. Back in the car, for five minutes we didn't speak at all. What we had seen, as Lily was to write two years later in an article for her school magazine, "had left us with our emotions strewn and our mission completed."

Just before I flew back from New York, I had breakfast with Edie Lutnick. She is the sister of Howard Lutnick, founder of international brokerage firm Cantor Fitzgerald, which had occupied floors 101 to 105 of the north tower. They suffered the single largest loss of life on 9/11 – 658 employees, trapped above the point of impact with around 800 others. Howard was late getting to the office that morning, as he had to take his young son to nursery school on his first day. Their 37-year-old brother Gary, who worked with Howard, was killed.

I had emailed Howard the previous September about the project and he'd replied right away: "How can I help?"

Edie was the director of the CF Relief Fund for the families of their people; to date they had given almost $200m to help them.

Edie was very supportive. I told her it would be important for us to have their official support. She promised to talk to her brother.

Later, I took a yellow cab downtown to the New York Fire Department. I'd emailed Commissioner Salvatore Cassano the day before, a Sunday, to say I was in the city and could I meet him? He'd replied by return, saying he was flying to Boston later in the day but I could come over around 10am.

We met in his office. After I had spent five minutes explaining our plans, he asked, "How can I help you?"

"I want your support."

"You've got it, Peter," he said and that was that. He said he sincerely appreciated what we were doing in London. The NYFD had lost 343 officers that day. They had died trying to rescue all those trapped; they'd been going up the stairs with heavy equipment on their shoulders as everyone else was desperately trying to come down.

Finally, I visited an office overlooking Ground Zero, now a huge construction site, to meet a man I'd been talking to for the last six months who, from my very first call, had been enthusiastic and helpful and who, although we had never met, I now regarded as a good friend. He had told me that, if he could, he would put up the WTC steel not just all over America but around the whole world, to show people what happened that day.

Lee Ielpi had been a fire fighter all his life until his retirement and was now in his mid-sixties. Both his two sons had also become fire fighters and the eldest, Jonathan, then 28, had rung Lee on 9/11 to say, "Dad, we're heading over to the World Trade Center, a plane's crashed into the tower."

"We used to speak six or seven times a day," he'd once told me. "Every day."

That was the last time they ever spoke.

Lee and a group of other NYFD veterans had gone straight over to the site to volunteer – they all had lost sons – and for months they worked every day. Nobody found their sons. Then, on 11th December, they'd shouted for Lee. They had found Jonathan. Lee was one of just a handful of people who were able to bury their loved ones.

He was now the president of the NY-based September 11th Families Association.

Lee, a quiet, thoughtful man, took me for lunch in a nearby diner. He told me how strongly he felt about our project and how important it was to educate our children "if there is to be any hope for a better future." As we left, everyone we passed greeted Lee as an old friend.

He took me to the WTC Tribute Center they had created next to the site. It was only a small street-front museum, but extremely well done. They'd had millions of visitors since they opened three years previously, he told me. There were photos and films of the attacks and their aftermath but it was the first-person filmed interviews that had the most impact on me.

Before we left, Lee said, "Come over here, Peter." On prominent display was a steel beam from the towers.

Postscript:

I later learned from one of his former fire-fighter colleagues that Lee Ielpi was one of the most decorated officers in the history of the New York Fire Department. He had never once mentioned it to me.

How to discover you're a salesman
October 1964, London

In July 1964, I left school. I had failed my A-level physics and had to retake it; my place at the Royal Dental Hospital was held over for me, so unintentionally I had what is now called a 'gap year'.

In those days, you just went straight to university. I passed the exam on my second attempt in October and thought I would get a job and buy a Sunbeam Alpine to impress the girls at college. I saw an advert: 'International publishing company launching major new publication seeks young enthusiastic management trainees'.

I got the job, and the next day I was knocking on doors in Upminster, Essex.

Carl Lewis, a 28-year-old larger-than-life Texan in cowboy boots and ten-gallon hat, had interviewed me. "Next year, Peter, the Grolier publishing company of America is launching its new 24-volume Moroccan-bound set of encyclopaedias for the first time ever in Europe. They cost £240 a set. So we are doing an advance marketing campaign here in the UK to select a number of families to receive a free set! So they can tell everyone how good they are, so when we come to sell them we'll have a ready-primed market. Now, as well as the set of books, there is an annual information service and updated single volume to keep 'em abreast of new developments in the world. All we ask is that the selected families sign up for this service, which costs £12 a year for 20 years; but rather than have it round their necks for 20 years, like a mortgage, they can pay it over just 24 months at £10 a month. What do you think of that, Peter!?"

"Well that is really a fantastic offer," I said. "So they get the entire 24-volume set of encyclopaedias absolutely free?"

"You've got it! Absolutely free, Peter!" said Carl, drawing on his Havana cigar.

I was part of a team of about 50 young guys, mostly from England, but my group leader was an American in his mid-twenties called Dan Adolfson. And Hans Fitz, an Austrian in his mid-thirties, had been a pilot. Carl was the right-hand man for the Lacey brothers, Price and Kip, the Americans who ran the company. They had hundreds of salesmen all over the country.

Chapter 2

They were making a fortune.

Only, I didn't know I was selling anything. I thought I was selecting people to get a free set of encyclopaedias.

Every morning we had a pep talk which ended with us all standing on our chairs as Carl walked in, flanked by Price and Kip Lacey.

"Okay, guys. What have you got?"

"Enthusiasm!" we shouted.

"What do you want?"

"Money!" we shouted.

"What are you going to do about it!?"

"Rock 'em!"

"Okay, let's rock 'em!" Carl shouted.

Then we all ran down the small staircase out into the street, got into our group leader's car and roared off to Upminster or Slough, to whatever housing estate we were headed for.

If you were in Carl's team you got to go in his electric-blue Ford Thunderbird.

The first house I knocked on in Upminster I got invited into. We had had to learn a ten-page script, word for word. I was doing pretty well in the tiny living room of this young couple and just getting to the bit where I threw open my briefcase, took out the stuck-together concertinaed spines of the 24 volumes and hurled them across the room... when my mind went totally blank. I knew I was halfway down page six but I hadn't a clue what came next. "I'm terribly sorry, but it's my very first day and you are the first people I have done this to and actually, I have got a little stuck... but I have the script in my briefcase and if you don't mind, I can read the rest to you?"

Amazingly, they were very understanding and so I got out the script and hurled the dead encyclopaedia spines across their living room; it bounced off the wall.

And they signed up. I had earned £16.

By the end of the first week, I had signed up nine families and made £144. As the average income in 1964 was £15 a week, this was amazing! I got the top prize at the Friday morning meeting, a silver Dunhill lighter.

It didn't matter I didn't smoke. I felt fantastic.

And that's how I became a salesman... only I didn't know I was selling anything at the time.

In fact, another three months had gone by when I discovered I was actually 'selling' the encyclopaedias. I was angry; I felt I had been duped.

"How can they do this? It's wrong!" I said to Dan Adolfson, who had become a good friend.

"Look, Peter," he said. "You can't just knock on a door and say, 'Hello, I am an encyclopaedia salesman, would you like to buy one?' You have to make them feel they have been selected. Everyone wants to feel special. We selected you for this job, didn't we? And you felt pretty good, right!? It's exactly the same thing... Remember, you're saving their children from a life of ignorance, and therefore the yawning jaws of poverty." He smiled. "Let's go for a drink, my naive little limey buddy."

We were sitting in the Ad Lib club. I could see George Harrison and John Lennon at one table. PJ Proby was knocking back a Jack Daniels surrounded by a bunch of pretty girls. Pete Townshend was by the bar. And the dance floor was packed.

I waved at John Entwistle, the Who's bass guitarist. "Hi, John. Do you know Dan?"

"Good to meet you, John," Dan said, shaking his hand.

John grunted something and went to join Townshend at the bar. The band all lived in Acton and I had met them originally when they played Ealing Town Hall. John couldn't drive and I would borrow my father's car and take him into the West End. He was not very exciting company – I don't recall him ever saying anything, really – but I thought it was a big thing knowing one of the Who.

I was young and impressionable... just as I am now old and impressionable.

The Ad Lib was the first 'in' club of the 1960s. A private members' club for rock stars, models, photographers and clearly one encyclopae-dia salesman, soon-to-be dental student, it was run by Brian Morris, who was either Alma Cogan's brother or lover (I can't remember which, but definitely not both). Every day, it was in the papers... and I guess the first paparazzi were outside every night.

I had gone there early one evening, before it opened, started talking to Brian and he liked me and made me a member. This was a big deal. You generally had to be one of London's 'in' crowd. The club was above the Prince Charles cinema off Leicester Square, unusual as most clubs were in basements. After a night selling encyclopaedias I would often end up there with my team; Bernie Rose, an old friend from Greenford, and Dan and Hans Fitz. My friends couldn't believe I hung out with the Stones and the

Chapter 2

Beatles. In fact, I never met any of them. It wasn't cool to go up and say hi, so you'd just ignore the most famous people in the world... even if they were sitting opposite you.

The only problem was, I was far too enthusiastic to be cool. I just couldn't say, "Yeah, man..." with the right lack of enthusiasm.

One night, the manager asked John, Paul and George to get off a table because "it's reserved for Peter". I couldn't believe it! But they just got up and moved to another table. I am a 17-year-old encyclopaedia salesman from East Acton, getting the world's biggest stars moved off my table!

I got the top salesman award again for the third month running. I now had a collection of two silver Dunhill and one gold Dupont lighters, pretty unusual for a non-smoker. At the award meeting, Carl asked all the other salesmen, "Okay, so what has Peter got that all you guys don't have? How come he's always number one? He is definitely not any better looking, that's for sure!" Big laugh. "He isn't any smarter, or better dressed... so what is it?"

"It's his smile. He smiles when he talks!" someone shouted out.

Now, this was funny, as I had always been self-conscious about my smile, ever since Ted Reynolds said that when I smiled, I looked like a monkey.

I couldn't stop smiling after this.

I had been selling encyclopaedias for five months and was now making £250 a week, a fortune in those days, when one morning we were called to a special meeting in a Kensington hotel.

Carl got up and stood on a chair – making him about seven feet tall, excluding his Stetson. The Lacey brothers sat smiling on each side of him.

"Guys, we have some big news! And I mean big... fact is, ain't going to get any bigger. The reason not everyone is here today is 'cos this is only for you, our very top guys. You are being selected to go on this exciting new journey. Guys, we are going to hit Germany! And we are going to hit them tomorrow!"

Germany!? 'Is he nuts?' I thought. 'I don't speak a word of German. I hate the Germans! I am Jewish, what do I want to go to Germany for? It's the last country in the world I would want to go.'

Everyone started to talk – no, make that shout – all at the same time.

"Hold on, guys!" Carl said. "We will answer all your questions at the end, but let me continue, okay?"

He explained that a new UK consumer protection law had come in that allowed customers a seven-day cooling-off period, where they could change their minds about any hire purchase agreement they had signed up for. This had resulted in a huge number of cancellations and so they had looked for another country, which didn't allow cancellations.

And Germany was that country.

He tipped the brim of his hat. "Well guys, is that great news or is that great news!?"

There was a murmur. "It's definitely good news," somebody said. "We are definitely getting murdered here!"

"Now, you might be thinking, 'Whoa there one minute, Carl baby!'" Carl continued. "'There's a little bitty thing called the German language and we don't speak it,' am I right? Well, you ain't going to need to, 'cos we are going to sell to English people just like we do now! We are going to sell to British Army bases all over Germany! Now, is that great news, or is that great news!?"

The room went crazy, with whooping and cheering. Although I did notice the team leaders seemed a little more enthusiastic than the regular sales guys.

Outside, I went for a coffee with Dan and Hans. I really wasn't sure about this.

"Listen, Peter, you want that beautiful sports car when you go to college?" Dan asked.

"Yes, I really do want it."

"Well old buddy, you ain't going to get it without a lot of money. Isn't that right Hans?"

"Ya, Dan eez right, we are a team, you are the great salesman, you ave to come, okay?" Hans gave me his twisted smile, showing a row of yellow teeth. "It won't be so much fun without you, Peter. You are a crazy guy, it's true Dan?"

"He is one crazy guy," Dan agreed.

I thought, 'Why not? I have no reason to stay in London, I am making a lot of money, having a lot of fun, maybe it would be good to find out what Germany is really like for myself?'

"I'm coming!" I said. As I always say, the only way I ever know what I am thinking is by stopping and listening to what I've just said.

Chapter 2

My parents were fine about it. Dad just said, "Have fun, phone us if you need anything."

The next morning, we met outside the Hilton in Park Lane and, as the top salesman, I had the honour of travelling with Price and Kip. I got in the back of Price's brand new silver Aston Martin DB5 – the same one as in James Bond movie *Goldfinger*, which had just come out. Off we went in convoy; the Aston led the way. It was like we were on a wartime mission.

On the ferry to Calais, I opened the briefcase we all had been given. "Wait a minute! What's this?" I had pulled out the sample encyclopaedia we showed the families we were selling to... sorry, selecting. How great the illustrations were, how detailed the subject text; most had never seen an encyclopaedia before, let alone held its Moroccan-bound spine.

The problem was, I wasn't holding a Grolier encyclopaedia. The name in gold print on the cover said 'Caxton Encyclopaedia'.

I had never heard of the Caxton Encyclopaedia. What was it doing in my briefcase?

"Dan, what's going on here?" I flung it in his lap, nearly knocking over his Jack Daniels.

"Oh yeah... we are selling Caxton's encyclopaedias now," he said calmly.

"What are you talking about?" I shouted, getting worked up. "I don't work for Caxton encyclopaedias! I've never heard of them and I doubt anybody else has either, apart from the Caxton who invented the printing press, and I'm pretty sure he didn't do an encyclopaedia in his spare time!"

"Peter, cool down, man! It's not a biggy." He took a gulp of his drink.

"Cool down? I don't know anything about this encyclopaedia, except that it looks crap compared to the Grolier." I flicked through it. "Look, there's none of those great transparent colour illustrations. How can I sell this, Dan? I'm a Grolier man."

Dan looked me right in the eyes. "Look, it's real simple, Pete. When you get to that page of the script when you say, 'Let me show you the new Grolier 24-volume set of encyclopaedias?'... Well, all you do is say, 'Let me show you the new Caxton 24-volume set of encyclopaedias! Think you can manage that?" He winked at me. "That's all there is to it."

And it's true, that's all there was to it.

After driving all day we arrived in a British Army garrison town in northern Germany that I had never heard of, Osnabruck. I climbed with great difficulty out of the back of the Aston. I couldn't stand up straight. For two days, I walked around like the Hunchback of Notre Dame.

I was pretty paranoid during the first days with the Germans. I was sure I matched the old stereotype of the caricature Jew I had seen reprinted from articles in *Der Stürmer*, the anti-Semitic 1930s Nazi rag. "Do they know I'm Jewish?" I asked myself. I didn't think I looked Jewish, whatever that meant. Nobody in England had ever said, "So you are a Jew, aren't you?"

Well, apart from our rabbi. But he didn't count.

The next evening we set off to sell our encyclopaedias to the British soldiers. I was nervous; I was sure they would spot I wasn't really a Caxton man. The married soldiers lived in big blocks of flats with their families. The officers were in detached houses outside the perimeter fence in wooded enclaves, like Surrey stockbrokers.

I knocked on the first door; Bob, a corporal, invited me in straight away. 'Maybe he thinks I'm an officer?' I thought. I knew I sounded like someone from one of the minor public schools that army officers mostly came from.

His young wife appeared with their two young children. I sold them a set of Caxton encyclopaedias and they were delighted, although I held my breath when the word Caxton popped out of my mouth. But they didn't seem to notice anything out of the ordinary.

They signed up for the information service and updated volume, and as I was leaving Bob said, "Peter, if you have time, could you go next door and see our friends Ron and Tracey? They've got young kids too."

I said I thought I could squeeze them in.

An hour and another cup of tea later, I had made another sale. I was on a roll. I knew now that beyond any doubt, Caxton was a great encyclopaedia, far superior to the old American Grolier.

Every night we went to the local club, the Rheingold, and try to pick up the local girls. I was still very shy with girls and still a virgin, much to the merriment of Dan and Hans. But Dan, a good-looking Swedish-American, was very confident around girls, had the knack of making them laugh and would often end up taking a girl back to the hotel. "Tell them you're a friend of the Beatles," he would say.

But I couldn't do that. "I've never even talked to one, you know that Dan."

"Yes Pete, but they don't!" he winked.

Chapter 2

After two months in Osnabruck, we moved to Berlin. Now, this was exciting. The big city! The divided city; the wall had only been up a few years.

The train went through West Germany and then East Germany to West Berlin, before continuing on to Warsaw. The ticket master told us to be sure we got off in West Berlin. The idea of going to East Berlin – behind the Iron Curtain – didn't sound too great.

It was a long train ride and very cold in the carriage. We hunkered down and fell asleep. At 5am we were woken by a large German soldier with a rifle pointed at us, shouting in German. We woke up Hans, who was snoring away in a corner.

Hans spoke to him in German. "We are in East Germany!" he said. Apparently, the soldier wanted us to get off the train immediately.

"That's what I thought he wanted," I said. "My German is coming along quite nicely."

We grabbed our suitcases and climbed down from the train. It was freezing cold. Everything looked as grey as the soldier's uniform. The surrounding streets were deserted; I couldn't see anything that looked like shops, just large granite-grey buildings.

Next to us was a sign 'Friedrichstrasse'. We were in East Berlin all right! We had missed our stop; not great news. The thought of a few years in an East Berlin prison, to be eventually exchanged for a Russian spy at Checkpoint Charlie, did come to mind.

But Hans explained we could just cross the tracks and catch the next train back to the Western sector. Easy for us, but if an East Berliner had tried that he would have been shot.

Two hours later we caught a train; one stop later we were in West Berlin. It was now 9am and as if a huge electric switch had been clicked on. The streets here were ablaze with lights, with gaily-coloured shop windows full of the latest fashions and with every food you could think of. We took a taxi to our hotel on the Heerstrasse, not far from Berlin's main shopping and entertainment street, the world-famous Kufurstendamm.

Later in the morning, we walked along the 'Ku'damm'. It blew our minds. It was as if all the luxury goods from the Champs-Élysées, Fifth Avenue and Bond Street had been shipped to West Berlin and put in the one street. It was the West's showcase and the ultimate 'Fuck you!' to the empty shops across the other side of the wall.

It started to snow heavily and the huge old bomb-ruined church, left as a monument to the war at the end of the street, took on a ghostly appearance.

That night we were in the wildest nightclub I have ever been in my life, in a side street off the Ku'damm. The place was jumping when, as a large naked blonde woman was leading a baby elephant on to the stage, a GI at the next table said to Hans, a little unkindly I thought, "Hey man, is that your head or has your neck blown a bubble?"

Hans reacted rather badly and a huge fight broke out, ending when we were thrown by two massive German bouncers out into the deepest snow I'd ever seen. It came up to my waist. Dan wanted to go back in, finish the fight and then drink the vodka he had paid for.

I didn't think it was a good idea.

We somehow made our way back to the hotel through the unbelievably deep snow. I felt like Shackleton trying to find his way back to civilisation, across the frozen wastes of Antarctica.

How to survive a game of chemmy in Soho
1964, London

I had been back by taxi to my grandparents' flat four times since arriving at 10pm for the chemmy game at the Mississippi Room, above the Whisky A Go-Go in Wardour Street.

I kept going back to take more money from my grandpa's wallet. He was in hospital for an operation and I was meant to be staying at the flat to look after my grandma.

Before leaving, he had shown me the secret compartment in the spare bedroom where he kept his valuables and his money in an old leather wallet. There was also a Colt revolver he had brought back from World War One.

I had now taken a total of £500 on the trips back and forth... and the wallet was empty. It was 4am. All the other players had gone home and there was just one man left at the table sitting across from me, next to Billy the croupier.

Suddenly, in just five minutes, I won it all back. I couldn't believe my luck. I could go back, put it back in the wallet and my grandfather would never know.

But I was reckoning without Curly.

As I got up to leave, the stocky little man with the mass of curly ginger hair stood up. "Where do you think you are going, sonny? Sit down."

"I am sorry but I really have to go. I've won my money back you see, I'm quits," I said.

He came and stood right in front of me, his face inches from mine. "I said, SIT DOWN! It's my fucking money you've won and I fucking want it back."

Joe, the Jordanian manager, quickly stepped between us. "Curly, he is just a kid. Let him go home. I will play you... for the house."

"It's not even my money, it's my grandpa's," I said.

"I don't give a fuck if it's your fucking grandpa's, grandma's or the fucking Pope's. Just fuck off out of here before I get really fucking angry," he said.

I thought it was a good idea to go.

The next night I did exactly the same thing. Only this time I lost it all and didn't win it back. I had to tell my father. Then I had to tell my grandfather.

And that's how I went to Gamblers Anonymous for the first time, as a compulsive gambler. I am truly my father's son.

I was 18 years old.

How not to destroy the finest mouths of a generation
October 1965, London

I think I really quit dental school on the very first day I went there.

I registered at St Bartholomew's Medical School in Charterhouse Square. First-year dental students did the same courses – anatomy, physiology, biochemistry – as the medics. Bart's was one of the oldest, and certainly poshest, medical schools in the country. The students were almost all public school educated, and mostly from the very top end; Eton, Harrow, Winchester. Latymer Upper, my direct-grant grammar school, although academically one of the top schools in the country, was not exactly in the same class... the upper class. Many of the students, I soon came to discover, had private incomes and career ambitions that extended far beyond medicine.

As I walked in I saw a blackboard, filled in with a typical new undergraduate's details: Father's occupation – landowner; School – Eton; Hobbies – hunting, shooting and fly-fishing; Ambition – to be a cabinet minister.

I felt a little out of place. I thought of filling it in: Hobbies – blackjack, roulette, chemmy; Clubs – Charlie Chester's casino, the Mississippi Room, Wardour Street... but then I thought it was probably not a great idea.

Heading to the student bar with Chris, a first-year medic I had met at registration, the first person I saw was Graham Chapman of Monty Python fame. I didn't know he was a medical student. He was in his last year at Bart's. He was wearing a well-worn tweed jacket, smoking a pipe and having a pint with a couple of other students.

We would spend most days at Bart's and only go to the Royal Dental for a weekly lecture. These early trips to Leicester Square quickly convinced me there was no way I either wanted to or could ever become a dentist. The idea of looking down people's mouths for the rest of my life appalled me. Teeth! Why hadn't someone ever told me it involved teeth?

At a time when it seemed like the whole of London was busy tuning in and dropping out, becoming pop stars, opening boutiques in the King's Road or Carnaby Street, styling hair in Mayfair salons... I was going to spend five years studying teeth!

You might reasonably ask, "How come you hadn't thought of this before? During all those years since you shot up your hand aged eight in prep school to answer the teacher's question, 'Does anyone know what they want to be when they leave school? Rose?'" – for I was the only child who had raised their hand.

"I want to be a dentist, sir."

Over the years that followed, it always seemed as if I was the only boy in the class who knew what he wanted to be.

"Now, boys, why can't you be like Rose? Have an ambition and work towards it?"

There was also the fact I was hopeless with the instruments. I was totally cack-handed; scissors had always defeated me. I had visions that, if by some miracle I managed to qualify, I would almost certainly destroy some of the greatest mouths of my generation.

So, after all those years of being the one boy who knew what he wanted to be, who had done all the subjects he didn't like – biology, chemistry and physics – just so he could pass the right O- and A-levels, on the day

Chapter 2

I started my dentistry course I knew it was just a matter of when I was going to leave.

We were gathered round the dissecting table, looking down on the body of a very old, emaciated Indian man that Professor Cave had just sliced open. We all had a good look inside, poking around with our scalpels. The smell of formalin was overpowering.

Now we came to the viva, the weekly oral tests he gave us. I was pretty hopeless at them. He went round the table one by one. He finally came to me. "Right, Rose, I am sure you are better prepared than last week, aren't you?" (Referring to my enthusiastic identification of the prostate... in a woman.) "Perhaps you would care to point out this gentleman's... just to put you on the right track here, Rose... levator labii superioris aloquae nasi?"

"Of course, sir. Okay, let's see... the levator aloquae labii nasi, you said?" I bent over and shoved aside a few feet of the large colon with my hands. I could see a few of my friends trying not to crack up, but not doing a very good job of it. David made a 'no' sign with a shake of his head. I moved in the direction of the penis.

"Rose... exactly where do you think you are going?"

"Just checking everything is in order, professor. Make sure it's all there, you know, nothing missing... now let's see, the levator... nasi superioris... wasn't it?" I pointed in desperation to something shiny I'd found by scrummaging around inside the poor bugger, under a lot of stuff on the right of the small intestine. "That wouldn't be it, would it?"

"Now, Rose, I could be wrong of course, but that would appear to me to be a kidney. Close, but no cigar, I am afraid."

The class couldn't stand it anymore. Mike collapsed with laughter; Marlene, David and Tony all cracked up too.

Professor Cave pointed to the space between his own upper lip and nose. "In fact, nobody here would be able to laugh or even smile right now if it wasn't for their levator labii superioris aloquae nasi. It is in fact the smallest muscle in the body, and you will also be interested to know, Rose, that it has the longest name of anything in the body."

"Really, professor?" I said. "Fascinating... so I was close then?"

I spent that year doing all the things medical students do, which in my case meant gambling with my old school friend Richard Wilkie, now studying medicine at the Middlesex Hospital, and going to disco clubs every night.

The Scotch was the hot 'in' club for a year or so from 1965. One reason was its location; not in Soho but in St James, in a cul-de-sac off Duke Street. The double-sided doors were solid oak with a little grille, and always closed; when you rang the bell, the doorman would slide the panel open and if he recognised you, open the door. The candle-lit room held a hundred people at most, with tables and seating around the walls. In the middle was a dance floor and tiny stage area.

One night, after a hard day slaving over a dead body (I was never convinced why I had to be able to identify someone's liver in order to take their teeth out), I was sitting with my girlfriend, a pretty, bright student from Sierra Leone called Celia Demby, when Daisy Williams, also from Freetown, sat down next to us with a girl and two guys. "Hey, you don't mind if we join you, Peter?" she asked.

One of the two guys shook my hand as he sat down. "Hi, I'm George," he said in a Liverpudlian accent. "This is Pattie."

I think I would have just about recognised one of the four most famous men in the world.

They'd only got married the day before. The other man sat down. "Hi, I'm Chris Denning of Radio Luxembourg!" he said in the mid-Atlantic voice all the radio DJs had in those days.

Despite having seen them in clubs many times since the Ad Lib days, I'd never actually met any of the Beatles until now. The nearest I'd got was a few months earlier at the Scotch. I'd been chatting up two stunning mixed-race sisters who were in a new group from Liverpool when Paul McCartney, with a huge beard at the time and wearing a long black fur coat, had walked up and they'd gone off with him without even saying goodbye.

I could never understand that. What did they see in him? I was a 19-year-old dental student living in East Acton with my parents, and he was one of the Beatles.

At the end of June, before the first year exams which I had no intention of even taking, I wrote to the dean of the dental school explaining that I knew it wasn't the right thing for me.

And so I resigned from a life of teeth. This was definitely a good move.

Whenever things occasionally haven't gone too well in my life in the years that followed, I have always raised my glass and said, "Thank God I am not a dentist!"

Although recently I met an eminent obstetrician, and after I'd told him about my short-lived dental career, he sighed and said, "You know, there are days when I wish I was a dentist."

Postscript:

In 2001, I was in Barbados for Christmas and read in the local paper that a British man had been killed on another Caribbean island; a psychiatrist called Richard Wilkie.

A man had been taken to the mental hospital after killing his dog and dragging it round town on a rope behind his truck. Richard had been assigned to examine him. He had turned his back for a moment and the maniac picked up a heavy object and hit him on the head with it.

He wouldn't have stood a chance if Richard had seen him coming. He was a good man and a great friend.

How to lose it
10th December 1966, London

The Speakeasy was the hottest club in London. The Beatles, the Stones and every big new band were there all the time; you had to be a member and of course, I'd been given a membership because I was a 'face' now. Okay, an unknown dental student face, but still a face; I'd been around the club scene since the Ad Lib in 1963.

The 'Speak', as everybody called it, was much larger than the Scotch. It was run by the irrepressible Jim Carter Fea and his manager Mimo and had a great restaurant run by an Italian called Dante who really knew what he was doing. It was packed with everybody who was anybody in London, in what was soon to be called the 'Swinging Sixties'. What was really special about it was its good size stage and terrific house band; whichever big happening band or singer was in the club, they'd get up on stage and jam around midnight. So you'd see Clapton on stage with McCartney or Eric

Burdon of the Animals or Zoot Money or Chris Farlowe (a Cockney who looked like a Smithfield porter but with an incredible black soul voice, and who finally had one huge hit record). Later, Chas Chandler brought Jimi Hendrix down and he would often get up with the band.

I was going to be 20 years old the next day, 11th December, and very conscious that I was still a virgin. I had been out with a few girls, but I was still very shy and self-conscious about how to go about the final moves that would solve this problem. Also, I had this romantic idea that I wanted it to be with a beautiful girl who I was madly in love with. But now I had literally only a few hours to go before saying goodbye to my teens forever, and couldn't stand the idea of being a 20-year-old virgin while everybody else in London seemed to be having sex with anything that moved.

So that night, when an attractive French woman in her early forties smiled at me at the bar and asked what I'd like to drink, I thought, 'Why not?' With a bit of luck I could sneak in just before the bell tolled. I looked at my watch; it was still only 10pm.

Marianne had married into a famous English brewery dynasty up north, and was sophisticated and rich with a husband from whom she apparently led a separate life when in London. An hour later we were back at her flat in Roland Gardens, where the bedroom walls were covered in red silk. I felt I'd stepped into an audition for the big seduction of a young English boy by a French femme fatale... which of course was exactly what I had done.

I was very nervous, and it took a lot of patience, gentle understanding and encouragement on her part before things got under way – only to be interrupted by half a dozen large black rats jumping up on the bed and running all over my back, just at the crucial point when I'd been sure everything was heading in the right direction.

"Oh, chéri!" she said. "It's just mes petites, my little Chihuahuas! Do not worry... zee are 'armless. Keep going, chéri, continuez! Do not stop now, please!" But it was too late... I'd come and gone at the same time. Those little bastards had interrupted my first night of passion with an older Frenchwoman.

'But at least I'm no longer a virgin,' I thought to myself proudly, whilst apologising to Marianne profusely. "I'm really sorry," I said. "I think it might have been the dogs jumping on my back..."

CHAPTER 3

How to open the world's most successful comedy club
The Comedy Store – 1979, Soho, London

In 1978, I went on holiday to Los Angeles. One hour after arriving, I'd decided to leave London and live there forever. I looked up an estate agent in the *Yellow Pages* and 20 minutes later I was up in the Hollywood hills being shown round a series of beautiful sun-drenched, pool-sided, Jacuzzi-integrated, Astroturfed, three-bedroom, six-bathroom homes by Morty "call me Mad Dog" Weinberg.

'Mad Dog' was definitely not one of the pinstriped, public-school brigade of London estate agents. This became even more apparent when around 9pm and half a dozen palatial homes later ("You just push this little button and the whole roof slides off!"), he said he was very sorry but he had to go, as he was auditioning at the Comedy Store later that evening.

In England, you just didn't often meet estate agents who were also stand-up comedians.

The next night we asked the hotel porter to recommend somewhere fun to visit and he asked if we had been to the Comedy Store. So we went along. The compère introduced the acts, all young comedians performing for about ten minutes, like a comedy conveyor belt. I had never laughed so much in my life. There weren't any comedy clubs in London. Where could you go to laugh in London? I'd spent too much time going to discotheques and I was fed up with the sight of 'cool' – i.e. miserable-looking – posers. I couldn't remember ever seeing anyone laugh in a disco.

I had always loved comedians. My father's grandfather's family were gentle Jewish fisher folk from Poland who'd set sail for California in the 1890s and by faulty navigation had landed up in Glasgow. My father came south after the war, with his war wound – a vivid scar running the length of his arm; a lorry overturned on a sand dune in Syria and everybody landed on top of him, their medical officer. He settled as a family GP in East Acton, West London – not exactly a centre of Talmudic learning. Our synagogue in Ealing was a converted church. We were very liberal Jews. My father was a great joke teller and would always be surrounded at parties by groups of laughing men.

The only comedians I'd seen in England were on TV. I'd grown up with Tony Hancock, Peter Cook and Dudley Moore, and later Monty Python. I was a big fan of Woody Allen, but I'd been too young to see Lenny Bruce when he came to the Establishment Club in the early 1960s. I had never liked the northern club comics and their mother-in-law jokes. After years of Benny Hill I'd had enough of double entendre jokes to last a lifetime.

The young comics that night at the Comedy Store were doing creative, intelligent comedy and I loved it. When we left the club, I said I must open a place like that in London, so I can have a place to go to laugh in.

I found the Nell Gwynne Club as my venue, through somebody who knew Don Ward, who ran the club together with a downstairs room called the Gargoyle. When we met, I explained that I wanted to open a club like the Comedy Store in Los Angeles. He had also heard of it and amazingly had once been a professional comic himself. He liked the idea and said I could use his premises on a Saturday night. The Gargoyle club's members were mostly businessmen only in town during the week and so he closed at weekends.

It was perfect. We shook hands on the spot. I would find the comedians and promote the shows and he would supply the drinks and staff. I had already decided to start off with Saturday and Sunday nights only and see how it went from there.

The Gargoyle had opened as the Blue Room in 1926 and was one of London's oldest nightclubs. At that time it was a favourite watering hole of the Prince of Wales. There was a mural by Matisse, who had also designed the beautiful staircase that led down into the club. The room itself was L-shaped and intimate, with a stage at one end and two raised tiers with tables and little gilt chairs, around a tiny dance floor. Walking into it was like stepping back into the 1930s, slightly faded but unchanged. Unlike most night clubs, usually in basements, the Gargoyle was three floors up and could only be entered by taking a tiny lift, which held two people wedged face to face, to the fourth floor, walking through the Nell Gwynne strip club and then down Matisse's staircase.

As a self-proclaimed promoter of non-sexist comedy, I had trouble explaining the topless barmaids to some of the aspiring comedians when they came to audition. "Look, they are nothing to do with me, they belong to the strip club and it's closed when we're open," I blustered. Don had other ideas, but after several heated discussions, during which I pointed out that it could seriously undermine any credibility we might hope to get as pioneers of a new kind of comedy, he finally agreed that the contentious boobs could disappear into the Comedy Store T-shirts I'd had made. But only after midnight, when we opened. A lot of people thought I was crazy to open there. "Who wants to go to Soho at midnight to watch a bunch of amateur comics in a sleazy strip joint?"

So it's February 1979 and I am sitting in an empty strip club in Dean Street at 6pm, waiting for 'any aspiring comedians, comedians or frustrated dentists' who had read my one-line ads in *Private Eye* or *The Stage* to turn up to audition for my new club which, I had announced at a press conference a week earlier, would be opening in April. I had never done anything like this before. I wasn't in 'showbiz'. I was a 33-year-old life insurance salesman.

I had been sitting in the Nell Gwynne every evening after work for nearly a month, waiting for an English Lenny Bruce or Woody Allen to walk in, and I was still waiting. My first mistake had been to put my ad in *The Stage*. I'd been besieged by every out-of-work Butlins Redcoat in Britain, as well as a lot of semi-pro northern club comics who sent me their glossy ten by eight photos (Kenny 'Cheekie Chappie' Smith), together with their own ads ('Dougal Donovan is back from his sensational tour of the Far East and has some unexpected dates free before his annual summer season on the Cunard Princess').

The *Evening News* had run a story about the club and now a lot of people were turning up whose friends had said, "Go on John... you tell terrific jokes down the pub. You're really funny after eight or ten pints." It seemed as if almost everybody wanted to be a comedian, although I don't think an estate agent ever turned up. Chauffeurs, builders, police-men, bank clerks. They were all terrible, but I didn't know that you didn't applaud at auditions and after every act I would clap enthusiastically. I started having nightmares about an opening night composed entirely of these unfunny people, hundreds and hundreds of them stretching off the stage into the distance... before a silent, appalled audience.

One morning I auditioned someone at my insurance office, in the training room. His name was Lee Cornes and he was the first aspiring comedian I'd met who actually did look funny. He reminded me of Marty Feldman with his crossed, staring eyes and manic manner. He did two mime sketches. The first was a surgeon performing an operation who removed every possible organ except the one he was meant to take out. In the other he finished up foaming at the mouth with rabies... and at that moment my boss put his head round the door. "This is Lee," I said. "He's thinking of joining us, aren't you, Lee?"

He made me laugh for the first time since I'd embarked on what increasingly seemed a hopeless enterprise. If England was full of bril-liant undiscovered comedians, they were doing a good job at remaining undiscovered. I told Lee he was booked for the opening night and not to leave the country without telling me! As the opening day drew closer, the auditions were getting worse and worse and I realised there must be few more depressing experiences than sitting in an empty strip club watching unfunny people, most of whom thought they were hilarious.

The procession was enlivened by the odd 'speciality' act – the 60-year-old housewife who sang 'I'm Only a Bird in a Gilded Cage' with her head in a birdcage. She followed it up after a quick change with 'Any Old Iron' in a dress with lumps of metal hanging from it. Then there was the man who called me about his saxophone act. He played 'I'm Forever Blowing Bubbles' while sitting at the bottom of a glass tank full of water. He didn't manage to audition because he couldn't get his tank into the lift. I've always thought that was a shame.

One evening in March, having sat through another dozen terrible acts with a frozen smile on my face (I'd stopped applauding by this time), there was only one person left and then I could thankfully go home. He was a stocky, tough-looking young man in a leather jacket with a Liverpool accent. He'd seen my ad in *Private Eye*. His name was Alexei Sayle and five minutes later, after a surreal and hilarious monologue involving a violent encounter in a cake shop, I knew I'd found my compère. Even if he had to introduce 20 of the world's worst comedians, I would definitely be opening as planned.

I'd always known the choice of compère would be crucial. I didn't want the traditional "A big hand, ladies and gentlemen, for the tremendously talented..." type. More the "That was John, taking another giant step from mediocrity to obscurity" school was what I was after. I instinctively knew I'd found it in Alexei Sayle. Physically he reminded me of John Belushi from the American series *Saturday Night Live*, one of the brilliant new young comedians whose work I admired.

As opening night loomed we were joined by Arnold Brown. He was a 40-year-old Scottish Jewish accountant working in the rag trade in London, and of course he wanted to be a comedian. "Why not?" he would ask; the question soon became his catchphrase. He was so nervous on stage that it was difficult to know whose ordeal would be the greater – his or the audience's. However, he had a very original way of looking at life and he'd head off in the direction of being funny, unfortunately mostly never quite making it. But he took the whole thing extremely seriously and would spend hours agonising over every word.

I'd sent out over three hundred invitations to the first-night party on 19th May 1979. The club was only licensed to hold 120 people, but I was told most people probably wouldn't come. They all did and it was packed. We had stocked up with an enormous quantity of champagne and a terrific buffet. I had invited the press and heads of all the television companies. A TV crew from the BBC's *Nationwide* programme and several radio reporters came. There was a lot of excitement as everybody waited to see these great new comedians I had discovered.

I was extremely nervous and was rushing about trying to marshal my 25 'comedians' – I use the inverted commas advisedly – into some kind of running order. I had asked them to wait in the kitchen (the dressing room was even smaller than the lift), but most seemed to have joined the party and I kept grabbing them and pushing them back into the kitchen. Ian Hale, a civil servant from Hanwell, arrived at the last minute with his bicycle clips still on, hauling a suitcase full of props that I never saw him use in his act. He bore an unnerving resemblance to Norman Wisdom.

So my motley bunch of chauffeurs, builders, housewives with birdcages on their heads and one accountant prepared for – in nearly all cases – their first-ever public performance before the cream of Britain's entertainment industry, most of who were getting pissed out of their brains.

I had realised I hadn't got a spotlight to flash from the back of the club to signal that the comedians should wind up their act and get off stage; somebody told me that comedians never leave the stage willingly and the spotlight was how they did it in the Californian clubs. I asked my friend, Ashley 'Billy the Kid' Roy, to pop out to a hire shop and rent one for the night. He arrived back, just before the first guests arrived, with what looked like the gong from Rank films. It was at least three feet across and hung from a solid wooden frame. A massive gong stick came with it. "What the hell is that?" I asked.

"They didn't have a spotlight," Billy said. "We can just tap it gently and they'll know it's time to go." It was too late to change it, so we set it up on the side of the stage.

The audience were sitting, standing, shouting, drinking champagne from the bottle and getting very impatient. I could tell because they'd started to chant "Why are we waiting?" and to stamp their feet. The whole place was a matchbox waiting to be lit. Sweating profusely, fearing some of the worst comedy ever was about to be performed, I reluctantly told an unnaturally relaxed Alexei to start the show.

The comics never stood a chance. The first one had hardly been on two minutes before somebody shouted, "Get him off!" The audience joined in and the poor man, a look of terror in his eyes, was totally thrown and seemed about to cry. I gestured desperately to Billy to tap the gong. A deafening 'GONG' rang out, as if Big Ben were in the room. The first victim, I mean comedian, slunk from the stage. Alexei brought on the next one. He didn't fare any better. "Good evening, ladies and gentlemen" is a strange line to finish on. This time somebody shouted, "Gong! Gong!" and Billy hit the gong again. It seemed impossible to strike it softly, and now everybody joined in, yelling, "Gong him! Gong him!" They were like cannon fodder, one after the other; on, off, on, off.

At the rate we were going, the whole 25 would be on and off in 15 minutes. It was a comedy massacre. *Guardian* journalist Tom Tickell was there to perform and then write about it in the next morning's paper (ironically, he was the *Guardian's* insurance reporter). He lasted longer than most – about three minutes.

A huge American restaurateur called Bob Payton was helping Alexei out as compère for the night. I'd met him when I was searching for venues. He was about to open his first restaurant, the Chicago Pizza Pie Factory, and had somehow persuaded me it would be very funny if he came along and read out his old High School book. 'Why not?' I now thought, as he proceeded to do just that to the incredulous mob. It was a crazy night. Amazingly, nobody was walking out. In fact they seemed to be having a great time! Unfortunately, as far as I was concerned, for all the wrong reasons. Alexei, however, was a terrific success, handling comedians and audience alike with equal contempt, unleashing his manically threatening stream of invective at both parties throughout. Without him, it would have been a disaster. Finally, we ran out of comedians and champagne and Alexei threw everybody out into a deserted Soho. It was 3am. Shattered and suffering from acute nervous exhaustion, I drove home.

Tom Tickell's column the next morning accurately captured the night's events. "All Rosengard has to do now to make the Comedy Store a success is find some comedians." Probably what saved us over the next few months was the fact we were only open on Saturday and Sunday nights. We were one of the first of the 'one-nighter' clubs that revitalised London nightlife over the next five years. Most of the old discos found the going very tough in the late 1970s, after *Saturday Night Fever* mania had run out of steam. Then along came punk, and kids were going to live gigs again. Many of the clubs were empty through the week, surviving only on their traditional Saturday night business. Now, a new breed of young entrepreneurs were approaching the disco owners and offering to fill their clubs for one night every week, with a new name and identity for the night, taking the door money and leaving the owner with the bar revenue.

It was difficult enough to find people to perform for two nights, let alone six nights a week! To my amazement, we got some good write-ups over the first weeks and people turned up for the shows. But every night I worried that either no comedians would show up or no audience. Sometimes the audiences were outnumbered by the comedians. It was touch and go for a few months. In 1979, Soho wasn't the hip area it was to become, it was still full of porno cinemas, rip-off bars and girlie magazine shops.

I tried to get well-known comedians down to try out new material, but their agents weren't enthusiastic. Jasper Carrott and Billy Connolly never came. Rowan Atkinson promised to, but went into a massage parlour by accident, asked if it was the Comedy Store, got punched in the stomach, was sick and went home. Les Dawson was an exception. He performed a couple of times and was very well received, even though his act was very different from the type of comedy the young audience was expecting. But he is a very funny man. Lenny Bennett came once, was heckled and sneered, "Listen, luv, when I drive home in my Rolls Royce, you'll be standing in the rain waiting for the bus."

Alexei gonged him off. "I'm not a violent person, but I keep being provoked," said Alexei.

We managed to survive the summer and then some new, very funny people started to appear. Tony Allen, Jim Barclay and Andy de la Tour all turned up at about the same time. Tony had been running an alternative cabaret at the Elgin pub in Maida Vale. Soon we had a nucleus of half a dozen regulars who were tremendous. Within six months they were joined by two brilliant double-acts, Twentieth Century Coyote (Rik Mayall and Ade Edmondson) and The Outer Limits (Peter Richardson and Nigel Planer). The place was now packed every weekend by word of mouth, people queuing round the block hours before we opened. We didn't have to advertise any more. The press loved the place and a steady stream of rave reviews appeared. It was the most talked-about club in London, the "hottest place in town".

The audience was young and from all walks of life – students to dockers, lords to dustmen. Everybody had to queue, even the celebrities who thought they could just walk to the front. There was always an electric atmosphere before the midnight show. People were crammed in, almost hanging from the ceiling. The first tables were only six inches from the stage.

The audience never knew who was going to perform and I was never sure either. The first night I wasn't there since we'd opened, almost a year earlier, American comedian Robin Williams walked in and did an hour of incredible comedy. I was his number one fan and I missed him. I'd followed his career since *Mork and Mindy* on TV and for me he was one of the top comedians in the world. The next Saturday he came again and did another hour of brilliance. It was the first time he had ever performed in England. I had an audience spot at the end of every show where anybody could get up and perform for five minutes, and every week three or four people tried out, sometimes just to tell their only joke. After some months I couldn't stand the stress of hoping the comedians would just drop in, so I started booking them a week ahead.

Early on I realised two important things were helping our success. Firstly, it was okay – in fact, essential – to have very bad performers along with the few good ones, not only to fill the show out but also because the audience took a perverse pleasure in watching the people who were embarrassingly bad.

Secondly, the gong. From the first night when the audience had screamed "Gong!" it was a great audience participation device, and became enshrined in Comedy Store legend: "Have you been to the club with the gong?" Just as the early music halls had a man with a shepherd's crook pulling the unwilling performer from the stage, the gong was our crook. Alexei was the gong master. At the beginning of every show, he would explain the rules. If you couldn't stand the comedian any more, you shouted "Gong", and if there were enough people shouting, a clear majority, then Alexei would strike the gong and the comedian had to leave immediately. This was Christians versus lions all over again and it had to be the toughest club in the world to play. If you could survive the gong at the Comedy Store, you could definitely play anywhere. Incredibly, the comedians kept coming back for more, and so did the audiences.

One night in early 1980, during the 2am audience spot, a short, stocky young man with a severely cropped haircut got up and unleashed a blisteringly aggressive monologue of surreal brilliance on the packed room. Alternating between seemingly on the edge of violence and an icy calm, he gripped everybody with his mesmeric presence. Driven by an "intense hatred of Max Bygraves", Keith Allen performed many times over the next year, becoming a Comedy Store legend. Always unpredictable, he didn't seem to care whether he was funny, but there was always a unique air of danger. Once David Hancock of the *Evening Standard* came to see him; Keith turned the fire extinguisher on him. Undeterred, Hancock came back for more the following Saturday.

In autumn 1980, Ben Elton came down from Manchester University, and by early 1981 had joined Manchester graduates Rik Mayall and Ade Edmondson at the Store. He soon became one of the regular compères. His super-fast hectoring delivery combined with prolific writing ability quickly made him one of the most popular acts.

From the beginning, like the original in Los Angeles, the Store was to be both a showcase for new talent and a place for professional comics to try out new material. None of the performers got paid, though I was very tempted to charge some of them! Alexei as the compère got £5 a show. I had hoped that agents and TV producers would regularly come to discover new people. This didn't happen. The showbiz establishment regarded us as a threat. They didn't see any wider audience for a bunch of foul-mouthed amateurs. TV was out of the question. One exception was a young BBC producer called Paul Jackson.

It took us almost a year just to get back the cost of the opening party! One of the biggest start-up expenses had been the enormous Perspex signs bearing the club's logo – a huge laughing mouth. Before each show we would hang the signs over the strip club ones. Occasionally, the strip club members would turn up and sit through two hours of comedy, waiting for the girls to come on. This usually led to demands for a refund of their £4 entry fee.

At the pre-opening press conference, I had been asked whether there would be any censorship. I had replied that anything went, as long as it wasn't racist or sexist! Of course, the audiences decided for themselves what they wanted and the gong became the ultimate censor. Heckling was a phenomenon from the start, veering wildly between being funnier than the comic on stage to drunken abuse of the 'Why don't you fuck off?' variety. "It's the kind of place where even the bouncers heckle," read one article. Actually we never needed any bouncers, but we did have Joe, our 72-year-old doorman. A 40-year Soho veteran, Joe was immaculate in dinner jacket and bow tie and unfailingly courteous to the queues waiting to get into our tiny lift.

We only once had a fight, when Andy de la Tour decided to explore the doubtful comic potential of a discussion on a TV programme on Auschwitz. A group of National Front-type skinheads, who had found their way in, suggested, "They should have gassed more of them." They were standing next to a large group of North London Jewish kids and a tremendous punch-up followed. The police arrived and broke it up, but seemed mainly interested in warning me about a "sweet, sickly smell" they had observed in the club atmosphere!

At the end of the first year, I decided to do an act myself, liberally 'borrowing' a few lines from American comics I'd seen. I attempted to talk about premature ejaculation for ten minutes. I was gonged off in record time. I kept trying and finally beat the gong. But the general consensus was, "Don't give up the day job, Peter."

After about a year, Peter Richardson wanted to do an early evening show five times a week featuring the best of the Store's acts, but it would have interfered with the operation of the Nell Gwynne and Don turned him down. Richardson went round the corner to Paul Raymond, who had been along to the Store, and started the Comic Strip shows at the Boulevard Theatre, which gave them a whole new audience at 8pm of people who didn't want to come to Soho at midnight on a Saturday.

Within a few months of opening the Comedy Store, I'd felt that we were doing for comedy what the Sex Pistols had done for rock 'n' roll. Thirty years later, I think that for perhaps six months in 1980 it was true. It certainly beat selling life insurance! Being a stand-up comedian is one of the world's toughest jobs. I had a poster printed that I stuck up on walls all over Soho. It read: 'What's the difference between skydiving and appearing at the Comedy Store? In skydiving you can only die once.'

When I was a teenager, whichever Saturday night party I was at, I always felt there must be a better party going on somewhere else. For about a year in 1979 to 1980, for a lot of people the Comedy Store was that somewhere else.

In April 2009, the Comedy Store celebrated its 30th anniversary.

Theo, a young Claridge's porter, asked me a few years ago: "Sir, any chance of you getting me tickets for the Comedy Store? It's my birthday in a month... they are fully booked."

Unfortunately, the answer was no.

Postscript:

In November 1981, my partner Don woke up one day and decided he didn't want a partner any more.

Only he forgot to tell me himself. I received a letter from his solicitor. 'Your business relationship with Mr Don Ward is dissolved as of today. You are not allowed to enter the club.'

If you get nothing else from reading this book, remember this – never go into business with a Soho strip club owner. A gentleman's word is his bond, but it's better to have it in writing.

My father once told me, "When you bear a grudge, you let that person live rent-free in the attic of your mind."

I know I could never have spent the rest my life in a sweaty Soho club; I love to be free... no office, no staff, no overheads, no admin. The truth is I could never have run it as brilliantly as Don clearly has for the last 33 years – they are still queuing round the block to get in.

For me, the real excitement has always been getting an idea in the first place and acting on it... making it happen. That was the buzz.

And I've always gone for the buzz.

How to talk to strangers (1)
November 2010, Marylebone High Street, London

It was a cold, rainy night and I was sitting outside Providores restaurant bar having a glass of red wine, when suddenly the pavement opened up next to me and up popped a black head, like a jack-in-the-box. It was a head belonging to a man in his mid-twenties.

"Good evening!" I said. "Who are you?"

"I'm Siddiqi," he said.

I reached down into the hole. "Hello Siddiqi, I'm Peter Rosengard," I said as we shook hands. "Very nice to meet you, Siddiqi. I like surprises, and I like meeting new people. This seems to fit the bill all right. What are you doing down there?"

"I work down here, in the kitchens. I do the washing up." He flashed me a huge smile.

"Really!? I used to wash up dishes as well; in fact, I got the sack as a dish washer once in Sweden in 1968... I kept breaking them! It must be pretty hot down there."

He laughed. "I'm from Sierra Leone!" he said.

He began heaving onto the pavement lots of large bags of rubbish. Still all I could see was his head and shoulders in a white jacket.

"Not Freetown?" I asked.

"Yes, how do you know?" He looked delighted.

"My first girlfriend was from Freetown, in 1965, when I was studying to be a dentist: her name was Celia Demby. A very pretty girl. You don't happen to know her by any chance?"

"Demby? That's a big name."

"I think her father or uncle might have been prime minister once. Any idea, Siddiqi, what's she up to these days?"

"You know something? I think she was in the government once... What do you do, Peter?"

"I'm a life insurance salesman."

"Have you got any jobs in your business?"

"Can you sell, do you think?"

"Really, I think I'd like to be an actor. Can you help me?"

"Well, you know something, acting's very similar really to being a salesman. I do know a few people in the business... you haven't done any 'stand up' have you? Or in your case, pop up! I'll certainly let you know if I hear of anything going."

"I like Shakespeare a lot. But I am sorry... I've got to go now," he said, swinging the trapdoor down again. "I hope we meet again Peter."

"Yes, so do I. Great to meet you Siddiqi, see you soon." The door slammed and he was gone.

I sat back in my chair. 'Yes,' I thought, 'it is a funny old world!' You really can make new friends in the most unexpected places. I'm going to keep on doing it until the day I die.

Postscript:

Siddiqi has since popped up at regular intervals when I am there and we've had interesting conversations on all kinds of things. Politics, the arts, the politics of the kitchen. My friends are always surprised when he shoots up! And he always has that enormous, dazzling smile.

How to volunteer for a six-day war
5th June 1967

I was on the Central line going to work. I had left Dunbee-Combex-Marx – well, I got the sack for falling asleep at my desk at Jean Sorrell's bubble bath company – and I had taken a temporary job with De La Rue, the famous banknote printing company.

They had developed a prototype for the automatic cash dispensing machines that, in years to come, were to be in every street in the world. I was part of the team whose job was to find flaws in the machine; essentially, to find out how people could steal the money. This involved everything from hitting them with pickaxes to hauling them out of a window, or driving a bulldozer at them... anything at all. I don't think electronic scammers and the like were invented, so we just focused on brute force.

I had only been there a few weeks and that morning on the tube, I glanced at the paper being read next to me: 'MIDDLE EAST IN FLAMES... ISRAEL INVADED FROM ALL SIDES'. Huge banner headlines. It said volunteers were being recruited to go to Israel at Rex House, the Zionist Federation's head office in Regent Street.

I got off at the next stop, went to a phone box and called my office. "I am sorry but I won't be coming in today, I am going to Israel to fight."

I had grown up in the post-war years, learning from my grandfather and from books and television what had happened to the Jews, about the concentration camps, the Holocaust, the murder of six million innocent people just because they were Jews. Grandpa was so proud of Israel. They were the new Jews, tough Jews, soldiers... they fought back.

And I was too; I didn't want to be asked by my own grandchildren one day, "Where were you when Israel was destroyed?" I went to Piccadilly Circus and joined a queue of young people at Rex House, all wanting to volunteer. A lot of them weren't even Jewish.

On 8th June I somehow managed to get on the first planeful of volunteers to land in Israel since war had broken out by telling them I was a medical student; they'd said that they were only taking people with medical or military experience. (Well, I had studied dentistry for about a week. And Dad was a doctor!) The evening newspaper ran a story about the volunteers and I was quoted: '20-year-old Peter Rose, the son of a London doctor, says, "They are sending me out in the next day or so."'

My parents had taken the news very well. Dad was fine about it: "Good luck son, look after yourself." Mum had insisted on immediately taking me to a photographer's studio in Shepherds Bush to get my portrait taken. Clearly, she wasn't optimistic about the chances of ever seeing me again.

I landed at Lod Airport early on the Thursday morning. The Boeing 707, donated by Marks & Spencer, had been blacked out on our final approach, just in case there were any enemy planes left. Also on the plane, as passengers, were Topol, the Israeli star of *Fiddler on the Roof*, which was playing in London, and Daliah Lavi, the beautiful Israeli film actress.

At Lod, we were divided up into groups and I was put in a truck for Erez, a kibbutz on the Gaza strip. With me were three other English guys; none were Jewish. I got talking to Robin Piper; he was a policeman and just wanted to help Israel win the war.

We were greeted at the kibbutz by a giant of a man with flaming red hair and beard, and an Uzi in his hand. Ammunition belts crisscrossed his chest. 'The new Jew!' I thought proudly.

"Hello, I'm Sean Armstrong from Dublin," he said. "Welcome to Erez."

He had been working on the kibbutz when war broke out and was now one of the guys in charge of the kibbutz defences; all the young kibbutzniks had been called up and were in the army, fighting.

The tens of thousands of volunteers pouring into Israel from all over the world were needed to fill the jobs of the guys who had been called up and keep the country going until the fighting was over.

I was given a small bare room with bunk beds to share with Robin and another guy, in one of the original kibbutz accommodation blocks built when it was founded in the early 1950s.

The next morning at 5am, we got in a tractor trailer and were taken out to a field to pick peaches. We went back around 9am for a massive breakfast of fruit, cheeses, tomatoes, olives, salads and eggs in the communal dining room, with all the older kibbutzniks and the teenagers too young for the army, and then back to peach picking for a few hours. By 1pm, we were exhausted and finished for the day.

Everybody had a transistor radio clasped to their ears all the time as the news came thick and fast. Jerusalem had fallen the day before I arrived, the Wednesday, and the Egyptians had been routed. The talk was of a massive battle in the Mitla Pass earlier in the week. It looked as if the war had been won on the first day when Israel launched a massive pre-dawn pre-emptive attack on the Egyptian airfields, destroying their entire air force on the ground.

On the Saturday, the Syrians were defeated after the Israelis stormed the Golan Heights and the war was over.

If you are going to volunteer for a war, make sure it's a six-day one. I could have got stuck in Vietnam or the Hundred Years War.

A week later, a group of us went to Jerusalem for the day and made our way to the Wailing Wall.

There were hundreds of people there: ordinary Israelis of all ages, young soldiers and Hasidim looking like they had just stepped out of Lodz in the 1870s, with their black clothes and broad-brimmed fur hats. I wrote a prayer on a piece of paper given to me by a beaming orthodox rabbi, standing nearby with a stack of paper and pencils.

I wasn't a big expert on praying but I asked God to make sure Israel could now live in peace forever. And then, as a 'ps', I asked him to please make Dad never gamble again and for Mum and Dad to be able to start their life together all over again and to always be happy.

I folded it into a little square and stuffed it into a crack in the wall. I looked round and saw that Robin had a Yarmulke on the top of his head as he wrote on his bit of paper. "What are you praying for?" I asked.

"Newcastle are playing Man United at home tomorrow!" he said.

I soon transferred from picking peaches – it was too hot out in the fields – to washing dishes. If any Arab Fedayeen fighters attempted to get into the kibbutz from across the Gaza Strip, I was going to throw plates at them.

One night, crossing the 100-yard strip of scrubland from my room to the dinner hall, I heard a burst of automatic gunfire. I instantly jumped into a ditch. It was pitch black. I had never heard a gun fired before. It had sounded very close, but could have been half a mile away. After five minutes, I thought it was safe to make a run for it, and got to the hall. Nobody else had heard it. "Probably just one of our sentries, letting off a few rounds," I was told by one of the young kibbutzniks.

It was at Erez that I first came into contact with drugs; marijuana to be exact.

"Peter Pumpkin," my mother had said when I was about 17, "don't ever try marijuana," (pronouncing the 'j' as in judge).

"Why is that, Mummy?" I asked.

"Because it will inevitably lead to hard drugs, like Marlboro."

Most of the people on the kibbutz were in their early twenties, from the States and all over Europe, and a lot were hippies who had been travelling in Jordan or Egypt or Lebanon when war had broken out and had fled into Israel for safety. When they weren't working they were smoking dope in their rooms and didn't mix much with the kibbutzniks. The Israeli kids were not into drugs at all.

I didn't smoke cigarettes, let alone grass. "I am fine thanks," I said when they passed the joint round. "I am high on life."

This didn't make me universally popular and I felt a little isolated. But they weren't much fun anyway. They just sat there, saying, "Far out man... cool... right man," and then fell asleep. I was still much too enthusiastic to be 'cool'.

Actually, I don't think I have ever been cool for a minute in my entire life. A girl did once say to me, "Peter, you are really cool." Okay, what she really said was, "Peter, you are not so hot." But I knew what she meant.

After a month, I went to Tel Aviv and stayed in a small hotel. It was a scruffy old place, but cheap. I would go for breakfast at the five-star Dan Hotel up the road and sit listening to the conversations of the wealthy American tourists, who were flooding back into Israel now the war was over.

It was good to be on the winning side. I'd contacted Carl Lewis again and suggested they open an encyclopaedia operation in Israel, which I could head up. They had sounded excited by the idea, but after a few weeks nothing had come of it. So one day, I called home and my mother sent me the money to fly back.

At the time, it seemed as if the whole world loved plucky little Israel, the tiny country that had beaten all their enemies in a brilliantly executed short war.

When I got back home to London I felt seven feet tall, I was so proud to be Jewish.

How to end up on a small island off the coast of Sweden
Summer 1968

I had met Annika at the Fledermaus club in Carlisle Street in Soho. It was always full of the au pairs who had flooded London in the mid-1960s from all over Europe, particularly Sweden and Germany.

So in January 1968, I had got myself a job there, as a DJ.

It was a tiny club. The bar was upstairs with the dance floor and a roulette table downstairs. I had got friendly with Mike, the croupier, who by day managed a Dolcis shoe shop in Golders Green. Mike was a slim, good-looking guy about ten years older than me, and he had a string of beautiful Swedish girlfriends that he met at the club.

Annika Nillson was a 19-year-old slim Swedish au pair with short blonde hair, blue eyes and a big white smile, who told me she had been in London for a year. I offered her a lift home one night, after the club closed.

Two days later, I was on a small island off the coast of Stockholm. I thought she lived in Golders Green.

My father was not happy, as he needed his car to visit his patients. He sent his young assistant, Dr John Foran, a big, gentle Ampleforth-educated Irishman, out to Sweden to get it back.

The island was called Gotland and Annika lived in the only town, Visby. We had got off a ferry from Stockholm late at night. We went to her home, and fell asleep.

I woke up very early and, letting myself out, went for a walk. I could see people dressed like people did a hundred years before, the women in long dresses and the men in tall stovepipe hats. Horse-and-carriages full of people trotted past me.

I turned the corner and was suddenly blinded by huge spotlights. An American voice shouted, "Cut... take six!"

I had walked into a huge film set. They were filming *Monte Carlo or Bust!* with Tony Curtis.

I looked around. I was standing in a totally medieval town, surrounded by thousand-year-old, 20-feet stone walls. Even Hollywood couldn't copy this place. They had to come to it.

I stopped at a kiosk. The little old lady was selling hard-core porn magazines alongside the chocolates and cigarettes. Incredible... I picked one up and leafed through it. I had never seen anything like it. I was in the home of the permissive society. I had read about it, but now I was here, 21 years old and right in the middle of it.

I went back to the house and went back to bed. An hour later there was a knock on the door. "Annika wake up! Someone's knocking on the door," I said.

"Oh, it's just my dad," she said.

"What? He will kill me. I am in bed with his daughter!"

"Relax. This is Sweden... don't worry."

The door opened and the Duke of Edinburgh walked in, carrying a tray with coffee, boiled eggs and toast. "Good morning," he said in a strong Swedish accent. "Welcome home." Her dad was the double of the Queen's husband. What were the odds of that? He shook my hand and didn't seem to notice I was in bed with his only daughter.

Only in Sweden. My parents would have killed me had I even dreamed of taking a girl back to the house in East Acton.

How to spend a day with the Doors
20th September 1968, Stockholm

The three surviving members of the Doors – John Densmore, Robby Krieger and Ray Manzarek – would, years later, look back on the final concert of their 1968 European tour at the Stockholm Opera House as one of their best-ever performances.

I had spent the day before showing them around... minus Jim Morrison.

"Jim's holed up in bed at the hotel with some new friend, and he's not coming out of there," Densmore told me.

I'd met them in the morning at Tetley's Teahouse, in the garden by the Opera House.

I was working as a DJ at the Golden Circle Club. They got me a ticket for their show that night in the beautiful Opera House with red and gold tiers of boxes all the way up to the ceiling. It was an incredible venue for Morrison, the most controversial and wildest lead singer on earth; he had been arrested for obscenity at their recent US concerts. That night, when he finally made it onto the stage, 2,000 stoned young Swedes went so crazy, they nearly took the roof off the centuries-old hall.

As he launched into 'People are Strange', I wasn't finding it too difficult not to think about the letter I'd received from my grandfather, asking me to come home to become a life insurance salesman.

In his previous letter, it had been an accountant and before that, a lawyer. Clearly he was getting desperate. Life insurance salesman? He was scraping the bottom of the barrel.

A few months later, I was woken up by three policemen in the flat I'd been renting in Grevgatan, in the posh Östermalm part of town.

"What are you doing here?" they asked.

"What am I doing here?! What are you doing here?"

One of them threw me my clothes. "You have to leave immediately," another said.

"What are you talking about? I live here, I rent this place."

"No. You have broken in here," the detective said. "Nobody should be here, the owner is living abroad, and he has called us."

I always wondered why I had to put my hand through the broken glass in the front door to get in. "I lost the key," had been the explanation of Steve, my English friend I had met in Stockholm, who let me share the flat.

"We will arrest you if you are not gone by one hour," the policeman said.

I thought about it. My life in Stockholm wasn't going anywhere, and I was hanging out with a group – Hungarian Andy, American John and a few other English guys – who were basically ducking and diving. They were always up to all kinds of money-making ideas, none of them legal. These included selling hash to naïve young Swedes, except they never gave them any drugs and just disappeared with their money, sometimes thousands of krona. Or, under assumed names, they kept insuring suitcases full of clothes and valuables and claiming off the insurance when they lost them, which somehow they always managed to do.

That night, I was on the ferry from Gothenburg to Tilbury.

The next day, I was back home in East Acton.

In the morning, I borrowed ten pence from my mother and caught the tube to the West End for a job interview to be a life insurance salesman..

Postscript:

Five years later, 'Hungarian Andy' took a heroin overdose and choked to death on his own vomit. He was 26. 'American John', real name John Dowling, almost lost a leg a few years later when he was drunk and got hit by a car. He'd become an alcoholic and died just before he was 50 when he was stabbed to death in a drunken fight over a woman in Stockholm.

CHAPTER 4

How to jump into life
May 1969

On 6th May 1969, I turned up at the Oxford Circus office of a new insurance company called Abbey Life, for my interview to become a life insurance salesman.

Derek Barnard, the manager of the Central London branch, leapt up from behind his desk as I entered his huge office.

"Peter! Come in!" He was in his late forties, maybe five feet five inches tall in his Cuban heels and smartly dressed in dark blue Italian suit, white shirt and bright red tie. A silk handkerchief flowed out of his breast pocket. I noticed he was also wearing a black Beatles-style wig.

He flashed me a huge white smile. I had never seen anyone with such big white teeth before. "You can earn a £1,000 a week, starting today! How does that sound, Peter?"

As the average UK income was now about £20 a week, it definitely sounded okay to me.

"Look! Do you like this?" He picked up a large silver-framed photo of himself, standing next to a large white Rolls Royce. "Two years ago, I was a beach photographer in Brighton. Now, I live in a luxury flat in Belgravia and drive my own Rolls Royce. Not bad going, eh Peter?"

"Not bad going," I agreed.

"Derek... call me Derek. Please!" He looked me right in the eyes. "Tell me, Peter. I know we've only just met, but can I ask you a personal question?"

"Sure, Derek."

"What's your dream car, Peter?"

"An E-Type Jaguar, Derek."

"Right! Fantastic. The silver convertible. I can see you in it now, Peter. The biggest bird puller in existence!" He jumped up and down. "Well, Peter, six months from today you can be speeding down the King's Road with a blonde bird in a miniskirt next to you... and one in the back! What do you think of that?"

"That sounds great, Derek. What do I have to do to get it?"

"You just go out and tell your story to five people a day, Peter."

"Oh right, okay. But where do I find these five people, Derek? I've just got back from Sweden and am a bit out of touch, if you know what I mean."

"I'll show you! Come over here." He trotted over to the huge window overlooking Oxford Circus. He pointed down; there were hundreds of people queuing to get into the tube station, and hundreds more walking up and down. "Down there Peter! Down there!"

As he said this, he actually jumped in the air with enthusiasm; his wig rose an inch off his head and he caught it like he was heading a football as it came down.

"Talking to strangers. Think you can you do it, Peter? I think you can, but at the end of the day it comes down to whether you really want that E-Type badly enough, doesn't it?"

"Oh, I want it Derek," I said.

I got the job.

Later I realised that if you could mist a mirror, you got the job, but that afternoon I was fired up with enthusiasm, like I had caught it from Derek. I was ready to go.

He gave me a ten-page script – "Learn this word for word by tomorrow morning" – some application forms and a rate book.

And that was the training. It took about 60 seconds.

I borrowed a pound for a taxi from him, picked up my briefcase – a plastic carrier bag with Superman on it – and went down into the street.

"Taxi!" I shouted. A black cab stopped immediately. I jumped in.

The driver was a skinny guy in his twenties. "Where you going, guvnor?"

"I'm going wherever you're going," I said. "Just keep driving." I slid open the glass partition. "Can you save £20 a month for a good investment?"

Chapter 4

"Yes, no problem."

I opened my bag and got out my ten-page script. "Great! What's your name?"

"Ray."

"Hi, Ray, I'm Peter Rose and I'm a salesman with Abbey Life. Recently I've been showing a very exciting new investment plan to successful businessmen like yourself, they've found it very valuable and I am sure you will too. If you are accepted for this Planned Investment Endowment Plan, you will be able to invest in hundreds of the most successful UK companies without having to find tens of thousands of pounds of capital and, through the unique pound-cost-averaging system, create tax-free capital to enable you to do all the things you have always dreamed of. I am sure you agree this sounds like a valuable concept, Ray?"

"Yes it does, Peter," Ray said as we drove towards Marble Arch. "By the way, where exactly are you going?"

"Oh, just turn left down Park Lane. I'm not taking you out of your way, am I Ray?"

"No... You see, the way it works is, I go wherever you want me to go. That's what taxis do." He gave me a funny look in the mirror.

I carried on reading at probably twice the recommended speed, putting as much enthusiasm into my delivery as Olivier playing Hamlet at Stratford. If there was a speed limit for selling, I was breaking it. Ray didn't seem to notice I was actually reading every word.

"Ray, you wouldn't mind having a medical exam, would you, as we also build in absolutely free life insurance so that if anything happens to you, your family would get all the money you would have saved over the next 35 to 40 years."

"No, I wouldn't mind having a medical, Peter. Shall I go left into Hill Street?"

We drove round Mayfair for another 15 minutes until I got to the last page. We stopped outside the Red Lion pub off Berkeley Square. I handed him the application form through the partition. "If you'll just fill in your medical details and okay it where I've put the big cross at the bottom, we can apply for you to be accepted, Ray."

He filled it in and handed it back through the opening. "There you are, Peter."

"Congratulations on becoming my client, Ray. Now, all I need is your first month's investment of £20." He got out his money box and gave me two crumpled ten pound notes.

"How much do I owe you Ray?" I looked at the meter. It came to 17 shillings and sixpence; I gave him the one pound note in my pocket. "Keep the change, Ray."

"That's very kind of you," he said.

How to have so much life insurance you run out of beneficiaries
Across the breakfast table – 16th March 1982, Claridge's

I was waiting for David Dein to come in for breakfast. We'd met a year previously at the Comedy Store. He was a successful young commodity trader – sugar from Nigeria, or maybe sugar to Nigeria... anyway, he was definitely big in sugar. He is a charming, dynamic guy four or five years older than me and we get on great.

He had called me six months before. "Peter, you sell life insurance, don't you? Come round to the office. I want to buy a £1m policy."

As he had always told me a joke whenever we met and my biggest-ever policy at that time was for £100,000, I had said, "Very funny! So, what's new with you David?"

"No, really, Peter, I want a £1m life insurance policy. Do you want to sell me one?"

"Okay, David, a joke's a joke... So how's business?"

We went on like this a few more times, until he said, "Peter, I'll tell you what. If you are not round here in five minutes, I will call someone who wants my business."

Suddenly, something told me he was being serious. "I'll be right over," I said. I ran like an Olympic sprinter all the way from Claridge's, through Berkeley Square and down to his office in Pall Mall.

Five minutes later, I signed him up on the spot for a £1m policy. The biggest policy I had ever sold, and my first £1m sale. And I had almost talked my way out of it!

David arrived. "So tell me, David, what's new?" I asked as he drank his orange juice.

"Nothing much," he said. "I've just bought 15% of Arsenal and been invited to join the board."

"Okay, you're not serious are you? This is a joke right?" This was at a time when soccer hooliganism was at an all-time high, and England's football reputation at an all-time low. Most people thought that buying into a soccer club was akin to standing on a street corner and setting fire to twenty pound notes one after another.

"I'm really serious, Peter. I've been an Arsenal fan all my life," he said.

David Dein was the first person in my entire career who had ever asked me to sell him a policy!

That's the great thing about my life in 'life'; everybody needs it, but nobody wakes up and says, "I feel really great today! I think I'll go out and buy a life insurance policy!" The marketing genius of all time has to be the guy who, one day 400 years ago in a coffee house by Lloyds of London, thought of renaming death insurance... *life* insurance! Without him I would have spent the first 30 years of my career calling people and saying, "Hi, it's Peter Rosengard from Abbey Death...!"

People don't like to think about dying. It's a bit of a downer... Incredibly, it took me 38 years before, in the middle of a speech to 2,000 salesmen at a Zurich Openwork sales convention in Birmingham in 2008, I suddenly said, "I've just realised something I've never thought of before. I love life! And I sell life!... I love selling life!"

So life insurance has to be sold, and nothing can ever replace the face-to-face sale. It hasn't been invented yet... and it's definitely not the internet! I could sit at a desk anywhere in the world and wait for people to knock on the door, and not only would I be waiting forever... I'd also starve to death.

Over the 30 years since we first met, I sold David 29 different policies. When he goes, the Zurich Insurance Company goes!

When he saw me with a client at breakfast one morning, he came over to my table and said to my guest, "Excuse me, my name's David Dein, you don't know me but Peter's the greatest salesman in the world... I know this, as he's sold me 29 different policies. In fact, I've got so much life insurance I've run out of beneficiaries! So if you'd like to be a beneficiary of mine, here's my card... just write to me and I'll mention you in my will!"

Postscript:

David Dein was vice-chairman of Arsenal for 25 years and helped to transform it into one of the world's greatest football clubs, bringing Arsène Wenger in as manager and signing Thierry Henry and many other star players. More recently he headed the international effort to bring the World Cup to England in 2018.

According to press reports at the time, he had paid £220,000 for his stake in Arsenal.

In August 2007, he sold his remaining shares in the club for £75m.

How to act enthusiastic and become enthusiastic!
May 1969, John Lewis buyers' office, Oxford Street, London

I was just entering the grand finale of my sales presentation.

"Mike, so to summarise... This policy is so fantastic!... so great!... so important!... that you and your family's dreams will always be protected throughout all the years your children are growing up. Their future will never be threatened because of this great decision you are making today. It's incredible isn't it!?"

I got so excited, I punched the wall... and my fist went straight through it and got stuck!

"Excuse me, I am really sorry! Can you give me a hand?" I said, wanting to crawl into the hole I just made.

He got up from behind his desk and helped me pull my arm out of his wall.

"Don't worry, it's all right, we needed redecorating soon anyway," he said.

He then still went ahead and bought the policy. I couldn't believe it.

"It's because you are the most enthusiastic salesman I have ever met! It has to be good!" he said.

2am, July 1969, the Revolution Club, Mayfair, London

"Bo, listen man! It's just a dinner once a month!" I said. "You won't miss it."

I slid the application form under the Gents' toilet door and pushed a pen after it. "Just sign it where I've put the cross, man!"

I took a long pull on the joint. The form reappeared under the door. He had signed it.

"Glad to have you as my client, man!" I said.

"I don't believe I've just bought a life insurance policy in the Gents' at the Revolution," Bo said.

"You have definitely made the right decision, man." I stood, poking at my hair in the mirror. "Congratulations. See you upstairs."

I headed back to my friends. Wilson Pickett was in town and coming on at any moment, and the place was packed. I waved at Eric Burdon, lead singer with the Animals, who was sitting nearby with Hendrix's manager, Chas Chandler. Chris Farlowe was at another table and Keith Moon and John Entwistle were with a group of girls in a corner.

Everybody seemed to be in the club tonight to catch his act. Many had seen him when he'd got up on stage a few months before at the Scotch and sung 'In the Midnight Hour'.

August 1969, Kensington Market

I put my foot down in the silver E-Type and zoomed past the Albert Hall, shot straight across the amber traffic lights at Queen's Gate and stopped on a double yellow line outside Kensington Market. Life's too short to drive round looking for a parking space. I had my own personal parking attendant, anyway; she dropped by the flat once a month for a cup of tea and a joint. I would end up paying about one in 20 tickets.

I was in my usual life insurance salesman's uniform of knee-high snake-skin boots with four-inch Cuban heels, dark green velvet jacket and tight blue jeans. For years I thought I was six feet two.

I picked up my briefcase; still the carrier bag with the Superman emblem. I ran up the stairs to the first floor. The place was full of stalls and little shops, selling the hippest clothes in London. I stopped outside Cockell and Johnson, the hottest boutique in town.

"Peter! Act enthusiastic and you'll become enthusiastic!" I shouted, punching my fist hard into the palm of my hand. "BE BIG!" I punched my hand again. A tall Swedish-looking blonde in a tiny miniskirt gave me a weird look.

I went into the shop. I recognised the skinny guy in red velvet flares, with shoulder-length blonde hair. He was sitting in a gold throne-like chair. It was Lloyd Johnson, one of the two owners.

"Hi, Lloyd man," I said, sticking out my hand. "I am Peter Rose, and I'm a life insurance salesman with Abbey Life." He now had a strange kind of appalled look on his face. He didn't say anything.

"Listen man, I've recently been showing our new Planned Investment Endowment Plan to a lot of other successful boutique owners like yourself along the King's Road; it's been very valuable to them and I think it could be for you too. In fact, I'm pretty sure I can get you accepted on it... and you only need to put in £25 a month to start. That wouldn't cause you any problem? It's just a dinner once a month, isn't it?"

He still didn't say anything. I took this as a "yes".

I pulled up a chair, sat down opposite him and opened my plastic bag.

Twenty minutes later, I was back in the car, with a signed application form for a £50-a-month policy in my pocket.

How to say 'No!'
Across the breakfast table – 20th December 1980, Claridge's

I had just managed *not* to sell a policy to a potential new client. It felt pretty good, too.

This was a first for me. He was a young stockbroker at Cazenove and probably the single most arrogant person I had ever met. An Old Etonian and ex-Army officer – Blues and Royals – he had looked at me over his porridge as if I was a lesser species. But for some unfathomable reason, he had seemed intent on buying a policy from me.

I usually found Etonians totally charming and I had developed quite a niche market, selling insurance to them in the City.

I had got as far as the question on the application form, 'Do you drink alcohol?'

"Yes, three or four glasses of wine a week, I suppose," he replied.

"Oh, I am terribly sorry, Johnny."

"Sorry about what!?"

"They are very strict these days and that's just over the limit for us, I'm afraid."

I picked up the form and tore it in half, then in quarters. I threw the pieces up into the air. They landed all over the table. Some pieces went into his empty porridge bowl.

"What are you doing!?" he said.

"Maybe if you can cut down in the future, we could consider you again, who knows? I'm sorry but I have another appointment now." I rose from the table.

I had always wanted to do that.

How taking LSD before entering a casino is a really bad idea
5am, 15th March 1970, London

I was flying along the Western Avenue, heading west out of London, in the dark green Rolls Royce Silver Cloud I'd bought a few months before. The Beatles and Stones had all recently bought Rolls Royces, so naturally as a life insurance salesman I'd had to have one too.

At East Acton, I passed the corner with Old Oak Road, where I lived. I looked at the speedometer; I was doing 70mph. The Doors were blasting out of the cassette player speakers.

"I am the Lizard King. I can do anything!" Jim Morrison was chanting.

"I am a king, I can do anything!" I shouted back at the top of my voice as we shot along.

I closed my eyes and took my hands off the wheel.

I may have thought I was a rock star in the life insurance business, but it probably hadn't been the greatest idea in the world to drop a tab of acid before going into Charlie Chester's in Archer Street earlier that night.

I had no idea who I'd given chips to, but I don't think I knew any of them. Word had spread quickly around the tables that I was in a generous mood. Gamblers appeared at my side every few minutes; "Hey, can you lend me some chips?"

"Sure man, how many do you want?" I would reply, dropping a few red and yellow £50 chips into their hands.

After ten hours, I was the last gambler left in the place. And when the casino closed, I had lost every penny I had... over £1,000.

Left - 1949 East Acton: Mum and Dad and brother Stuart. I am on the tricycle. I won the 1947 East Acton Bouncing Baby Competition: 35 years later I discovered my father had been one of the judges.

Top left - December 1952: me aged 6.

Top centre - Summer 1960: In the back garden East Acton - modelling my first hairstyle: it was a present from my uncle Ernie.

Top right - 1969: I'm posing with a postbox off the King's Road, Chelsea.

Below left - May 1975 London: Author giving speech to life insurance salesmen.

Below right - 25th October 1976: *Left*, Abbey Life agency director David King, me and *right*, Robert Sheridan. I'd just sold 100 policies in a month.

Top left - 1971:
Selling life insurance
on the King's Road.
I'm the bearded
bloke on the *right*.

Above - 19th May
1979: Opening night of
the Comedy Store, Soho.
Brother Stuart is front
row, 3rd from *right*.

Top right - 1980:
Ben Elton on stage
at Comedy Store. I
made him the compere
after Alexei Sayle tried
to strangle me.

Right (2nd from top) -
Summer 1981 London,
West End: Robin Williams
at 4am after the Berkeley
Square Ball.

Right centre - 1980:
Arnold Brown on stage
at Comedy Store.

Right (below centre) - 1979
London: Rik Mayall performing his poem "Vanessa!
Vanessa!..you made...a
messa...my life... Vanessa."

Right - 1980: Rik Mayall at
my flat, South Kensington.

CHAPTER 5

How kidnapping the one you love is not a good idea
August 1970, Cornwall

I now realise that trying to show a girl how much you love her by kidnapping her is probably not a good idea. (Make that, *definitely* not a good idea.)

I had met Solveig in Stockholm in December 1968, when I was a DJ there. I had got the job by accident as I'd just been fired as a dish washer and in Swedish, they sound the same; diska... disk-jockey. Anyway, being an English DJ in Sweden in the late 1960s was like being in heaven. Every girl you saw could have been Miss World, but very importantly they didn't seem to know it. I was like the kid who's let loose in a sweet shop and it relaxed me about beautiful women for the rest of my life. When I came back to London to start my new life as a life insurance salesman, as we'd been going out together for over four months and I liked her a lot, I'd asked Solveig to come with me.

Unfortunately, almost as soon as I got back to London I also began my career as a compulsive-gambling, grass-smoking lunatic, and after a few months she walked out on me.

I couldn't understand why.

"So you have tried everything to get her back?" my American friend Johnny asked me one night, as he passed me a joint.

"Yes, everything," I said.

"Well Pete, you've just got to kidnap her then, haven't you?" he said, exhaling.

"Kidnap her!? Are you crazy!?"

Chapter 5

"Look man, you just rent a cottage some place in the countryside for a weekend, give her a lift to work and instead, drive there and woo her all over again. You know, buddy, turn on the famous old Rose charm... remember, you are a king, you can do anything."

"Isn't that a line from the Doors album?" I said.

The next day, I rented a cottage in Cornwall and that evening, went over in the Rolls to the flat in Charlotte Street where Solveig was living. I waited until she came out to go to work. She had got a job at the Valbonne discotheque in Kingly Street, a quarter of a mile away.

"Hi. Do you want a lift?" I asked. She got in.

I picked up Johnny round the corner, and she sat on the big leather bench seat in the front between us.

I drove through town. "Where are we going?" she said. "That's not the way to the club."

"Look relax, it's okay," I said. "I just want the chance to talk to you quietly somewhere. So I've rented a place in the country for the weekend, so we can talk. Just you and me."

She went nuts. She started shouting: "Let me out! Stop the car now!"

I just kept driving, and she stopped shouting.

Soon I was running low on petrol; I hadn't planned things very well. I stopped at a garage outside Guildford. As I went to pay, Solveig jumped out of my side and ran away across the dual carriageway. I raced back to the car and drove after her; but to do so, I had to bump it over the central reservation and nearly broke the car in half. So I got out, ran after her and by the time I caught her up, she was talking to a middle-aged couple sitting in two folding chairs, eating their sandwiches and drinking tea out of a thermos on a verge by the side of the road.

"It's okay, she's my girlfriend. We have just had a row," I said to the man.

"It's not true, we have finished... I don't want to be with him!" she cried.

"We mustn't get involved dear, it's nothing to do with us," the man said to his wife.

"I don't know, she does look very upset, doesn't she?"

I took Solveig's arm and led her back towards the car.

"Look, please calm down. You know I would never hurt you or make you do anything. Just give me a chance to show you I've changed, that I really love you, that's all. Is that so much to ask, after all we've been through together?"

She just looked at me, said nothing and got in the back of the car.

I felt she was now going to give me a final chance.

That night I drove into a field near Exmoor and we all fell asleep in the car.

We were woken by an angry farmer, wanting to know what I was doing in the middle of his land.

A few hours later, we were just outside Penzance and almost at the cottage, when I saw in my rear-view mirror a little Noddy car coming up behind me, blue light flashing. He pulled in front of me and I stopped behind him. The policeman walked up and leaned into the back where Solveig was sitting.

"We had a report of a young woman in distress yesterday near Guildford. That wouldn't be you young lady by any chance, would it? Do you want to be with these gentlemen?"

"No, I don't," she said.

He opened the back door and helped her out. "Follow me please, sir."

I had never been in a police station before, let alone locked up in a cell. Johnny was in a cell next door. After four hours they let me out and I was bailed to appear, on suspicion of kidnapping, at Albany Street police station in London in a month's time.

"They will decide whether to charge you or not by then," the desk sergeant told me.

After a very anxious month of waiting, and having had to tell my parents, I was told I wasn't going to be charged.

"We know you didn't intend to harm her, but it's not the way to go about it, is it Peter? We're letting it drop this time, but if you kidnap anyone again we will throw the book at you," the inspector said.

I faithfully promised my kidnapping days were over.

As I was about to leave, he said, "Just remember this Peter, you might think you can persuade a lot of people to do lots of things, but you can't make someone love you."

I have kept my promise: I have never kidnapped anyone again.

Chapter 5

Postscript:

Two years later, I was in Stockholm and Solveig called me. We spent a very enjoyable evening together and left as friends.

How to talk to strangers (2)
21st July 1969, Mount Street, London

Doug Hayward had just called to say, could I come in for my fitting for the two dark blue suits he was making for me? (Since 1969, I have only ever worn identical dark blue suits; it saves so much time in the morning! I don't have to think, 'shall I wear the grey one or the brown one?')

I'd left the flat at No. 125, jumped in the silver E-Type and drove at speed the entire 100 yards along Mount Street to his shop at No. 95, pulling up with a screech of brakes.

As I opened the door, I bumped straight into a distinguished-looking man in his mid-sixties coming out backwards, a large surgical collar round his neck.

"Oh I'm so sorry!" I said.

"No dear boy, it was entirely my fault. For it was I who was coming out backwards. I was gladly glued to the television set! A man has just landed on the moon!" He turned his whole body round to face me and looked me in the eye. "Can any of us mere earthlings truly conceive of this monumental voyage into the vast unknown? Isn't it remarkable? You, I and Doug and countless billions around the world are, at this very moment, on this very day, witnessing history being made... and not just our suits. Goodbye, young man!"

He walked briskly but stiffly off down the street towards Berkeley Square.

Doug, as always sitting in the large wing-backed brown leather armchair, was intently watching a small black and white TV on the table in front of him. "Who was that Doug? His voice sounded a bit familiar."

"Peter, you just got the news of the moon landing from the greatest actor in the world. That was Larry... Sir Laurence Olivier."

Over the following years until his early death at 73 in 2008 (he never looked more than 48), I would almost never pass the shop without dropping in to see Doug, who was always sitting in that chair. It was Doug's club and on the right days you'd meet every big star in the world there: Kirk Douglas, Sir John Gielgud, Terry Stamp, Clint Eastwood, everybody who was anybody. Doug made their suits and they invariably became his friends as well. His best mates were Roger Moore, Michael Caine, Michael Parkinson and Terry O'Neil.

He had more good friends than anyone I've ever met. I wasn't ever a close mate but I liked him and I think he liked me. He was a handsome working-class boy from West Kensington, a well-built six feet four inches, with a dry sense of humour and great charm combined with a natural intelligence and curiosity. Never a loudmouth or show-off, he had humility and that gift, as in Kipling's 'If...', of being able to walk with kings and paupers, and treat them just the same.

Lots of people loved Doug, especially women. I first met him in May 1969, when I walked in the shop as a 22-year-old stranger, having just joined Abbey Life, and he not only got me somewhere to live, the Mount Street flat, but also made me a member of Tramps, the most exclusive of the 'in' clubs of the 1970s and where I was to spend almost every night for the next ten years. I developed this very sophisticated chat-up line; "Would you like to come to Tramps with me?" and that was it! Thank you, Doug!

Whenever I came through the door, he would start singing: "There's no one with endurance like the man who sells insurance..." Believe it or not, it had been a hit song in the 1930s!

How to get to Stockholm in a Rolls on a fiver
September 1970

One day, I decided I'd take my brother Stuart to Stockholm for a week's holiday.

He'd just turned 21 and was trying to earn a living as an actor. He'd also gone to Latymer but left school before his GCSEs and gone to Ada Foster's stage school. He wasn't getting any acting work and seemed to have inherited the Rosengard gene, spending any money he got hold of in betting shops and getting into a lot of drugs.

He'd been living in a commune squat in Bristol Gardens in Maida Vale and I thought this trip would be good for him. He'd never been to Sweden before and when I told him how beautiful and friendly the girls were, instantly he said he'd come along.

Chapter 5

The idea was we'd drive there in the Rolls. I'd never seen one in Stockholm. I bought tickets for the overnight boat from Tilbury to Gothenburg. From there it was a straight road, all the way to Stockholm.

I'd done the same trip in January in the E-Type, when there was snow all the way. I'd skidded at 120mph and the car spun 360 degrees; luckily it was 3am and the road was deserted. I'd miraculously ended up unhurt in very deep snow, missing the canyon walls on either side of the road; I had to be dug out by a passing lorry driver. Amazingly, the car also was undamaged and I drove at 50mph the rest of the way. I was still trembling when I got to Stockholm three hours later.

The night before we were due to leave, I thought I'd go to Charlie Chester's and double up the money I had for the journey, but by 4am, I'd lost the lot playing blackjack tables.

How were we going to get to Stockholm now? I'd lost everything I had – except, I remembered, £25 back at the flat. But that wouldn't last a day in Stockholm.

The next morning, I went to see Stuart.

"Sorry Stu, got a bit of bad news..." I told him what had happened.

"What? You lost the lot... everything!? How much!?"

"£350... £400. I was up a lot at one point as well! I'm sorry, mate."

"How much have you got left?"

"Nothing! Well, £25. Why?"

"Well, there's a horse running in the 2.30 today at Kempton. And it's a cert... at 10-1."

"How do you know it's a cert?" I'd never bet on the horses.

"Trust me... I got a tip. Okay?"

I went with him to a betting shop on the Edgware Road. I handed over five fivers.

To my amazement, our horse won! We ended up winning £300... we could still go to Stockholm!

Now, this is the incredible bit. I went straight back to Charlie Chester's and lost every penny all over again.

We were due on the ferry that night. Stu already had all his stuff at my place. But this time we were really screwed!

Then I had a brainwave. I remembered the week before I'd received a Diners Club card in the post. I don't know why I had it, but it was obviously the answer to our problem.

I found the credit card amongst dozens of mostly unopened letters I'd just left piled up on the kitchen table. I grabbed my passport, threw some clothes in a bag and we set off. Stuart had a fiver. "That's enough to get us to Stockholm," I said. "Once we're there we'll just pay for everything with the Diners card!"

"See you in a few days, Tommy!" I shouted to my Geordie butler/housekeeper/bass guitarist as we left. I'd met Tommy, who had hair halfway down his back and a great sense of humour, and his girlfriend Angie a few months before in a club and they were looking for a place to stay. So they'd moved in to look after the huge flat... and me.

We put our bags in the boot of the Rolls and set off.

"I'd better fill up with petrol first," I said, stopping at the Blue Star garage on the corner of Gloucester Place.

"Fill it up please... to the very top," I said to the pump attendant.

A few minutes later, he came round to my window to get paid. He dropped the Diners Club card as I handed it to him and bent down to pick it up.

"That's strange," he said. "It's not on the ground."

"It has to be there! You just dropped it!" I climbed out, got on my hands and knees and looked under the car. It wasn't there.

I looked inside the car. It hadn't fallen inside either. I suddenly realised where it had to be. It must have fallen down the side of the window and was now stuck somewhere in the door! A million to one chance.

We looked at the huge, heavy Rolls door with walnut panel finishing. There was no other option – we had to take it apart. All our holiday was in the card wedged somewhere inside.

"Have you got a mechanic here?" I asked him.

"Nobody's around today. And a Rolls door is a very complicated bit of work, you've got all the electrics in there mate... you'll need a Rolls specialist to do that."

I looked at my watch; we had two hours before the boat left Tilbury. We had to get going.

"Okay, we'll just have to get the door taken apart in Stockholm! There's got to be one Rolls Royce dealer there." I've always been a bit of an optimist.

Chapter 5

We drove down to Tilbury and loaded the Rolls aboard the ferry. We had enough cash left for a drink each and a couple of cheese rolls and then went to our cabin.

The next morning we woke up in Gothenburg.

We headed in the direction of Stockholm. We finally got there five hours later with just a few drops of petrol left and somehow I managed to find the only Rolls Royce distributor in the city. After two hours the car was up on a ramp, the door stripped down but still no sign of the card.

"It'll definitely be there!" I said to the mechanic.

"Okay, if you say so... you try and find it," he said, handing me a torch.

I slid under the Rolls and put my hand up inside what was left of the driver's door. I felt around blindly for a few minutes – nothing – and was about to give up when I felt something.

"I've got it!" I shouted, pulling a piece of plastic wedged in the bottom corner of the frame.

I jumped to my feet and triumphantly held up one very greasy Diners Club card.

"Okay! Now, we're in business! Let's rock 'n' roll big brother!" Stuart said.

One crazy week later, as we headed back to London, I added up in my head that we'd managed to spend over £5,000!

I'd immediately discovered that the only places that took Diners in Stockholm were the most expensive hotels and restaurants. We had to take a two-bedroom suite at the Grand Hotel. Everyone assumed because I had a Rolls, I must be an English rock star, and I didn't like to disillusion them... especially the girls we met. After all, it would have been silly not to live up to it.

It didn't bother me at the time as I didn't have any money to pay the Diners bill anyway. It just went in the pile with all my other unpaid bills and debts.

How to stop gambling
November 1970 – 21st March 1971

If I only dropped into four or five clubs, it was a quiet night. The West End had dozens of discotheques at this time. In the early 1960s, Louis Brown had opened one of the very first, Le Kilt, in a Greek Street basement. Now, he was chauffeured round in a black Rolls Phantom and had over a dozen clubs, including Samantha's in New Burlington Street, which famously featured a white E-Type Jaguar in which the DJ sat and played the records.

I'd usually get home, often with a new girl I'd just met, around 4am. This was the time when I forgot to go to work every day, selling life insurance... for a whole year. Which is probably why I had ended up heavily in debt and with the Rolls repossessed.

Samantha's was, as usual, full of pretty girls and the dance floor crowded as I walked to the bar. I saw a beautiful blonde girl sitting with another girl. I gave her a big smile and walked over. "Hi! I'm Peter Rosengard!"

Her name was Irmeli, but she said everyone called her Irkku. She was Finnish, from Helsinki. Her English was excellent, and she was bright and funny. She'd been in London a few months and was working in a hospital in North London. She was 20 years old, petite and had a very special smile. I immediately asked her for her number.

Irkku moved in with me after a few weeks, leaving her job. The lease was up at Hanover Gate Mansions and I found a new flat in Mount Street, across the road from the Connaught. I rented it from Jill Bennett, the actress; Doug had introduced us one day, in his shop down the street. She was married at the time to John Osborne, the original 'angry young man' playwright who, by the time I met him with her one afternoon, was an angry and overweight middle-aged man.

I was gambling every night, and losing heavily. I couldn't stop when I was winning and I couldn't stop when I was losing. I'd gone to Gamblers Anonymous when I was 18, after 'borrowing' money from my grandfather's wallet, and stopped completely for a few years. But I'd stopped going to the GA meetings and soon started gambling again. Sometimes I didn't gamble for a few months, only to fall back into it; either because I was celebrating something, or had been upset by something. Any excuse was good enough. I just got the feeling I had to gamble, and I'd head off to Charlie Chester's, where I'd first gone when I was still at school.

Christmas Day had been particularly bad. I'd promised Irkku we'd have a real Christmas lunch somewhere great, but told her I just had to stop off and give some money I owed to a guy... at Chester's. I promised her I'd be five minutes. She was to sit outside in the car.

After an hour, I was sitting at the blackjack table when she stormed in, screamed, "You're a fucking bastard, Peter! I've had enough, it's Christmas Day!" and stormed out again.

I felt terrible... but only because I'd been found out. Did I think she'd sit quietly in the car for two or three hours and not guess I was gambling? I shrugged and said, "Sorry about that," to the other people at the table.

I finished playing my hand and, drawing a king on 14, promptly went bust.

I ran out after her and caught up with her just before Shaftesbury Avenue. She was running, but it wasn't easy in 6-inch platform-soled shoes, very trendy at the time. When I grabbed her arm, she kicked out at me but missed, her shoe flying off, up in the air and landing on the roof of a boutique. It would have been hilarious any other time. I eventually calmed her down by swearing I'd never gamble again.

She had to walk back to the car with the one foot still wearing the shoe in the road, and the other on the pavement to keep balanced.

By early January, I was gambling again.

One morning in March, I left the flat as soon as the banks were due to open and went to Oxford Street.

I had now got hold of a cheque card which allowed me to take £30 from any bank. It's hard to believe, but in 1971 there were over 150 bank branches along and just off Oxford Street.

So that morning, by running between them, I managed to get to more than 100 of them by 2pm, when Chester's opened. At each cash machine I took out £30. I had 100 bundles of £30 each; £3,000 was a lot of money in 1971.

I went to the casino toilet and took the paper wrappers off the brand new notes. Then I went into the club, sat down at the blackjack table... and lost it all.

I did this every day for four days. And lost £12,000. I was now in big trouble, as I'd only had £10 in the bank when I started on the Monday morning. I felt exhausted and full of self-loathing. I'd known for years I was a compulsive gambler. I was just like Dad. If I didn't stop now, I knew

I was going to end up in the gutter, in prison or in the river.

I had a choice: somehow borrow more money and try and win it all back, or go and see the bank manager and tell him the truth.

I finally knew I could never win. I decided to go to the bank.

I'd only had the account at the National Westminster branch in Sloane Square a few weeks and the manager wouldn't know me. He would either call the police or give me one last chance.

The manager, Mr Trim, was an ex-army major with a bristly moustache, and I could see he lived up to his name. I sat down opposite him in a big leather armchair and, taking a deep breath, I started talking. After an hour, during which he said not one word, I'd told him my whole life story; about my father, Gamblers Anonymous, my own compulsive gambling and finally about the events of the last four days.

He would be receiving cheques for over £12,000, but I only had £10 in my account. I told him I knew he could call the police, and my life would be ruined; I'd have no job, and would probably go to prison. But if he could possibly let me have one last chance, I would promise to go back to GA and stop gambling permanently, and I'd work hard and pay back every penny, no matter how long it took.

After I finished, he sat there looking at me, saying nothing. He put his hand in his suit pocket and, pulling out his tobacco pouch, filled and lit his pipe and puffed on it steadily.

He finally said, "Peter, I am going to give you one last chance. I don't know why, but I am. Don't let me down, will you?"

I felt at that moment as if I'd won the pools. I felt far happier than I'd ever felt at the tables... even when I'd got a 21 at blackjack, or my number had come up on roulette.

I promised I wouldn't let him down.

That was 21st March 1971.

It wasn't difficult not to gamble, as I had no money: not that this had ever stopped me before from borrowing it or coming up with schemes to get hold of it. But actually I was now so 'sick of being sick', in the GA mantra, that the last thing I wanted to do was gamble. But I also knew this feeling wouldn't last forever, and sooner or later it would come back: the feeling that just one huge win would solve all my problems – to hell with years of repaying everybody, when I could do it in one spin of the wheel!

Dad was very supportive, and for the first time it was great to have a father who was a compulsive gambler! He had done everything I'd done and understood what I was going through, as I struggled to get back on my feet. He was powerful motivation for me to see that I really could stop destroying my life. Every day since he'd stopped gambling he wore a fresh red carnation in his buttonhole, to celebrate! "Since I stopped gambling, every day is a birthday now! A winning post! And every night's a honeymoon!" he would tell his fellow GA members. "I'm Lady Luck's lost lover!"

The fridge at home was always full of milk bottles with carnations in them.

I now had a choice. And I chose not to gamble. I was on the 'up' escalator. Before, it had only gone in one direction... down. As a friend said to me, "Peter, you parachuted out before the plane crashed!"

I had to start my life again. Gambling had given me the greatest excitement I'd ever known. I loved the atmosphere of the casino, mixing with low-lifes and millionaires, with gangsters and greengrocers. It was my drug. But the difference now was I really knew it would kill me. I thought of the terrible pain I would cause my family. I could understand it when GA members talked about other members who'd killed themselves after going back to gambling, and about others who, after years without a bet, had fallen off the wagon and gone back to the dog track, the horses or the casinos... and it was as if they'd never been away.

Once you're a compulsive gambler, I learned, you can never gamble normally. The only way to full recovery is to stop one day at a time, forever. But the idea of never gambling again, especially when you're young, is pretty hard to conceive and that's where the brilliance of the 'Just For Today' programme came in. Adapted from AA, it was the same 12-step programme, only that the word 'alcohol' was substituted by 'gambling'.

Irkku had also given me another last chance. I went back to weekly GA meetings, where the understanding and compassion shown to me by my fellow members was a great strength as I started my new life.

But first, I needed to hold off my creditors... there were lots of them, apart from Mr Trim at the National Westminster. Bernard Phillips, a senior partner of a firm of West End accountants, was definitely more used to dealing with company liquidations than 24-year-old compulsive gamblers, but he soon put forward a plan on my behalf, whereby he'd receive all my income from Abbey Life and guarantee to pay all my creditors a proportionally small amount every month. The programme would last five years and by the end of it everyone, including the bank, would be repaid in full.

To my great relief, a fortnight later all of my 20 or so creditors, including Diners Club and several other banks apart from National Westminster, agreed. Every month Bernard sent me enough money to live a reasonable life on, pay the rent and eat, and so on, and the rest went to the creditors.

In all, I owed a total of just over £20,000 – an awful lot of money in those days.

Five years later, I had not gambled once and had paid everyone back.

How to get run over by a one-eyed driver
28th August 1972, London

I decided it was about time I learnt how to ride a motorbike, and so I went out and bought one; a second-hand gold Honda 250cc. I was sure it couldn't be difficult; after all, I knew how to ride a bicycle, so I felt pretty confident. "Just remember, keep looking ahead. That's all you need to know," the salesman advised me.

The next morning, I got on it to ride over to the office in Oxford Circus. I was doing rather well, I thought, and I'd got as far as the Connaught, 50 yards from the flat, when a red Mini came at terrific speed from behind me, round the bend of Carlos Place and crashed straight into me, sending me flying. He didn't stop, and left me lying in the road. When I tried to stand I felt a sharp pain in my shoulder.

"Don't worry, sir. Looks like it's just a broken collar bone," the commissionaire said as he and a porter carried me into the lobby. I'd always wanted to go to the Connaught, but I hadn't planned on being carried in.

As I lay there waiting for the ambulance, the hotel clients carried on as normal, going for breakfast or reading their papers in the lounge. Either I was invisible or it was the most natural thing in the world for a man in a motorbike helmet to be lying in the hall. "I'd like to check out, please," an elderly American said, stepping over me to get to the cashier.

Chapter 5

After getting my arm put in a sling, I decided that I couldn't go back to work until I felt 100% better and pain free. So I stayed at home for a month and watched the Munich Olympics. I was watching on 5th September as the Palestinian Black September terrorists attacked the Israeli athletes' quarters, followed by the hostage-taking and ending with the murder of the 11 Israeli athletes and the deaths of the terrorists at the airport.

Incredibly, the games went on as if nothing serious had happened. Mark Spitz, the Jewish American swimmer, won seven gold medals in the Olympic pool, more than anyone had won in any games before, and I was so proud that he was Jewish. But the innocence of the Olympics was destroyed forever.

The attack had a huge effect on me. They were killing Jews again, purely because they were Jews... and it had happened in Germany.

A week later, I decided to change my name from Rose to Rosengard, my father's family name.

He'd been born Jack Rosengard in 1915, the third of eight children of Rebecca and Harry Rosengard. In the 1930s the whole family changed their names to Rose – except the youngest, Ernest, who kept the Rosengard name. My parents are Jack and Sally Rose.

When I was growing up, the only word I'd ever had a problem pronouncing was my own name! "Rhodes?" people would say. "Ross?"

When I told my parents, they couldn't understand why I would want to be Rosengard. But I thought it was a great name, a beautiful name – it means 'garden of roses' in German – and so I have been Peter Rosengard ever since. When I tell people I was born Peter Rose and changed it to Rosengard, they always ask, "Why did you do that?"

"I wanted to sound more Jewish," I always reply.

A couple of months after the hit-and-run incident, I had to go to court. A witness had jotted down the Mini's number plate and the driver had been prosecuted for dangerous driving and failing to stop after an accident.

When I gave evidence, I looked over at the driver in the dock, a well-dressed man in his thirties, and was amazed to see he had an eye patch over one eye.

I'd been knocked off my bike and nearly killed by a one-eyed driver!

But amazingly, nobody mentioned it during the whole case; not the magistrate, or the prosecution counsel. Nobody thought to suggest that just maybe he shouldn't even have been driving in the first place because clearly he could only see out of one eye.

He got disqualified for six months and fined £100.

Not deterred, one month later I passed my bike test and went straight out and bought a huge 750cc Suzuki. The first time I went on it I took Irkku on the back; we got about 200 yards down the Finchley Road from the flat and fell off as we went round the Lords roundabout. We were both okay. "Sorry darling, there must have been some invisible grease on the road," I said.

That was the first and last time she ever came on the bike. It was stolen soon afterwards and this time I thought someone was trying to tell me something.

I stopped riding motorbikes.

How to 'Keep Strong!'
1973, Istanbul, Turkey

The guy must have done 50 lengths of the pool in an effortless crawl.

I was exhausted just lying there watching him; even in the shade under my umbrella, it must have been 95 degrees. Behind him, the turquoise-blue Bosphorus glistened. He was a Burt Lancaster lookalike, a big, tanned guy with muscles everywhere. He finally got out of the pool and started towelling himself down. It was like Charles Atlas was right there in front of me. I couldn't wait for somebody to try and kick sand in this guy's face.

He looked over towards us. "Hi, how you guys doing?" he said in an American accent.

I was sitting there by the side of the Hilton pool, with Irkku, my friend Robert and Ulla Britt, his latest Swedish au pair who he'd brought to Istanbul for the Abbey Life sales convention.

I stood up. "I'm doing very well thank you, how do you do?" I said.

He stuck out a huge hairy hand; it nearly crushed mine. "I'm Brad, but most people call me Big Brad. Or BB for short."

"Hello, Big Brad. So, what are you doing here Big Brad? By the way, let me introduce myself. I'm Peter Rosengard. I'm a life insurance salesman from London."

"Great to meet you. Well, Peter, you see that tanker out there in the harbour?" He pointed towards a huge ship lying half a mile off shore. "Every morning this week I have been driving an E-Type Jaguar straight off its deck at 100mph, into the sea."

"Why do you do that Brad?"

"I'm a stuntman, Peter, and we're filming the new Bond movie here." He finished drying himself off. "Well, got to be going. Good to meet you, Peter."

"Goodbye Big Brad," I said.

He turned round. "Keep strong, Peter!" he said.

And I have been telling people to 'Keep strong!' ever since that day. I never sign off a letter or email 'yours faithfully' or 'yours sincerely', and never hang up a phone either, without saying, "Keep strong!"

"It's a good life, if you don't weaken," Graphic Seth wrote. Every day's a battle. You have got to keep strong!

How to make the Million Dollar Round Table
June 1973, Seattle, USA

I was on my first trip to America, for a meeting of the Million Dollar Round Table.

I'd heard about this legendary life insurance salesmen's convention from a couple of the salesmen at Abbey Life, who'd been attending them for a few years. They came back raving about the new sales ideas they'd picked up and the great salesmen they'd met. They told me it was the most motivational and inspirational thing I could possibly do. So I decided I had to qualify and attend the next meeting.

The idea was this: 5,000 of the top life insurance salesmen from all over the world met for a week in June every year, usually in a different city in America.

To qualify, you originally had to sell $1m of life insurance. This was an enormous figure in 1927 when a group of American salesmen had first thought of the idea of forming a 'club' where they could share the ideas and sales techniques that had been successful for them. Over the years, it had grown into a huge annual convention and the minimum qualification was now $5m of life insurance. You had to pay all your own membership fees and travel expenses; your company was not allowed to fund your attendance.

The 1973 meeting was being held in Seattle and I qualified easily on my 1972 sales. I sent off the application forms and a few weeks later got a letter saying I'd been accepted as a provisional member, and inviting me to attend the meeting in June. As it was my first time in America, I decided to go to Los Angeles for a few days before flying to Seattle and, on the way back home, to spend a week in New York.

I didn't know anyone in LA, or anywhere else in America apart from one extremely distant relative, a Great-Uncle Sydney, who must have been at least 95 years old and lived in Brooklyn. I rang MDRT headquarters in Chicago, to see if they had a member living in LA who might like to show me round the city. "I'm 24 so it would be great if he was a young, single guy as well," I told the woman at the other end of the line.

She called back. "We have a member called Frank Nathan who lives in Beverly Hills. I've just spoken with him and he'd be delighted to show you around when you arrive."

Two weeks later, I was sitting in the huge lobby of the Beverly Hills Hilton. It was crowded with incredibly tall, good-looking people with tans, any one of whom could have stepped off the set of *Gunsmoke* or my 1960s favourite TV show *Rawhide*. But I hadn't spotted anyone in his twenties who might be my host Frank when I noticed a distinguished silver-haired handsome man in his early seventies who had just come in; he paused and looked round the room. I watched as several equally successful-looking men, who I guessed were either businessmen or movie executives, greeted him warmly and, clearly, with great respect. 'He must be the boss of a studio or the president of an oil company or bank,' I thought.

I looked at my watch; it was exactly 2pm, the time I'd been told Frank would meet me. I glanced down at the copy of the *LA Times* I'd found in my room.

"Peter?" a soft voice by my side said. I looked up, into the eyes of the man I'd been watching for the last five minutes.

"I'm Frank Nathan. Welcome to America, Peter." I stood up and we shook hands.

I was a little disappointed as I followed Frank out to his car, as I'd asked the MDRT for someone around my own age. Somehow I didn't think we'd be hitting the discos together.

As we drove off in his gleaming white Cadillac convertible with red leather seats, Frank told me he'd been a 'life insurance salesman' for over 40 years.

He was the first person I'd met who called himself that: in England everyone was a 'financial adviser' or 'investment planner' or 'broker'. He told me he'd spent his whole career as an agent for New York Life, one of the oldest of the large American insurance companies, and was never going to retire.

I'd told him I'd like to see where the stars lived. "Well, we're in the heart of Beverly Hills right now," he said as we drove down a palm tree-fringed avenue. I felt I was in a Hollywood movie. He pointed out beautiful homes on either side; "Ella Fitzgerald lives over there... and you see that house on the other side? That used to belong to Cary Grant." I'd never seen anything like it. The lawns were green and immaculate and the houses were magnificent. I immediately fell in love with Los Angeles, or more precisely, Beverly Hills. East Acton was nothing like this!

Frank took me for lunch at Nat 'n Al's, the famous deli on Rodeo Drive, where our Reuben sandwiches were mountains of corned beef the size of small houses. The waitresses all seemed to have worked there forever and had great put-down remarks for everyone. The place was packed and loud, full of regulars. Frank told me about his career, the great people he worked alongside and the people he sold to; many had been clients for over 30 years. He'd had the same branch manager, a close friend, at the Beverly Hills office for over 25 years. He had recently retired and the new manager was a young guy who he liked a lot.

Frank was very different from the extrovert salesmen I'd always imagined Americans to be. He wasn't a loud, showy guy, but had humility, something I'd never come across in the salespeople in London (and not one of my characteristics), and it was only afterwards that I realised he'd never once talked about his own achievements.

It was later at the MDRT meeting, when I mentioned I'd been shown round by Frank Nathan, that people's eyebrows shot up. "Wow! Frank Nathan? He's a living legend, Peter! Did you know that? He sold the largest NY Life policy ever," they told me. "Just a couple of years ago." Frank had never mentioned it.

After lunch, Frank took me to his very luxurious offices on Wilshire Boulevard. The other salesmen all greeted him with the same affection and respect as the people had in the Hilton lobby.

We went to his private suite; an outer area where his secretary sat led to his own office. On his desk were photos of his wife Eleanor and his children, all in their thirties now and married with children. "I'm a lucky guy, Peter. I have been married to the same beautiful woman for 45 years, and we've brought up a wonderful family together. I love selling life insurance and I've managed to help a lot of people... and made so many great friends along the way. You are so lucky, you're a young man, you have it all ahead of you."

He insisted on driving me back to my hotel and as we drove along Ella Fitzgerald's street, I asked him where he lived. "That's our home there," he said, pointing out a beautiful white Spanish-style house with a red tiled roof across the street, in a driveway surrounded by two large oak trees. He would never have shown it to me if I hadn't asked him.

The next night, he invited me to his house for dinner. Once again, he insisted on picking me up. I couldn't believe how hospitable they were and how interested in hearing about my life and family in London. We had a terrific evening. His wife Eleanor told me she'd been an actress and had given up her career to raise their family. She now served on Beverly Hills city council.

Frank was going to Seattle too; he'd never missed qualifying since the year he started in the business. Attending the meetings over these years, he told me, had changed his life. "And I don't just mean it's taught me how to sell more, Peter, but I've learned so much about life as well. But I think you'll find out what I mean next week." He told me he wanted to introduce me there to Ben Feldman, a friend and veteran fellow agent at NY Life.

I'd heard of Ben Feldman. Universally recognised as the greatest-ever life insurance salesman and now in his late sixties, he'd lived his whole career in a small town called East Liverpool in Ohio and regularly sold over $100m of life insurance a year; an unbelievable amount when a good salesman's ambition might be $1m or $2m of insurance.

Nothing anyone had told me back home prepared me for the MDRT opening ceremony in Seattle. I'd never seen anything even vaguely like it.

The convention centre was the biggest hall I'd ever seen, with 5,000 people inside; the stage was so far away they had huge screens along the side to show what was happening onstage. Little golf-type electric buggies ferried people around and there were hundreds of volunteer staffers, all of whom were MDRT members themselves.

It was like a Hollywood spectacular, with dancers, orchestra and singers, all in glittering costumes. I felt I was at the Oscars. Then hundreds of salesmen, all the overseas attendees, marched on stage: "And now, please welcome... Australia! Please welcome... China!... Denmark!... Israel!... Malta!" And finally, the PA boomed, "Please welcome... the United Kingdom!" All proudly held their national flags on long poles, often wearing their national costumes. I counted 30 different countries represented.

The compère, Lyle Blessman, was six feet seven inches tall and must have weighed at least 240lbs. He wore a large white Stetson and cowboy boots. Lyle had to be from Texas, I thought. He bounded on stage like a runaway train, to enormous applause and a standing ovation. He was, he told us right away, "Proud to be a life member of the MDRT, the greatest organisation on the face of this earth!"

He continued, "We have a show for you this year that will be the best you've ever seen! The greatest speakers in our industry are here to share their secrets with you, and whether you've been in the business one year or fifty, I promise you'll find something to take back home that will transform your selling... and your life!" Another huge standing ovation. In fact, I counted five standing ovations – all 5,000 people on their feet every time – in his five-minute opening speech.

This was repeated continuously over the next five days. Every speaker got at least half a dozen standing ovations in his 30-minute presentation; I'd never got up and then sat down so many times, it was like doing PE at school.

I met so many great people from all over the world that week. But the Americans had the biggest effect on me, with that unique combination of warmth and white-toothed smiles and always the instant offer of hospitality, together with an optimism and enthusiasm, a sense that anything was possible. They'd all grown up wanting to be president, or at least knowing they could be. Everyone in Seattle greeted me as a friend. It was as if I was part of a huge family of distant relatives whom I really liked but had never known existed!

The main platform speakers were not just top life insurance salesmen but people who'd achieved outstanding success in all walks of life. There was a black basketball star cum teacher, who had turned a failing gun-ridden ghetto school in the Bronx into one of America's biggest educational success stories. I asked him afterwards if he had 'the butterflies' addressing 5,000 people; "We all get butterflies Peter, it's just a question of teaching them to fly in formation."

And a decorated Korean War army veteran, who'd saved his comrades' lives and had more bravery medals than any man in the US Army, also told his story.

One day, Hans Selye, a world-famous psychologist from Vienna and top authority on stress and how to deal with it, gave an afternoon Q&A session.

I put my hand up to ask a question. "Professor Selye, what is your definition of success?"

He thought for a moment and then said, "Success is a journey and not a destination."

I thought, 'That's right!' It's not about who has the most money or sells the most insurance. It's about those little successes that happen every day. Making a child smile, making someone laugh, saying or doing something that leaves the person you've just met feeling better about themselves, lifting people up rather than putting them down.

It is 40 years since I heard those words but I never forget them, and many times since have said them out loud to myself and in answer to people who ask what success means to me.

Selye had gone on to say, when asked how to deal with stress, "Always aim for the highest achievable gain... but never put up resistance in vain."

"Do you ever get stress, Peter?" someone once asked me.

"No, I don't get stress... I give it!" I delegate it; why keep it to yourself? Share a bit of stress!

Chapter 5

It's not like happiness. As one of my father's GA aphorisms goes, "Happiness is like perfume, you can't sprinkle a drop or two over someone without getting a bit on yourself."

It was a whirlwind week. I loved every moment of it... and forever fell in love with America and Americans. Talk about having my batteries recharged... I felt as if I'd been plugged into a million watts of electricity! It made me think I'd been living in a black and white photo all my life, and now everything suddenly was in colour.

I'd never had any experience that came close to it. As one of the speakers said, "We're living the real American dream every day, we tell our story to those five people a day, honestly and with sincerity," quoting Frank Bettger, who wrote the life insurance salesman's bible, *How I Raised Myself from Failure to Success in Selling*. I still have it by my bedside today.

I learned that selling was an honourable profession in America, and if you put your clients' needs ahead of your own, you got the same respect that other professions enjoyed. They were all proud to be salesmen. This was so different from the attitude of the salesmen, and the image people had of them, back in Britain.

For the first time, I really understood that what I did for a living was important and valuable. That what I sold – security and peace of mind – helped people.

The day before the meeting finished, I got a call from my mother to tell me my father had had a heart attack. "But he's fine Peter, please don't worry and don't fly back early."

They were on their first holiday since he'd stopped gambling, to Lake Como where an old patient of Dad's ran a small hotel. They'd gone out on the lake in a small boat one morning and that's where Dad had his heart attack, in the middle of Lake Como.

If you have to have one, there are not many more beautiful places to have it in. It certainly beat the Central line in rush hour or the White City dog track.

I remembered a story that Dad told at GA meetings, especially to new members, to get across how he was the same as them, just how addicted he'd been.

"I'm a GP. But once I was in a packed betting shop in Shepherds Bush, one of the few where they didn't know me, we were all cheering the big race, the Gold Cup at Cheltenham, and I had to have a winner. I was in trouble, as always, and as they came round the bend, my horse was right there, neck to neck with two others... suddenly one of the punters had a heart attack and collapsed on the floor. Everybody crowded round and were shouting, 'Is there a doctor in the house!?', and I just stood there, glued to the screen, cheering my horse on, ignoring it all until they passed the finishing post, before I said, 'I'm a doctor,' and went over to help. My horse won by the way, and he survived. Gambling was more important to me than a man's life! That's how sick I was. I've never been so lucky since the day I stopped gambling. But for many years I had eight extra letters after my medical degree to my name: 'NYSOBAMN'. Not yet struck off but any minute now!"

Once more his luck was in. June Leone, his former patient, had been a nurse and knew what to do. He was rushed to hospital and after a few days, was told to take it easy for three weeks before he could fly back to London. So they had an extra three weeks' holiday by the lake.

My sister Tabetha flew out from Bali to be with them, but my mother was adamant I should stay on in America as planned.

You don't argue with my mother.

June 1973, New York, USA

On the way in from JFK, bouncing off the potholes, the cabbie was talking to me about his time in Europe during the war. He half turned and said, "Yeah Hitler... nice guy, a little aggressive though!" He gave me a big wink. His licence gave his name as Hyman Silverschlitz.

I'd flown from Seattle immediately after the meeting had finished on a bang with a grand finale. At one point Big Lyle Blessman rode onto the stage on a white stallion surrounded by as many dancers and singers as at any Las Vegas show.

I'd then said goodbye to literally hundreds of my new American best friends.

The New York heat was incredible: "We're hitting the high 90s today," one of the 100-plus channels on the TV in my room told me. The humidity was right up there too; before I'd even got to the corner of the first block, I was dripping with sweat and had to go back to change my suit. I decided to take an air-conditioned yellow cab to a restaurant on Madison for lunch.

That evening was a little cooler and I felt it safe to walk the street again. I was just passing a guy selling watches from a box. "Wanna buy a watch brother?" he asked, holding one out.

"No, thank you," I said, adding for some inexplicable reason, "I'm English."

I carried on and had got 20 feet further when I felt something fly past my ear.

"You limey motherfucker!" He'd thrown the watch at me!

Welcome to New York!

I went out that first night to a few singles bars along First Avenue. One, called Thank God It's Friday, had been recommended by the hotel concierge.

"I just love your accent!" a girl next to me at the bar said, hearing me order my drink. "Speak some English for me!"

She asked me what my star sign was. I thought it might be Sagittarius. Apparently this was the wrong sign, for she turned back to her friends almost immediately.

New York was electric. I'd never seen so many people all walking so fast, looking like they were going somewhere. I walked with my head craned up at the skyscrapers, until I couldn't move my neck and spent the rest of one day unable to look round without turning my entire body.

Despite the heat wave, I loved the city. I had the feeling I must have really been born a New Yorker in an Englishman's body. Years later I met a guy in Manhattan who said to me on parting, "See you in Jul, Peter."

"Jul?" I asked.

"Yeah, July! But I'm in a hurry... it saves time."

CHAPTER 6

How to stay clean and get married for the first time
December 1976, London

It had been five years since I gave up gambling and I'd finally paid back all my creditors. I felt pretty good about myself.

I'd been going along every Friday with Dad to the same GA meeting that he'd helped found, all those years before. On the 13th August 1975 he had celebrated 11 years without a single bet. Nobody else in GA had stopped gambling now as long as Dad; many had fallen off the wagon along the way. It really was a miracle. He and Mum had rebuilt their lives together and those miserable years of my childhood seemed like they'd never happened; but of course, we knew they had.

From the very first days, they'd put all their energy and enthusiasm into making GA a success, not just for Dad but also for all the other compulsive gamblers. They knew that for it to be a permanent success, they had to hold meetings up and down the country and not just in London. And so, every other weekend, they would set off in the car, with three or four other members, to Bradford or Bournemouth, Manchester or Sheffield, to start new GA groups from scratch, giving interviews to local papers and radio stations as 'Jack R', a recovering compulsive gambler, to announce that a new group was being formed at the church hall or Quaker meeting room or wherever they'd found a room. One day, they'd flown up to Glasgow and opened the first GA group in Scotland.

In 1974, I'd taken on the role of national PR officer for GA, and set about treading the fine line between introducing GA to people who wouldn't know it existed, in those days the great majority, and promoting and advertising it, which wasn't allowed under GA principles. One day, I was invited on a new London radio station called LBC. The idea was that Brian Hayes, the interviewer, would talk to me about my experiences as a compulsive gambler and after 20 minutes, he'd throw it open for listeners to call in. The 'call in' was a new broadcasting concept that had recently come to Britain from America, and as to be expected, the shy, retiring Brits of the stiff-upper-lip stereotype were finding it difficult to get into the spirit of things.

The interview had gone well and, after taking half a dozen calls, mostly from women concerned their husbands might be compulsive gamblers, I settled back and relaxed to take the last call of the programme. A cockney voice said, "'Ello Peter. My name's Frank and I'm calling 'cos my wife's been losing the housekeeping at bingo... regular like, week in, week out. I've 'ad a word with 'er, know wot I mean, but she keeps at it. So what you fink?"

I replied that it certainly did sound like she had a gambling problem and maybe she should come to GA if she really wanted to stop. I asked if he had anything else he wanted to tell me and he said, "Yeah, I do... you're a fucking cunt!" Actually, he shouted it at the top of his voice and nearly blew the headphones off my head.

"That was a funny line to end on," I said to the show's producer afterwards in the Green room. "Lucky you have that 30-second delay button."

"What button?" he asked.

"The one that stopped that nutter telling me I was a 'fucking cunt' being broadcast!"

"Oh, we haven't got one of those yet."

Terrific! My whole family had been proudly listening on the radio at home to their son, grandson, nephew being interviewed for the first time, and they'd have heard that nutcase saying... what he thought of me. I'd never once heard my mother utter a swear word, not even a 'bloody hell!' in my entire life.

That evening, my mother called me. "So Mum, how did you think it went this afternoon?" I said, hoping she might somehow have missed the last caller.

"Whatever did you say to that man to make him so upset, Peter?" she said.

In 1976, I bought my first flat in a brand-new block in Swiss Cottage – and Irkku and I moved in. We'd been together for six years, and now she wanted to get married.

We were going to get married the year before in 1975 but I'd got cold feet a few weeks before. Irkku had told me she was pregnant, and I was thrilled with the news, but at the same time as usual I was thinking of myself; and after a few weeks part of me felt I was being rushed into marriage and that I wasn't really ready to settle down and be a husband and a father. But I was also very happy... so it was a confusing time.

Sadly it turned out to be an ectopic pregnancy and Irkku had to have a termination.

We finally got married on 10th December 1976. I'd always told people I'd never get married before I was 30: the Marylebone Registry Office ceremony was one day before my 30th birthday. I wonder if things would have turned out to be different if I had waited that one extra day.

The wedding reception was held at our flat, with about 40 family and friends. Irkku's father, who I'd never met, came over from Finland with her sister and brother; her mother had died when Irkku was 12.

It was a great party. It was the middle of the 1970s streaking craze and so, of course, I was dared to streak through the middle of the party. Whatever happened to the shy boy, who just stood in the corner at parties and wouldn't speak to anybody?

We went on honeymoon to St Lucia. It was our first time in the Caribbean. We stayed at a wonderful relaxed hotel called the Halcyon Beach Club.

One evening, strolling along the beach before dinner, we met an English couple, Dave Cash the DJ and his wife, and their friend Lionel Bart, the composer of *Oliver!* Over the next few days we had drinks and dinner with them a couple of times. Lionel was a very sweet man. We said we'd keep in touch, but it was ten years before I met him again... at a Narcotics Anonymous meeting in Chelsea.

Irkku had started modelling and I was selling lots of policies for Abbey Life and making lots of money. She got lots of advertising work; one TV commercial was for Norska bubble bath, but instead of heading to her home in Finland to shoot it, or the Norwegian fjords, they took the whole crew to New Zealand and shot it near Christchurch.

Life was pretty good. We went on holiday two or three times a year, in addition to all the Abbey Life company conventions, which were always held in exotic locations around the world – Bali, Rio and many other places I might not have gone to in those days, when two weeks in France or Greece was still wildly exotic for the average Englishman.

How to confront Gordon Ramsay over the scrambled eggs
Across the breakfast table – 2nd June 2002, Claridge's

"Excuse me... what is this?" I asked after Marco had whisked off a silver dome to reveal a towering yellow jelly-like thing that was doing a good impression of the Leaning Tower of Pisa. "Is this some kind of Italian joke?"

I spotted some burnt pieces of bacon and one large mushroom in the vicinity of the wobbling tower, so I knew exactly what it was meant to be.

"It is your scrambled eggs, Mr Rosengard."

"No, Marco, this is not my scrambled eggs. My scrambled eggs don't look like this."

"This is Mr Ramsay's way of expressing scrambled eggs, Mr Rosengard."

"Is that so? Where is he? I am going to give Mr Ramsay Mr Rosengard's way of expressing how I want my scrambled eggs."

Gordon Ramsay, in a blaze of publicity, had just taken over the legendary Claridge's restaurant, in the process destroying one of the most beautiful art deco dining rooms in the world and replacing it with something that looked to me like Helsinki's airport lounge.

As part of the deal, he had to continue to provide breakfast for the hotel's guests. Today was his first morning.

"Do you know what he looks like?" I asked David, another regular, at the next table.

"There he is," he said, pointing to a blonde-haired man wearing a dentist's tunic, who had just come in.

"Are you sure that's not the Claridge's dentist?"

"No, that's him all right."

I threw down my napkin and shot off across the room. I headed him off just as he got to the kitchen door.

I hadn't noticed the deathly hush that had descended on the entire room.

I hadn't seen the knives and forks suddenly suspended in mid-air, the open mouths full of kippers and cornflakes, the boiled eggs balancing on their tiny silver spoons.

I had never seen Ramsay's TV appearances. I didn't know anything about him, other than that he was a famous chef.

"Are you Gordon Ramsay?" I asked, planting myself between the kitchen and the dentist.

"Yes," he said.

"Can I have a word with you?"

"What's it about?"

"It's about your scrambled eggs."

"What about my scrambled eggs?"

"I don't like them."

"What's wrong with them?"

Suddenly I realised something was different. The silence. The normal buzz of conversation, the noise of knives and forks on plates, cups being put down on saucers... it had all gone.

I glanced round. The whole room had stopped eating and talking about the latest share deals, takeovers and derivative trading. Ileen, at her regular table on my right, was no longer promoting her new film production to a leading young actor. Harvey wasn't discussing his Springsteen summer Wembley Stadium concerts with his aide-de-camp.

Everybody was looking at us.

It was like the scene where Gary Cooper is facing down the bad guy in *High Noon*.

I looked him right in the eyes. "I'll tell you what's wrong with your scrambled eggs."

"Go on then," he said, jutting out his chin.

"They are like a towering jelly. That's what's wrong with them!"

There was a pause while he digested this. "How do you like your scrambled eggs?"

"Soft and fluffy."

Another long pause.

"Okay," he said. He went on into the kitchen.

I went back to my table and sat down.

Five minutes later, Marco was back with a plate of soft and fluffy scrambled eggs.

Chapter 6

How not to pay your tax bill
15th December 1980, London

I got a brown envelope through the door one morning. It was from the Inland Revenue. I owed them £10,000.

I had paid off all my debts four years before, but I had forgotten about my income tax. And I always had spent everything I earned. I rang my accountant, my friend Mike Saunders, who I'd first met in 1967 at the Fledermaus, as he was, like me, a devotee of Swedish au pair girls. "What's all this, Mike? Please tell me it's a mistake!"

"Peter, I've told you a thousand times, but you never listen. You have to put money aside every month for the tax man. That's how it works. The government needs some of your money to keep the country going... you're self-employed, so they don't take it automatically. You have to pay it."

This was a bit of a blow and had come right out of the blue.

I hadn't any money put aside. Mike said I had to pay it immediately or they would seize my chattels. I wasn't entirely sure what a chattel was, but I was pretty sure I didn't have £10,000 worth of them. I started to think how I was going to find the money, and the more I thought about it the more the little voice, after years of silence, started to whisper in my ear: "Why don't you gamble?"

I tried to ignore the tax demand at first, hoping they'd forget about me, but I got a second letter with 'Final Demand' in big red letters on it. As the days passed the voice in my ear got louder... and more insistent. Why don't you go just for one hour? You'll be lucky again after all these years of not gambling... you'll have beginner's luck, like that first time you went to Charlie Chester's when you were 14. I thought, 'I'll win £50,000, pay the tax man off and still have a fortune. Then never gamble again. Nobody will ever know!'

I was booked to fly to Florida with Billy the Kid and Lance, a mate of ours who worked in the rag trade. Irkku and I had split up a few months before; we'd been having a bad time for most of the last year, I just wasn't ready to be married. This wouldn't have been so bad if we hadn't already been married for over three years. I still wanted to meet other girls, which, I'd discovered, never goes down well with your wife. She'd been back in Helsinki to see her family and had come home a day early... to catch me in bed with a German girl I'd picked up in a club.

She wasn't happy... in fact, she'd gone totally mad! She attacked me with a chair and stormed out. I got rid of the girl and caught up with her as she walked down the Finchley Road.

"What's wrong? Nothing happened," I said.

"There's a girl in our bed!" she screamed. "That's what's wrong, you fucking bastard!"

"What girl!? What are you talking about? Have you been drinking Irkku?" I carried on like this, as if she'd imagined the whole thing.

I knew it would be a miracle if I could talk my way out of this one. But I remembered a guy, late one night in a bar, once telling me, "Peter, the golden rule is never, ever admit it. Never... not even if she catches you in bed having sex with another girl. Always deny, deny, deny... and keep denying. Never give in."

So I'd put it to the test.

Unfortunately, it doesn't work.

Irkku left me.

Or rather, I'd moved out and was now living in a little basement flat on the corner of the King's Road, owned by a friend from Abbey Life.

The day before we were due to fly to America, I got in the blue Rolls convertible and drove to Bruton Street, where there was a car dealer. On the way I thought, 'This is crazy Peter, take the money and go straight to the bank and pay the tax man.'

I'd been told the car was worth £15k but he only offered me £10k, for a cash deal on the spot. I took it.

I called Robin, a young guy I knew, whose father owned Annabel's. Robin was a member of a casino called Aspinall's in Knightsbridge, and didn't know about my gambling history. He kindly agreed to sign me in.

I went over in a taxi. I changed the entire £10,000 into 20 £500 chips. And sat down at the table to play roulette. I'd never had a clue how to play roulette, other than red or black, odd or even, and trying my luck on numbers.

In two hours I lost the lot... every penny. I felt nothing: cold, numb. I got up from the table and went back to the flat. I had £1,000 under the mattress. I took it out and looked at it for a long time. In the old days, I'd have gone straight back to the casino to try and win it all back. But this time I didn't.

Something had changed.

I knew I'd lose it.

The next day I went to the airport, met up with Billy the Kid and Lance and flew to Miami, en route for Fort Lauderdale.

Postscript:

That day was the first time I'd gambled since 21st March 1971. And looking back in 2013, it's the only time in over 40 years.

Over the next year I paid the tax bill off in monthly instalments, plus a lot of interest!

Many times over the years that little voice has come back to try its luck with me... to make me gamble just once more. The voice of self-destruction... and every single time, I've responded that it's now wasting its time with me.

I have always just told it to "Get lost!"

And it has!

CHAPTER 7

How life isn't Hollywood... it's Cricklewood
August 1981, Hollywood, Los Angeles

I am driving up into the Hollywood Hills in the 1961 pink Cadillac convertible with the huge chrome fins that I had collected from Rent-a-Wreck on La Cienega.

I was running late as I'd had to take back the first car they gave me, after going just half a block. The seat was flat on the floor and I couldn't see above the steering wheel. I'd felt like a baby trying to drive a tank.

"Oh yeah... you got Marlon's car," the clerk said.

"Marlon?" I said.

"Yeah, Brando. He gets all his cars from us; this happens all the time."

Marlon Brando must have weighed 300lbs at this time. I met a guy in the Whiskey A Go-Go on Sunset a few days later and told him about this. He didn't seem surprised. "You know where all the fat goes from the 55m Americans who at any one time are on diets?" he said.

I had to confess it wasn't something I had spent a lot of time considering.

"Every Thursday night, thousands of US army trucks collect all the fat from these fat people's homes and drive through the desert in the middle of the night till they get to Palm Springs, where they all converge at Brando's house. And they pump it into him."

I didn't want to arrive late as I was on my way to meet Don Arden, the toughest, most feared manager in the music business on both sides of the

114

Atlantic. "He held his accountant out of a 12th floor window once..."; I'd heard the same story from at least six people in London, sometimes it was his solicitor, other times his dentist, sometimes it was the 6th floor window, but everyone agreed he had dangled a middle-aged Jewish professional person from an office building in London, until he'd agreed to write him a big cheque that he thought he was owed.

Don, who I'd never met, had invited me and Jimmy Grierson, my new discovery, to dinner at his LA home. Don had just signed Jimmy to his own record company. He was managing Electric Light Orchestra, the biggest selling band in the world and he was making millions.

Jimmy was a brown-haired, blue-eyed, gentle 28-year-old Liverpudlian singer-songwriter, who had been recommended to me as a future star by Pete Brown, a small bearded bald guy I'd met in a club in the West End one night.

"Trust me, Pete," he said, as I sold him life insurance. "He's going to be big. Mark my words."

And I did, especially when I found out a few days later that Pete Brown had been a key collaborator with the 1960s supergroup, Cream, co-writing with Jack Bruce and Eric Clapton some of their biggest hits, including 'White Room', 'I Feel Free' and 'Sunshine of your Life'. I thought, 'He must know a star when he sees one,' and if I could spot a comedian with star potential, how difficult could it be to find an unknown songwriter and turn him into a pop star?

Jimmy was the first person I'd ever met who told me he was gay. In fact, he hadn't been off the train at King's Cross two minutes when he said, "By the way, Peter, I am gay you know."

"Good, Jimmy. Good," I said, giving him my strongest handshake and deepening my already bass voice. "Okay, that's terrific, good... welcome to London, Jimmy."

"I think this must be it," I said to him after 30 minutes of hairpin bends and death-defying curves, as I pulled up outside a set of huge electronic gates. I pushed the buzzer.

"Peter Rosengard and Jimmy Grierson from London, for Mr Arden," I said. Up the drive I could just make out a large California-ranch-meets-French-chateau-style house.

Two large men in black uniforms, carrying pump-action shotguns, came out of the house and walked up to the gates. They gave us the once over, twice. One of them held a remote control in his hand and the gates swung open.

"Mr Arden is expecting you two gentlemen," he said. "Keep going up the drive for a quarter of a mile to the house. He will meet you there himself."

"This isn't the house?" I pointed towards Chateau Hollywood.

"Hell no!" he laughed. "That's just our guard house."

A heavily-tanned, short, thickset man in his mid-fifties, with his white shirt opened halfway down his hairy chest, came out to greet us. He had a heavy gold bracelet on one wrist and a large gold watch with crescent moons in diamonds on the other. Don Arden was no more than five feet six inches tall, but he was as wide as he was tall.

Behind him, and all around him, was the biggest house I'd ever seen. It looked as if it could have belonged to the Warner Brothers, Gary Cooper or Errol Flynn... all at the same time.

"Peter, Jimmy. Welcome to LA. I hear it's your first time in the States, Jimmy," he said in a throaty American-Cockney-Leeds accent as we got out of the car and shook hands.

We followed as he scuttled off at great pace though a pair of massive oak Cotswold Manor House doors and found ourselves in a huge stone-floored hall, by itself bigger than our whole house in East Acton had been. I noticed it had a minstrels' gallery.

"Like me to give you a tour of the house?" he said. It was clear this was an offer we couldn't refuse.

One hour later... "We could have gone round Buckingham Palace quicker," I whispered to Jimmy as we arrived back in one of the five reception rooms.

Don had taken us into every one of the 25 bedrooms and shown us all their ensuite bathrooms. I wasn't quite sure of ensuite bathroom etiquette, so I had gone into each in turn and walked slowly all the way around, casting admiring looks into the showers and gazing down the toilet bowls and their matching bidets with their solid gold fittings, as Don stood by like a proud father closely watching our reactions to a newborn baby.

"This is a really lovely lavatory, Don," I said in ensuite bathroom No. 9.

"Thank you, Peter, I like this one myself," he said. "When I grew up in

Leeds, we just had one outside one."

"And now you have got 25 toilets. You've done well, Don. Congratulations. You do know Prince Charles collects lavatories, don't you?"

"You are kidding me!"

"Not a lot of people know that Don. Keep it to yourself, will you?" I said.

After dinner, when he had laid out his plans for Jimmy's first album, he got up from the 20-foot refectory table ("Bought it off a skint Oxford don, didn't I?") and said, "I want to show you something very special."

He walked to the French windows and pushed a button in the wall. There was a whirring noise and the entire roof of the house slowly slid open. 'He must have bought the house from 'Mad Dog' Weinberg,' I thought to myself. It was amazing.

It was now dark outside; we looked down into the San Fernando Valley, a million twinkling lights shimmering below.

"This is living, isn't it?" Don said, glass of champagne in hand.

"It certainly is Don," I said.

"Wow!" Jimmy said.

Don stuck a big Havana in his mouth. "One day, Jimmy, this can all be yours," he said. I am not making this up.

Postscript:

Jimmy made his album. The record company released one single, called 'This Way Up'. Together they sold just a couple of hundred copies. He was soon dropped by Don, and a few months later I let our management agreement expire.

Jimmy, as 'James Wraith', later went on to be the new singer in Roxy Music after Brian Ferry left the band.

Don's son, David, who naturally I'd sold life insurance to, went to prison for beating up his dad's accountant. Or maybe it was his lawyer? Later it turned out he was innocent; he had taken the rap for his father, who had done the beating-up bit.

Don later somehow lost all his money, then got Alzheimer's and died penniless. His daughter Sharon married Ozzy Osbourne (Don had also managed Black Sabbath), turned them both into US reality TV stars and became famous as a judge on *Pop Idol*.

How to give Prince Charles a lavatory for his birthday
November 1981, London

My friend Peter Byfield was running a very successful restaurant in Baker Street called School Dinners. He had young pretty waitresses, dressed in school uniforms; short skirts, stockings and suspenders. He was the headmaster, with cape and mortarboard, the head girl had a cane... you can imagine the rest. It was full every lunchtime, with bank managers and businessmen demanding to be caned. The 'English thing'.

I was looking for a place to open a new comedy club after my partner Don Ward had kicked me out of the Comedy Store. I had unfortunately taken the advice of a solicitor I'd met one night at a Gamblers Anonymous meeting and sold my half share in the Store to Don for £500. He had just got kicked out of the Dean Street premises when the lease was up, and the club was closed at the time. I had asked him for £10,000.

"Look, Peter," my solicitor said, "he hasn't got a business any more. He hasn't got the money. Take the £500 he's offered and go back to selling insurance."

There are probably times when you should never listen to a compulsive-gambling lawyer... and this was one of them. But I did, and took the £500. I must have been mad.

Peter Byfield offered me his premises on a Wednesday night to start my new club, The Last Laugh. I was so eager to get back in the comedy business that I didn't stop to think that Wednesday nights in Baker Street, in a vast room that could hold 500 people, spelt disaster. North of Oxford Street has never worked for restaurants, let alone clubs. But at the time, it seemed like a good idea... I needed a great publicity stunt to launch it. But what?

I have always been a news fanatic. "You were the only one of the children who read the morning papers," my mother said recently, when I asked her what she remembered of my childhood. That was it? That's all she remembers!? It's weird, but there are only about three photographs of me between

118

the ages of one and 18. (I feel like Woody Allen in *Annie Hall*: "There is no documentary evidence that I ever existed before the age of 32.")

I opened the paper one morning and leafed through it. And that's when I got it. My stunt!

There was a tiny news piece hidden away about Prince Charles visiting a factory somewhere; it mentioned that he had said he collected lavatories. I couldn't believe it. Nobody had picked up on this... it should have made the front page: 'Future King Collects Toilets!'

What kind of person collects lavatories? It was amazing... and nobody knew about it. It was as if he had said he collected stamps or matchboxes. I knew immediately I was going to give him one for his birthday, which I had read was coming up in a week's time.

I looked up 'bathroom supplies' in the *Yellow Pages* and made a few calls. There were a few shops selling old loos and naturally, they all had punning names: 'Clean and Pretty', 'Sitting Decent'. By the end of the day I had bought a Victorian loo; the selling point was that the bowl was embossed with Prince of Wales feathers. A bargain for £350.

I rang the Press Association. "I am going to give Prince Charles a lavatory for his 33rd birthday at Buckingham Palace tomorrow morning, at 10am... yes, he collects lavatories... send a photographer and you can have a world exclusive... the future king on his throne!" I couldn't resist it.

The next morning, I loaded the royal lavatory into my red Beetle convertible, put on my 'Elton John at Las Vegas' red glitter jacket and set off for Buckingham Palace.

When I got there, the whole pavement was full of thousands of tourists waiting for Changing of the Guard. I had no idea who the Press Association cameraman was; everybody had a camera. I drove round and round the memorial out front. It occurred to me the police might think a man in a red glitter jacket, driving round Buckingham Palace with a lavatory in the back seat, might seem a little odd... but nobody seemed to notice. Finally, I spotted a man in a raincoat and trilby hat with two cameras round his neck. He seemed to be looking for someone, so I pulled up next to him.

"Excuse me, sir, are you by any chance looking for a lavatory?" I asked.

"Yes, I am. I'm desperate and my kids need to go too."

"Sorry, wrong lavatory!" I drove off.

Two Japanese tourists later, I finally found the PA man. He helped me manhandle the loo onto the pavement, much to the crowd's amusement. I just managed to pick it up and stagger to the front gates.

"It's a birthday present for Prince Charles," I told the policeman.

"Please put the lavatory down, sir." He bent over, lifted the lid and peered down the bowl. His helmet fell off into the toilet. He retrieved it, to much applause.

"Is his Royal Highness expecting this lavatory, sir?" the policeman asked.

"No, it's a surprise. He collects them, you know."

The PA man was busy shooting away. In the end I had to put it back in the car and drive round to the tradesman's entrance, where they accepted it as if it was the fifteenth lavatory to arrive for Prince Charles that morning. "Right... One lavatory received, embossed with Prince of Wales feathers. Thank you very much, sir. If you'll just sign here, please sir?"

The next day, the *Times* carried a picture of me delivering the royal loo with the policeman looking down the bowl. 'Peter Rosengard, the Comedy Store founder, promoted his new comedy club The Last Laugh yesterday, by presenting the Prince of Wales with a lavatory.' The picture went round the world and I spent the morning giving interviews to radio stations from Sydney ("Well, Peter, you must be flushed with success, mate... so is he on the throne right now, do you think? The Royal Thomas Crapper, eh!") to Sacramento.

A week later, I received a letter from the Prince's equerry on Kensington Palace notepaper: 'Dear Mr Rosengard, HRH the Prince of Wales has asked me to convey his immense gratitude for your magnificent gift of a lavatory on the occasion of his birthday. It will be installed at his Kensington Palace residence, where no doubt it will be greatly admired.'

Admired?! Where was he going to put it? In the drawing room?

We haven't kept in touch since, but some years ago I did drop him a line, asking how the loo was working, if he would like to invite me over for dinner, and so on. I am still waiting for a reply.

Postscript:

When he moved from Kensington Palace to Clarence House, the newspapers reported that he had taken one of his favourite loos with him.

I think we know which one.

Chapter 7

How to avoid having breakfast with a life insurance salesman
Across the breakfast table – 1998, Claridge's

I am having breakfast with a client, the TV talk show host Clive Anderson. We've been friends since he appeared at the Comedy Store in 1979. He was one of the few comedians at the time to be making any money – he was a barrister – so naturally I'd sold him life insurance.

"You know that guy you suggested I call? A potential client? Well, I rang him up," I said, as I put my scrambled egg into my mouth.

"Oh, you mean Guy," he said.

"Yes, that's him... I invited him for breakfast. And do you know what he said?"

"No, what did he say?"

"He said, 'I don't believe in life insurance!' I said, 'That's okay, it's not a religion... you don't have to believe in it!' Come on Clive, that's funny, admit it."

"Well, go on... what did he say to that?"

"He said, 'I don't have to have breakfast with you, do I?', so I said, 'No Guy, it's not a law, you don't have to have breakfast with me, it's not mandatory. But what's the worst that can happen? We meet, we have a great breakfast at Claridge's, and you go away with one more new idea than you had before breakfast.'"

"So what did he say to that?" Clive asked, putting down his coffee cup.

"He said nothing. So I said, 'Do you have your diary handy?' And he said, 'No.' And so I said, 'Can you go and get it?' And he said, 'No, I am not going to get my diary. I know my rights; I don't have to get my diary if I don't want to. I am going to call my lawyer.'"

"You are kidding me? He was going to call his lawyer? Why? To see if he had to have breakfast with you?"

"Yes, Clive, he is a total nutter. I can't believe you told me I should call him!"

"Well, I am sorry, I just thought he was a potential client for you."

"Well, you thought wrong."

"So is that how you left it?" Clive asked, putting more marmalade on his toast.

"He asked me to call him back again, in 20 years: I've made a note in my diary."

How to sell life insurance to a Mafia hit man
March 1982, London

I got a call from my friend Alexandro. "Peter, I have a new client for you."

"Great, thanks man. Who is he and how do I contact him?" I asked

"His name is Francesco Di Carlo, but you can't meet him."

"What do you mean? How am I going to sell him a policy if I can't meet him?"

"Look, he is Italian, and he doesn't speak a word of English."

"So how are we going to do this?"

"Give me the forms, show me what he has to complete and I'll get them back to you once he has signed them."

"What does he do for a living?"

"He has a wine bar and small hotel... okay, it's a bed and breakfast... in Surbiton. He only needs a small pension plan for £100 a month and £100,000 life insurance."

"Okay, no problem," I said.

A few days later, Alexandro got me the forms back. Abbey Life issued the policy and that was that.

Three months later, I was walking through Berkeley Square in Mayfair, when outside Jack Barclay's Rolls Royce showroom I saw Alexandro with a very big man in a full-length camel-hair overcoat with the collar pulled up, broad-rimmed black fedora and wrap-around Ray-Bans. He had a large cigar in his mouth. He could have stepped straight out of casting for *The Godfather*, but would probably have been rejected for looking too stereotypically Mafioso.

"Hi, Alexandro, what are you doing here?" I asked.

"Peter, let me introduce you to your client, Francesco di Carlo."

"Buon giorno, Peter! Come sta?" Francesco beamed down at me. I shook his hand. It was huge and as hard as rock.

"Francesco has just bought this Corniche." Alexandro pointed to a gleaming blue Rolls convertible in the window.

"The wine bar in Surbiton must be doing very well," I said to Alexandro.

After a few minutes I had to leave to get to a meeting. I said goodbye to Francesco.

He blew a plume of blue Havana smoke into the air. "Ciao, ciao, Peter."

"Ciao, Francesco," I said.

Six months later, I bought the *Evening Standard*. The front-page head-line was: 'MAFIA HIT MAN JAILED FOR 25 YEARS FOR PIZZA PARLOUR HEROIN DISTRIBUTION RING'.

The story began: 'Francesco Di Carlo, otherwise known as 'Frankie the Strangler' and wanted by Italian police for 37 Mafia murders, was today sentenced at the Old Bailey to 25 years for masterminding the biggest heroin ring ever discovered in Britain.'

I rang Alexandro. "Hi, Alexandro, seen today's *Evening Standard* yet by any chance?"

"No, what does it say?"

"It says, Alexandro, that our wine bar-owning friend from Surbiton is in fact one Frankie the Strangler, a Mafia hit man wanted for 37 Mafia kill-ings, who has today been jailed for 25 years at the Old Bailey for a massive heroin operation in Britain... Alexandro, you introduced me to a Mafia hit man! I sold life insurance to a Mafia hit man!"

"I had no idea, I swear it."

"Alexandro!?"

"I promise you, Peter, I had no idea at all!" he said.

Two months later, I got a premium reminder notice from Abbey Life.

Francesco 'the Strangler' Di Carlo hadn't paid the monthly premiums for his life insurance and the policy was about to lapse: could I chase him for the premiums?

I made a split-second decision not to do that.

Anyway, I didn't have the phone number of Parkhurst Prison.

In 1998 I told this story to an insurance sales conference in Miami.

"Wait a minute. Your company, Abbey Life, accepted an application for life insurance from a Mafia hit man?" a guy in the front row asked incredulously.

"He didn't disclose it," I replied. "He said he was a wine bar proprie-tor. Funnily enough, on the application form, where they ask you for your health details, there isn't a box that asks, 'Are you a Mafia hit man?' But after this, maybe it would be a good idea."

Postscript:

After seven years in British jails, Di Carlo was transferred back to serve the rest of his sentence in Italy. In 1996, he became one of the 'pentito', the Mafia members who had turned informers. Over the following years, he gave evidence for the prosecution at a series of major Mafia trials.

He was also reported to have confessed to one of the most famous unsolved murders of the 20th century: the killing of the Pope's banker, Roberto Calvi, who was found hanging from Blackfriars Bridge in London in June 1982, just three months after I had sold Di Carlo his life insurance policy. He later retracted this alleged confession, saying that he had been asked to do it, but by the time he made contact with his would-be employer, Calvi was already dead.

A first inquest in London concluded it was a case of suicide. How many fugitive bankers, who having allegedly stolen millions of pounds, decide to hang themselves from a famous bridge over the Thames? After protests from his family, a second inquest decided he had been strangled before his body was dangled from the bridge.

In December 2005, 23 years after Calvi's killing, Di Carlo gave evidence at the trial in Rome of Calvi's four alleged killers (all of whom were later acquitted). As he left the court, it was reported he was wearing a full-length camel-hair overcoat, dark glasses and a hat with the brim pulled tightly down.

CHAPTER 8

How to sell life insurance to an African chief
1982, Lagos, Nigeria

The shortest flight I ever made was the one I took from Lomé in Togo to Lagos.

"Fasten your seat belts for take-off, please," the flight attendant said. "Okay, now unfasten your seat belts please as we have arrived in Lagos." The entire flight seemed to be no more than five minutes long... we had hardly cleared the runway.

I'd flown to Lagos to sell a multi-million-dollar life insurance policy to Chief Abiola, an African billionaire and philanthropist. A year or two before, he'd been a middle-manager accountant working for ITT when his best friend from school, an army officer called Murtala Mohammed, waved goodbye at the airport to President Gowon as he took off for an OAU meeting in Uganda, then turned to the assembled troops and said, "Right, chaps, I am now your new president."

It's good to be the president. But sometimes it's even better to be an old friend of the president.

A few weeks later, he awarded his old friend Abiola the biggest contract ITT had ever had, over $1bn, to put a new phone system in the country. As there were 100m people and only 20,000 telephones in the country, you could say a market opportunity existed. Two months later came a second, even larger order. The chief was appointed president of ITT for Africa and the Middle East. Within six months, he was the richest man in Africa.

President Mohammed decided one morning to dispense with his body-guards and presidential motorcade and drive to the palace. He was ambushed on the freeway and riddled with machine-gun bullets. A bad decision.

The airport is named after him. The bloodstained bullet-riddled car is today in the national museum, in a room adjacent to African bronzes.

I didn't know the chief and he had definitely never heard of me, let alone knew that I was flying out just to see him.

There must have been 5,000 people in the immigration hall. I landed at 5pm; it was almost midnight by the time I cleared customs. Nobody else seemed to be leaving the terminal; instead they were now lying on the ground, trying to sleep. A fellow passenger asked me how I was going to get into the city, and looked astonished when I said I was going to take a taxi. I was about to discover why.

I got into a taxi at the airport rank. "Take me to your chief," I said to the driver. I'd always wanted to say that.

"Which one?" he said. "We have a lot of chiefs here."

"Chief Abiola," I said. "Abiola Crescent, Lagos."

He turned round to look at me. "You know the chief!?"

"Of course I know the chief. Do you know the chief?"

"Everybody in Nigeria knows the chief. But we cannot go to his home now. It is too late to disturb the chief, he will be sleeping. Does he expect you?"

"No, it's a surprise."

"It is better I take you to your hotel first. Lie down on the floor please."

"Why?"

"It is better for you if you lie down on the floor..." He produced a wire coat hanger and hooked up the door locks with it. "You never know."

About five miles down the road, he suddenly braked to a halt.

"What's the problem?" I asked

"Road block," he said. "Don't be afraid. It's either the army, or armed robbers. Sometimes they are the same people. If they are robbers, please be polite and give them your watch and all your money quickly, please. Last week, they chopped a woman's arm off with a machete to get her watch;

she was too slow in doing what they asked."

I peeked my head up from the floor of the cab. Twenty yards in front of us I could see a group of men with large guns, standing next to half a dozen blazing barrels of tar that were right across the road.

The door opened and a big guy with what looked to me like a little Uzi stared down at me lying on the floor.

"Good evening," I said. "I'm Peter Rosengard. I am a tourist from London. I've just arrived in Nigeria; actually it is my very first visit."

"Please get out of the car," he said. The driver took out my suitcase and put it on the road. "Please open it up," the man with the Uzi said.

"I have something for you," I said.

"What do you have for me?"

"Well, I have got some gold toothbrushes."

Before I had flown out, a Greek friend with business interests in Nigeria had told me to have some gifts ready in case of exactly this kind of encounter.

I opened my wash bag and took out two gold toothbrushes in sealed plastic cases. "Here, please take them, they are for you."

"They are really gold?" he asked.

"Absolutely, solid gold, they were a gift to me from the Queen of England."

He looked at them closely. "The Queen of England gave these to you? Okay, thank you very much, sir. Please, you can go now."

I repacked in record time. "Let's get moving fast," I said to the driver. "Before he opens them and finds out they are plastic."

The next morning I took a taxi to the ITT building in downtown Lagos.

"I have come to see the chief," I said to his male secretary.

"Chief gone shopping," he said.

"Chief gone shopping? That's okay, I'll wait."

"The chief has gone shopping in London. He left in his private Boeing 707 this morning, after breakfast."

"Any idea how long the chief will be gone shopping for?"

"Maybe one day, maybe a week, who can know?"

This was not great news. I had planned to surprise him. Now, he had surprised me.

"I will call you tomorrow," I said.

Seven days later, the chief flew back. I went over to his office.

The chief was a tall, very charismatic man in his mid-forties. He was wearing a colourful traditional robe over what looked like a Savile Row tweed suit; a huge gold wristwatch full of diamonds glittered on his wrist.

I handed him my letter of introduction. He read it carefully. "Ah, Dan Weadock! He is a close friend of mine. He says you have a big idea for me, Mr Rosengard."

"I certainly do, chief. May I call you chief, chief?" I said.

"Of course." He sat back in his chair and lit a large Havana.

I picked up a brown paper parcel from the floor next to me and, with a dramatic flourish, tore it open. I held the board inside across to him. It was a mock-up of the front page of the *Times of Nigeria* newspaper, dated two weeks ahead.

The main headline in huge banner print read: 'CHIEF ABIOLA ANNOUNCES 100M NAIRA GIFT FOR BENEFIT OF ALL NIGERIANS'. The chief was pictured at the UN in New York, announcing the creation of the Abiola Foundation. "I want this to be for all Nigerians, irrespective of their tribe or religion," he was saying, "to build universities and hospitals throughout Nigeria." Next to the main story was a picture of UN Secretary-General Perez de Cuellar: "This magnificent record-breaking gift by Chief Abiola ranks with the Rockefellers in the history of philanthropic giving."

I had got an advertising agency friend in London to mock it up before I left.

He beamed at me. "I like it, Mr Rosengard. You want me to give 100m Naira away? That is a lot of money you know." It was a lot of money; at the time, about US$60m.

"Yes, chief, but my company, Abbey Life, will pay the 100m for you! And you only pay 1% per year."

"How do I get this money?"

"No, chief, you don't get the money. You have to die to get it!"

He stopped smiling. "Who's going to kill me!?"

"You can choose. Anyone you like! No, I'm just kidding, chief. It's a life insurance policy, it lasts all your life, and many, many years from now, when eventually you do one day die, the Abiola Foundation gets the money. Let's hope you live to be 100, chief!"

I shut up.

Chapter 8

I had done my homework. I knew the chief's only goal in life was to be president of Nigeria. He also had a huge ego; I was told he thought there were only three people in the world, Jesus, Mohammed and Chief Abiola, and not necessarily in that order. He was already very rich; in less than two years of hard work, he had accumulated an estimated fortune of more than one billion dollars.

But he did want power. The one problem was that he was from the wrong tribe. He was a Yoruba, from the south, in a country where power had always been held in the north, by the Hausa people.

My idea was that, by launching the Abiola Foundation for the benefit of all Nigerians, he would increase his popularity among all the other tribes enormously. Basically, by selling him a life insurance policy, I was going to help him become president of Nigeria.

"A very good idea, Mr Rosengard. I like it. How do I buy this policy?"

"I just need the first monthly premium chief, if you can give me a cheque for £200,000? And I will arrange the medical exam. What's a good time for you?"

"I can do it at midnight tonight," he said.

"Fine, midnight it is then, chief," I said, as if all my clients always wanted their insurance medicals at midnight. He took out his cheque book and wrote out a cheque for £200,000.

I put it in my pocket.

My usual size sale at that time was about £25 a month.

I left his office thinking I had just earned a million pounds in commission, which was a very good feeling. Lagos was a great city!

Back at the hotel, I started to make calls to find a clinic that would stay open all night. I finally found a doctor willing, for ten times the normal fee, to open his clinic at midnight.

I went over to the chief's house – or rather, palace. It was enormous. He lived there with all his four wives. And his 24 children. And the staff, over 50 people.

We got into a Mercedes. After five minutes driving through empty streets, I noticed in the wing mirror another car close behind us, full of men with large guns.

"Chief," I said, "I don't wish to alarm you, but we are being followed by a car full of armed men. They are armed to the teeth, actually."

"I never go anywhere without them," he said.

A month later, the insurance company asked for the chief to have another medical in London. And oh yes, could I also just ask him to sign a statement saying he would never again go into politics? I told them this was not a great idea; he would never sign it. Well, then, he cannot have the policy, they said.

We were in the back of his Rolls Royce, being driven by Tommy, his ex-Grenadier-Guards chauffeur cum bodyguard, back to his London home in Regents Park from Harley Street, where he'd just had the new medical.

"Chief, I wonder if you could just sign this for me?" I said, passing him the sheet of paper.

He glanced at it briefly and then went absolutely mad! "Never, Mr Rosengard!" he exploded. "The whole thing is off!"

Postscript:

Some years later, newspapers reported that the chief had apparently claimed to have woken to find a man with a machine gun in his room. He had fired at the chief at point-blank range and miraculously missed.

In 1993, Chief Abiola won the freest Nigerian presidential election ever conducted, the first Yoruba to have ever done so. However, before he could be sworn in the election was annulled and he was later seized and put in jail by President Abacha, who had seized power.

On 7th July 1998, he was about to be freed finally, due to the efforts of President Clinton and UN Secretary-General Kofi Annan, but he suffered a fatal 'heart attack' the day before he was to be released.

A few years later, while lounging by the pool during an insurance convention in the Seychelles, I contacted the country's president, after looking up his number in the phone book (between 'plumbing' and 'pretzels').

"Mr President, I have an idea for you that has been very valuable to many other successful presidents like yourself, and so I'm sure it will be valuable to you too." (Thank God, he didn't ask me who they were: "Papa Doc Duvalier... Mussolini... Hitler..." Stick with the dead ones.) He agreed, but again Abbey Life would not authorise a policy: apparently the president had only recently escaped an assassination attempt.

Clearly, I was not having a lot of luck selling presidents life insurance; so I decided to concentrate on City investment bankers. It would be a lot easier, require less travelling, and as far as I knew, nobody had ever wanted to kill a banker...

How not to be rude
1982, London

My mother told me about something that happened in the early 1950s, when we had gone to Devon for our summer holiday.

We were staying in a very smart seaside hotel, and one evening at dinner the three of us kids must have been running around the restaurant or making the kind of noise that young children do, when a man came over and said, in a very public-school voice, "You bloody Jews, can't you keep your damn children quiet!?"

My father had just looked up at him and said, "Sir, pray desist."

I've always admired that response of Dad's. Over the years, I've come to believe that rudeness is the weak man's imitation of strength. But it would have ended very differently if it happened to an adult me because, in the words of my friend Alexei Sayle, "I'm not a violent person, but I get provoked." There'd have been an ugly scene, almost certainly resulting in my punching the anti-Semitic bastard on the nose, and the whole family being asked to leave.

My father had won the argument by staying calm and by doing so, show-ing a strength and dignity the other man clearly didn't possess.

The very few times in my life that I've either got into a fight, or been very close to one, have been when I've heard a racist remark or seen someone treated physically badly... usually a woman or a child. I find it impossible to walk on by on the other side of the road.

One night in early 1982 when I was still living in Chelsea, I was in the Admiral Codrington pub, a very trendy spot with a high quotient of 'Hooray Henrys' among its regulars, when I heard a guy in his twenties shout, "You're a fucking Jew boy!" to someone.

I turned round and said to him, "Don't say that again, because if you do, I'll beat the living daylights out of you."

"What's it got to do with you?" he said aggressively.

"Because I'm a fucking Jew boy too, that's why. I'll tell you what, let's go outside and we can settle it now." Unfortunately at times like this, the words 'Peter, keep your big mouth shut and get out of here now!' never seem to come into my head. Luckily for me, like all bullies, he was a coward; he said nothing and went to the other side of the bar.

A month later, I was in D'Aethusas, a club on the King's Road, with my pal Billy the Kid. I saw the guy from the Codrington across the room.

I told Billy the story, and before I knew what was happening Billy had gone over to him, had a few words and then hit him flush on the jaw, knocking him clean out.

Billy had a punch to go with his temper, and he was always very loyal to his friends.

Not long afterwards, I was driving my new red Mercedes convertible fast down Lower Sloane Street, on the way to make a sale. I had the hood down and, as usual, was reading a newspaper, talking on my mobile phone (the size of a small suitcase and weighing 10lbs, it was like the one Radar had in *M*A*S*H*) and listening to music on the radio, all at the same time.

At the red lights, a huge lorry roared up next to me.

The shaven-headed, heavily-tattooed driver stuck his head out the window.

"Oi! You! You fucking cunt!!" he shouted, his face contorted with fury, the blue veins in his forehead throbbing violently.

I must have cut in front of him.

"I do apologise... my fault entirely, old chap. I'm terribly sorry," I said.

"Oh... right, er... all right then, guv. No problem!"

As the lights changed to green, I shouted over to him, just before accelerating off, "By the way, how did you know my name!? Were we at school together?"

Rudeness is the weak man's imitation of strength.

And the one who 'loses it' loses the argument (and gets his head kicked in by lorry drivers).

Chapter 8

How to fight the battle of the breakfast table
Across the breakfast table – 1989, Claridge's

As soon as I walked into the restaurant this particular morning, I knew something terrible had happened. My table had disappeared. It had been there in the same place every morning for seven years. I had grown up with that table! It was *my* table. Nobby had given it to me. Now, it had gone.

A large red sofa stood in its place. Several other sofas surrounded it. There had never been sofas in the restaurant before. "Nasser!" I shouted.

I love shouting "Nasser!" When I was a volunteer in the Six-Day War, the Egyptian president was Nasser: after losing the war, everybody thought he had died. So you can imagine my surprise when he showed up at Claridge's as a breakfast waiter.

"Nasser!"

Nasser ran across the room, close to tears. "I am very sorry, Mr Rosengard. They have taken it away."

"What do you mean? Who has taken it away?"

"The management. They have redesigned the restaurant. They have taken your table away."

"Nasser, you let them take my table away?" Was this his final act of revenge for the Six-Day War, I wondered?

"There was nothing I could do, Mr Rosengard. They came at night."

"A night raid!?" I said.

He looked even more upset than me. "I can give you a very nice table in the corner. Maybe you prefer the alcove?"

"And what if David Frost comes in? He always has the alcove," I replied, numbly.

"I will tell him what has happened to you. He is a regular like yourself. He will understand." I followed him to the alcove and sat down. "Barbara Cartland always loved the alcove."

"Just bring me the coffee Nasser, please," I said.

"Why don't you have a kipper today Mr Rosengard? Maybe it will help." He was only doing his best.

That's when I had my 'out of breakfast' experience. It's true what they say: all my thousands of previous breakfasts passed before my eyes. One in particular haunted me. A couple of years previously, I had arrived to find that Nicholas Soames had occupied my table. He was minister for the armed forces at the time and, clearly having read some army manuals the previous night, had launched a pre-emptive strike. He was obviously still smarting from being pictured in all the papers the week before, stuck in a tank turret in Germany and so, desperately needing a quick military victory, he had invaded my breakfast table.

Another regular, David, rushed over. "Peter! Thank God you are all right! When I couldn't see you at your table, and just that empty sofa... well frankly, I feared the worst."

Marcus the porter brought over my shoes. I had left them, as usual, at the concierge desk to be polished. (Where else do you know where you can get bacon and eggs and your shoes polished, all for £30?)

"I am very sorry sir, we have just heard about your sad loss, please accept the porters' condolences," he said.

"This is worse than the Soames affair, Marcus. That was bad enough, then they gave my table away without putting up a fight, but now they have actually taken it away."

"You're not going to let them get away with it, are you, sir?"

"Certainly not, Marcus. I will never give in until I get my table back. This is just the beginning of the Battle of the Breakfast Table."

"It is incredible sir, isn't it? It was only just before last Christmas that you fought the Battle of the Marmalade."

I nodded. "Yes, Marcus, but that was just a battle. This is war."

One week later, following a series of skirmishes culminating in a successful early-morning ambush of the General Manager as he approached the main staircase from the east, the new layout was scrapped and I got my table back.

How to be a pirate in Wandsworth
February 1984, London

I went to Narcotics Anonymous meetings for about three months.

I didn't think I had a cocaine problem. All right, I couldn't think of going out for the night unless I had some with me, and if there was a gram in my possession I had to snort the lot. But apart from that, as far as I was concerned, I definitely didn't have a drug problem.

Chapter 8

I had gone to see Joyce Ditzler, a psychologist who with her husband ran a practice specialising in compulsive behaviour. I had been going through a bad patch since Kate, the girl I had been dating for six months, had dumped me.

"You are too obsessive," she said. Obsessive? Just because she'd caught me peeking through her letterbox at 4am, wearing a full pirate's outfit with thigh-high leather boots and cutlass.

I had thrown a fancy dress party for her 21st birthday, with a rock band I'd seen that morning busking at Tottenham Court Road tube station, in my flat. But I didn't have any furniture, as I'd only bought the flat three years before. So I rented everything for the evening from a theatrical props store; tables, huge modern-art paintings, chairs and large gilt mirrors. The place looked like a baronial hall, there must have been 150 people in the living room and I probably knew 20 of them; word had spread that I was having a party.

I managed to get rid of everyone about 2am. Then some of us had gone to Annabel's for an hour or so, and when we came back, the floral display above the mantelpiece was on fire. Two giant candelabras had been left alight and I'd also left the windows wide open, so a gust of wind had blown the flames onto the flowers. We were just in time to pour saucepans of water over the flames.

Then Kate had gone off with a David Bowie lookalike she'd been talking to earlier. I followed them in my car, and that was how I was crouching behind a hedge in Wandsworth, shouting, "Kate, if you don't come out immediately, I shall knock the door down!"

At that moment, a police car came along the otherwise deserted residential road. I ducked just in time and they didn't see me. I'm normally confident of talking my way out of any situation, but I didn't think it would be easy to explain why I was dressed as a pirate at 4am outside a stranger's house in Wandsworth.

I put my sword back in its sheath and drove home.

So I was now out of the third obsessional relationship I'd made a habit of getting into since breaking up with Irkku.

If there were 100,000 beautiful, intelligent, well-balanced women in Trafalgar Square, and only one of them was a pathological liar and all-round loony, and you put a blindfold on me... I had this uncanny ability to pick her. It was quite a talent.

Kate was a pretty, bubbly, blonde English girl from a Ukrainian family, and the relationship had taken the usual pattern. On meeting her I'd done my usual charming sales job and swept her off her feet with my humour which, combined with my astonishing generosity, I'd discovered was quite a successful formula.

As a surprise present, after we'd been going out a couple of weeks, I bought her a Yorkshire Terrier puppy from Harrods pet department. Which she loved, but her parents wouldn't let her keep so I had to return it. "But it's been used, sir," they said. Okay, it was a little scruffy and dirty (from running around Hyde Park), I admit. "We don't give refunds. But you can have a credit note; how about a cockatoo, sir? Or have you considered a python?"

I then bought her a red Beetle convertible. I parked it outside her house and tied a huge white ribbon round it, and a big bow over the bonnet. I rang the doorbell and hid when she came out. She was flabbergasted – I think that would be the right word. She loved it, but again, her parents wouldn't let her keep it either. I was running out of ideas. I took the car back and drove it myself.

We might actually have been engaged for a couple of days, until I threw that fateful 21st birthday party.

The problem with me and girls in those days was that once I'd got them, I took them for granted and ignored them. They'd naturally get fed up with this and go off with someone else, at which point I would immediately decide I was madly in love and couldn't live without them, and would go totally potty and do everything I could think of to get them back. Which, of course, never happened.

Ten years later, I saw Kate again. She was married by then, and I asked her what had happened with us. "You know, I really liked you a lot, but then you got obsessed with me. And totally changed," she said.

"What was that like? Being on the receiving end of my obsession?"

"It was like drowning."

I was so upset about her finishing the relationship that I was lying in bed all day. A friend suggested I get help and recommended the Ditzlers. I was fed up with the way my life was heading. These obsessions were exhausting, and I just couldn't do any work when I was in the middle of them so

Chapter 8

I was getting into debt again, as no sales meant no money.

I told them my life story, the gambling and the girls, and after listening for almost my allotted hour, they asked if I took drugs or drank a lot. I said I only drank a little champagne or red wine and that drugs weren't a problem; I could stop whenever I wanted to. But when they probed me, it turned out I'd been taking quite a bit more cocaine than I'd realised.

The Ditzlers asked if I thought the drugs were helping with the situations I got into. I thought how, a few weeks earlier, I'd spun my brand new Mercedes on the icy road as I'd shot out into Park Lane with Kate, a glass of champagne in my hand and having done a gram of coke as we headed for Tramps, did three complete pirouettes, miraculously without anything crashing into us, and ended up facing north in the southbound fast lane. I had to admit they didn't, really.

They recommended I went to Hazelden, a legendary addiction centre in Minnesota. I really didn't think my problem was drugs or alcohol, but when they said they dealt with addictive relationship behaviour as well, I agreed to give it a try.

"How long do I have to go there for?" I asked.

"Well, the course is six to twelve weeks."

"Are you mad?" I shouted. "She will have got a new boyfriend by then! Do they do weekend courses... you know, 'How to get the girl you love, who doesn't want to see you ever again, back' courses?"

"Unlikely to be quite so specific, but you could enquire if they do a general addiction introductory course. But this is really about you Peter, not her. This is not the first time this has happened, is it?"

Two days later, I was on a plane to St Paul, Minnesota. I had booked myself in for a four-day introduction to the 12-step recovery programme.

The first person I met was Ron.

Ron La Pread was the bass guitarist of the Commodores. A tall, gaunt black guy in his thirties, with an enormous, dazzling smile, he had only just come out of the detoxication unit after his arrival five days before. The band had given him a final ultimatum – quit the drugs or quit the band. He'd decided to have one last binge and had snorted so much coke before he got on the plane, and then more in the lavatory on board, that he'd passed out and been rushed to the airport hospital, having been stretchered off the plane on arrival.

"So, what are you here for man? Smack?" Ron said to me.

"Oh no, it's not drugs, although I do occasionally do a little cocaine. No Ron, I am a crazy about this girl, who has gone off. And I want to find out how to get her back again," I said.

Ron looked at me for a long time. "Oh man! Women! They drive us crazy, don't they?"

Hazelden was a huge, sprawling place; a couple of dozen low-level buildings set in 100 acres of countryside. We were divided into groups and I shared a room with Ron and a guy from northern California, Steve, who had a wry sense of humour, permanent slow-burning smile and an alcohol and drug problem.

The daily regime was very structured, with sessions all through the day starting straight after breakfast at 7am. We had to wash up for ourselves after meals and make our own beds, which was something a lot of us hadn't done in a long time, if ever. In some sessions we were addressed by staff members, almost all recovered addicts themselves, and in others we had group therapy sessions, almost identical to my GA meetings back home. We'd go round the room, sharing our experiences. There were over 200 'clients' staying there (we were strictly not called patients), and I soon discovered the vast majority were getting the six-week course paid for by their health insurance companies.

They were a great bunch of people and there was a lot of laughter during the sessions, mixed in with the horror stories. They made their serious points through humour, like I did naturally. At a very middle-class group therapy meeting I had once had been invited along to in Chelsea, I'd been criticised by one woman for turning everything into a joke ("Can't you ever be serious about anything!?"). But here my brand of self-deprecatory humour was the norm.

Everyone in my group of 20 guys (there were women there, but not in my group) had drug or drink problems of various degrees, ranging from those who'd hit rock bottom and had nowhere to go but up, to others who recognised their habits were changing their behaviour and wanted to stop before things got worse. There was a third category, those whose family or boss had given them an ultimatum and ordered them to attend. Their addictions had often already cost them wives, friends, careers, their children's love and reduced some to the gutter or prison, sometimes even to suicide attempts.

But interesting as their often-horrific stories were, I found it hard to identify with them. I just felt grateful I didn't have the same problems. When it came to my turn, my story, about how I'd get totally obsessed with girls, but only once they'd left me, sounded pretty tame compared with listening spellbound to Ron as he talked about his life of sex, drugs and rock 'n' roll with one of the world's biggest bands. But they pointed out that my behaviour was just another form of addictive self-destructive behaviour, just as my compulsive gambling had been.

Then one morning, I finally got it! I was just the same as them. Just as I used to be a mad gambler, a 'crazy suivi-er' at the chemmy table, always chasing a losing bet (if you lost one pound and suivied ten times, you ended up losing a thousand pounds), I was still suivi-ing compulsively 20 years later. Only this time, the game was women.

I'd just swapped addictions.

After the four days at Hazelden I flew back home.

I never touched drugs again.

How to meet Miss Dong
August 1984, King's Road, London

It was a lovely, sunny summer afternoon.

I'd just come out of a Narcotics Anonymous meeting and I was sitting in the garden of the Pheasantry on the King's Road, having tea with a few of the members.

Our waitress was a stunningly beautiful Chinese-Canadian girl from Vancouver, called Shirley, who was working that summer in London in her vacation from her university, UBC. She was not just beautiful but also very bright and funny. I was smitten at first sandwich.

The next day I called the Pheasantry and managed to discover when they changed shifts. So, just before 5pm, I was waiting a little way up the King's Road until she came out. I let her get 50 yards along the street... and then accidentally 'bumped into' her. She was wearing red clown-type leggings, held up with braces over a striped T-shirt.

"Hi. You're the waitress, from Canada! We met yesterday... look, I wonder if you can help me? Do you think my contact lenses suit the shape of my face?" I asked her.

She lowered her sunglasses and looked straight into my eyes.

"No... but I think they suit the shape of your eye ball."

'That's a pretty good answer,' I thought.

I invited her for a coffee and managed to make her laugh a lot. She was a third-generation Canadian, one of five children. Her father was a civil engineer running his own business and she told me her great-grandfather, a giant of a man called Yip Sang, had four wives and 19 sons! (They were called No. 1 son, No. 2 son, and so on.) She said early photographs showed him with a pigtail, sitting in the front row surrounded by his huge family. He had come from China and became one of the main labour contractors for the Canadian Pacific Railway that was blasted through the Rockies in the 1890s – one of the greatest engineering feats in history – bringing in thousands of Chinese workers to build the railroad.

I liked her a lot right away and apart from being stunning, she was full of enthusiasm for life. And she laughed at my jokes. I immediately fell for her in a big way... and luckily she seemed to like me a little bit too. We started seeing each other every day, and a couple of weeks later I somehow persuaded her it made a lot of sense to come and stay with me for the rest of the summer.

So Shirley moved in with me in Cranley Gardens.

How to create a world-famous pop group
Curiosity Killed the Cat – 1984, King's Road, Chelsea

I was having a pizza in Pucci's with Tariq, a client of mine. Tariq was in the clothing business, but was also a wheeler-dealer and had been managing Julian Lennon, John's son. Now, another manager had enticed Lennon away and he wanted to play me his new discovery, a heavy metal band.

"Sure, Tariq," I said. "But why ask me? I'm a life insurance salesman, remember. I haven't a clue about heavy metal bands, or any other bands for that matter."

Pucci's was the hot spot on the King's Road. It was regularly in the papers and fashion magazine columns and always packed with beautiful girls, and so lots of guys, naturally... a very good-looking, hip young crowd. It was basically one big party every night, fuelled by great music and mine host Pucci – a larger-than-life stocky Italian, who would table-hop, a beautiful new girl always on his arm. His waitresses were mostly young 'Sloane Rangers' or models.

So I am sitting there with Tariq and the place is, as usual, really jumping. He gave a cassette of his new band to Gianni the barman to play. It sounded to me like every other heavy metal band I'd ever heard. "Good luck with them, man," I said. "They sound terrific."

The wine was flowing and suddenly I heard, above the din, a great song playing – very different, catchy and funky, just guitars, drums and great vocals. I asked Gianni, "Who's this record by?"

"It's not a record Peter. It's a demo." He carried on shaking a cocktail.

I knew what a demo was; a tape made by an aspiring band. "Who are they?" I asked him.

He pointed towards the end of the bar. Three young good-looking guys were having a few beers, surrounded by half a dozen very good-looking girls, who seemed to be fascinated by them. Whatever 'cool' was, they were it.

I thought, 'If they have all these girls around them now, what would it be like if they had a hit record?'

I walked up to them. "Excuse me, guys," I said. "Was that your demo just now?"

"Yeah, we recorded it in my bedroom at my mum's house," the dark-haired one said.

"It's a great song. I loved it. Do you have a manager?"

"No, but we're thinking of getting one."

"Well, let me introduce myself. I am Peter Rosengard and congratulations! I am your new manager."

"Why should we let you be our manager, man?" the tallest and skinniest of the three said.

"Because I am going to make you the biggest band in the world." You can't say, I'm going to take you from mediocrity to obscurity in one giant leap, can you? And anyway, I meant it. Moderation and Peter Rosengard are mutually exclusive terms.

I bought them a round of tequila slammers and we drank to their future success. "Look, I am the best insurance salesman in the world, and the music business is all about selling. I will make you number one all over the world."

They liked the idea, and we agreed to meet at my flat the next day, to sort out a management agreement. After my experience at the Comedy Store, this was clearly a good idea.

I went back to Tariq. "You are not going to believe this, Tariq, but I've just discovered a band and I am going to manage them." I told him what had just happened.

"What are they called?" he asked.

"Oh... I forgot to ask. Hang on, I'll find out."

"So what's the band called?" I asked the dark Spanish-looking one, who'd said he was the drummer. His name was Miggy.

"Rydance," he said.

"That's a terrible name! We've got to change it, it sounds like a brewery. What's the name of the song I just heard?"

"Curiosity Killed the Cat," the tall one, the singer, said. His name was Ben. He reminded me of someone. I didn't know who though.

"Curiosity Killed the Cat!? That's going to be the name of the band. It's brilliant... nobody can ever forget it. See you tomorrow guys."

I went back to a thoroughly bemused Tariq. "They're called Curiosity Killed the Cat," I said, pouring myself another glass of wine.

"You are unbelievable, Peter!" Tariq said.

"I know," I said.

The next morning I called George and Petros, my Greek ship-owner friends. "I have just discovered a band and they are going to be huge. Do you want to come in with me?"

"Sure," George said. "Why not, it should be fun right? What's the deal?"

"Well I think a manager gets 20%. So I'll do the actual managing for half, and if you put up the money you take the other half... fifty-fifty."

"Okay, Peter, you have a deal," Petros said.

We were in business... the music business.

They came round exactly on time. Ben Volpeliere-Pierrot, whose dad was a fashion photographer, was the singer and wrote the lyrics; Nick Thorp, the bass guitarist, whose father had a successful King's Road fabrics business; and Miggy Drummond, the appropriately named drummer, who had co-founded the band with Ben; his father was head of design at London Weekend TV. With them they brought lead guitarist Julian Brookhouse, a quiet, intelligent guy, and who I later found out was the Jewish member of the band. This wasn't your usual group from a housing estate in Liverpool or Glasgow. They were a bunch of middle-class Chelsea kids. They were all about 18 and very polite and well mannered.

'This is going to be easy,' I thought.

An old music publisher friend, Eddie Levy, recommended a lawyer and the next morning we were all in John Cohen's office and signing a management agreement. I immediately liked John; very quick-witted and funny, he looked more like a bouncer than a lawyer. Still in his early thirties, he was already a partner at the firm, which specialised in the music business.

I decided the first thing we had to do was record some songs at a proper recording studio. Eddie introduced me to Nigel Frieda, who ran a studio in Great Russell Street. After a few weeks, we had a dozen songs on tape. I rented a flat in Olympia for them and gave them £100 a week pocket money each.

One day, Ben said he had been to my flat. Suddenly, I knew where I had seen him; he was this brilliant, totally original dancer, who had been a sensation at the huge parties I'd held over the last couple of years. Nobody ever knew how he turned up, but he always had lots of great-looking girls after him.

One night, I organised a gig in the Green Man pub in Stratford, East London. There were only about six people in the audience, or rather the bar; regulars who showed no interest in the band.

"It doesn't matter," I said. "I want to hear you play live. That's the reason we are doing this." The boys were fine about it and started playing.

Immediately, I saw that Ben was a star. He had a distinctive, soulful voice, but his stage presence and dancing set him apart. Nobody has ever danced like Ben. I can't begin to describe the moves, but they were his moves and nobody else's.

They clearly needed practice, but they seemed to play their instruments well. I had no idea if Julian or Nick were great guitarists or if Mig was a virtuoso of the drums. They looked great. Four good-looking cool dudes who played terrific songs they wrote themselves. I couldn't see anything that was going to stop them getting to the top.

Over the next few months, more recording sessions and gigs followed. We started doing regular gigs at Crazy Larry's on the New King's Road, where Rusty Egan was the DJ. Rusty had been in Visage with Steve Strange a few years before and knew the guys. It was a big barn of a room that had a regular crowd, so we quickly built a following among the young Chelsea set, particularly the girls.

Soon we started to do more gigs around London and the Larry fans would come along to support them. So we'd be playing at some dodgy pub in Wood Green or Shepherds Bush, and in would flock this bunch of trendy Chelsea girls who would start dancing as soon as the band played.

I was introduced to a bubbly young guy called Antimo. He was very keen on the band and I hired him to look after them on a day-to-day basis. I didn't want to hang around recording studios all day. I needed to sell life insurance! The band was a hobby, and I knew it would be at least a year until we could get them a record deal.

Petros and George were great partners; they never interfered and were happy to put in whatever money we needed to get the band in a position where we could mount our assault on the record companies.

After a year, we had a great demo tape of four songs and a growing repu-tation as a hot live band who were going places.

I had an idea. At this time, most aspiring bands just had a demo cassette, but I figured, as so much of Curiosity was about how they looked and Ben's dancing, why not show the record companies everything? So we made a video of the song that had started everything that night in Pucci's: 'Curiosity Killed the Cat'.

We shot it in a day at The Embassy Club in Bond Street. I got my friend Dario Poloni to direct it; he had done a couple of pop promos for success-ful bands. It was just a straight film of the band on stage and the boys wore what they always wore: jeans and T-shirts. Dario shot it in black and white and then made it look terrific in the editing suite, with great 1950s retro touches and lots of Ben dancing cut in.

I had for months been trying to get Ben to stop wearing his hat, a kind of blue Greek fisherman cap he wore back to front. "The girls will think you are bald." I kept trying to snatch it off his head before he went on stage. But he insisted on wearing it. And the hat became history. It shows what I know about pop culture!

I called up the heads of A&R (artist & repertoire) at all the major companies. Most bands just sent cassettes in the post and hoped for a response, but this was where I came in. I was going to get appointments with the top guys, play the video and demo, and sell the band. I had the enthusiasm and all my appointment-making skills, honed from selling life insurance.

"Will he know what it's about?" the secretary would ask.

"Not unless he's psychic!" I would say. "Just tell him it's Peter... Peter Rosengard."

"Where are you from Mr Rosengard?"

"Well I was born in Hammersmith, my family are from Glasgow and I live in South Kensington. But enough about me... is Dave in?"

"What's it about?"

"It's a surprise. I want to surprise him!"

"Hi, I'm Peter Rosengard. I don't think we have met but I am the guy who founded the Comedy Store and discovered Alexei Sayle, Ben Elton, French and Saunders and all the others who have become phenomenally successful." (Life's too short to be modest.) "Now, I have discovered my first band, Curiosity Killed the Cat, and they are going to be huge. I want to give your company the first opportunity to sign them... Have you got your diary handy? I can see you next Thursday at 11am or Monday at 4pm, which is better for you?"

Very soon, I had appointments with all the major companies.

At this time, it cost about £1m to launch a band, excluding a signing advance of anything from £50k to £500k. The band paid this back from future royalties, but if they flopped they didn't have to return a penny. So it was a high-risk business; every week over a hundred new records were released in the UK alone and only one or two became hits.

I was going to get the band signed up on the spot, as I did with my insurance sales. We arranged a showcase gig and invited all the interested parties. We packed the room with friends for the set.

The boys were now using horns and a keyboard, played by their pal Toby Anderson, who came with an attitude – the 'I don't like Peter Rosengard' attitude – and I just couldn't charm him. Apart from their music, their big selling point was that they were four good-looking cool guys: Toby wasn't exactly a pin-up boy; prematurely bald, he looked much older than the others, but he was apparently helping the boys on the writing side. As well as Toby, Molly Duncan, a brilliant sax player and former member of

Average White Band, was grey-bearded and in his forties. I wasn't very happy but the boys insisted on having them play, so they often went on stage as a six, or even at times a seven, piece!

Still, the showcase went very well. And I waited for the offers to flow in.

Well, I waited and waited... nothing was happening. Were they all blind and deaf?

Finally, Polygram's Mercury label made us an offer, but I had also brought a small but well-financed independent label called China Records into the race and, to some extent, we were able to play one off against the other.

Eventually, with the help of John Cohen we decided Polygram was the best place, so we signed with Mercury.

Then followed months of recording the first album at Island Studios in Hammersmith. It was produced by Stuart Levine, who had worked with Culture Club. He brought in an array of talent, including star Reggae producers Sly and Robbie, who did a couple of tracks. I was in the ganja-stinking studios for an afternoon one day, listening to them tell Ben how to sing "Love you, baby" like they wanted it, over a hundred times. I couldn't stand it any longer. Patience is not my strong point; when I make toast, I put it in the microwave and stand there shouting, "Hurry up!"

The boys were getting invited to lots of openings and premieres, and had already been on the cover of the ultra-hip magazine *Ritz*. There was a big media buzz that they were the 'next big thing'. One night, Andy Warhol was at an opening party at the Anthony d'Offay gallery off Bond Street; the boys had been invited along and Antimo scored a real coup by talking him into directing their first video.

"Listen, Peter," Antimo said one day, "I get on very well with the boys and am doing a lot of work, but I'm only getting a wage. I'd like a percent-age, a bit of your commission. What do you say?"

"Antimo, you are doing a good job. I'll talk to Petros and George and come back to you."

The boys went off to New York to film the video. We had chosen 'Misfit' as their first single, which I thought would be a big hit. I didn't go along, one reason being I don't think they wanted me to go, they seemed to be getting increasingly close to Antimo.

In the team was John Cohen, who had played a valuable role in negotiations with the record company and, crucially, advised us to keep America out of the deal, so if things went well we could do a US deal with a huge advance. We'd already got a £250k advance from Polygram, a very large amount for an unknown new band.

The band filmed the video with Warhol – who really liked the guys, but then went and died shortly afterwards. He actually appeared in it himself, doing a parody of the famous Bob Dylan video where he holds up a big artist's pad and tears off one page at a time with the lyrics and throws it on the ground.

I noticed a definite change of mood when they got back. Somebody said one day, "You do know Antimo is trying to get them to leave you, don't you?" It didn't surprise me; he hadn't even waited for me to get back to him about a stake in the band.

I sat down with him a few days later. "Antimo, you're fired," I said. It was the first time I'd ever sacked anyone – it's difficult if you don't actually employ anyone.

Loyalty has always been very important to me.

Things started moving very quickly. The company had set a release date, and now all the marketing meetings were being held. I got the feeling the record company were not used to dealing with someone like me. I wasn't your usual manager, often a friend of one of the band, sometimes the same age, that kind of thing. Maybe I was a bit demanding.

I was lucky because I could always get good advice from John or Eddie, who looked after the music publishing company we had formed. John had explained that the really big income came from publishing royalties. What, in retrospect, didn't make sense was that I didn't own a part of the company, but John was acting for the band and not me.

The big day came and 'Misfit' was released; and it flopped. "We knew we should have put out 'Down to Earth'," the boys said. "We don't know why you insisted on 'Misfit'."

"I've always been able to spot a hit record," I'd told them. "Trust me, I have got great ears!"

A month later, we released 'Down to Earth'. It went to No. 2 in the charts, and would have made No. 1 if a one-off song from a Levi's jeans TV advert, with hunky male model Nick Kamen, hadn't got there first. We did

Top of the Pops and the kids in the studio went nuts.

The album came out a few weeks later and went straight to No. 1, only the third or fourth time a new band's first album had done this on the day it was released.

Curiosity mania now broke loose. They were on the cover of every pop magazine and were pursued by thousands of screaming girls. Showing how much I knew, Ben's hat became a fashion icon; guys started wearing it in the street. The next single was a re-released 'Misfit', which also made the Top 10, as did the next one. They were easily the biggest new band in the country, and the album was number one in over 20 countries.

We had a phenomenon on our hands! George and Petros were very happy.

I started getting calls from American agents who wanted to co-manage them in the States. One, Robert Ellis, who'd managed a couple of big American bands, flew over just to meet me. At breakfast in Claridge's, he told me his wife was a singer.

"Oh really?" I was being polite. "Has she had any success?"

"Yes, a little," he replied.

"What's her name?"

"Diana Ross."

We flew to America to do showcase gigs in New York and LA and negotiate a US record deal. We went with Polygram America, but not before being courted by most of the big companies. We were taken out for lunch in Beverly Hills by Joe Smith, legendary head of Capitol Records. As we walked in, he announced to the packed restaurant, "Please welcome Curiosity Killed the Cat, from England!" Everybody stood up and applauded us to our table. 'Only in America,' I thought.

We ended up getting a $1m advance from Polygram, just for the US release rights.

Back in London, Virgin records were desperate to sign us for publishing. I kept saying no and one day I got a call. "Richard (Branson) wants you to come over to his house."

I went over to his big place in Ladbroke Grove. A blonde Scottish woman answered the bell; I thought she was the maid, I gave her my coat. She showed me into the living room.

A few minutes later he arrived. "Hi Peter, you've met my wife." I'd nearly made a big mistake.

He was wearing a big loose pullover and, as he sat across the coffee table, kept looking down at his feet with occasional glances up in my direction as he spoke hesitatingly about the band. He was very different from the extrovert showman I had seen on TV.

"Would you like some oysters?" he said. "I have just brought them up from Cornwall."

"That will be great, Richard," I said.

He then offered to pay £1m for the publishing rights. I told him I would let him know.

In the middle of the night I woke up; I thought I was dying. I had eaten a bad oyster.

A few days afterwards, he crossed the Atlantic in his balloon. I sent him a telegram.

"Richard. Congratulations on your record-breaking success. Sorry cannot accept your £1m offer... as you tried to poison me."

For a year all was going great, but I found it difficult to sell life insurance as I was so busy with the band and I was definitely ignoring Shirley, who was at home alone a lot while I flew off somewhere. We were nominated for a Brit award, went to the opening of MTV Europe, festivals in LA, New York and Montreux and the music biz annual convention in Cannes. We were hot.

I had introduced the boys to a West End accountant called Ronnie Harris and they had taken his advice and bought flats around town.

Ronnie had lots of frogs all over his office in Welbeck Street.

"What's with the frogs, Ronnie?" I'd asked at our first meeting.

"I just like frogs, that's all. It's not a crime, is it?" he said. I had to agree that having 250 frogs in your office was not, as far as I knew, a criminal offence.

To replace Antimo I had brought in a guy called Chris, who was recommended by Eddie. He'd managed lots of bands without any big success, but he seemed an amiable guy who knew the business. "I'll focus on strategy," I told him, "and doing the deals." I didn't have a strategy, beyond having lots of energy and enthusiasm in fighting the boys' corner with the record company, and as far as deals were concerned, I could rely on John, Eddie and Ronnie. Together, we made a good team.

After a year of non-stop frenzied activity, the boys needed a holiday and we sent them off with their girlfriends to the Seychelles. Chris and I had been working together for over six months when I was being told that he too was trying to get the band to go off with him. I heard this from too many sources for me to ignore it. "Peter's a life insurance salesman, he doesn't know the music biz," was the theme. I didn't recall Brian Epstein had much experience either before he met the Beatles. I certainly hadn't done too badly to date. Curiosity, at that precise moment, were probably the No. 1 band in the world outside America, which was of course our next big target.

We had agreed to give Chris 20% of our commission on the band's income. When the day came to sign the contract, I went along with it until we were sitting opposite each other.

"Sorry, Chris, you are out. I know you have been trying to get them to leave me."

I got up and left the room.

But now I had a big problem. He immediately rang the band in the Seychelles and they went absolutely nuts. My phone didn't stop ringing.

"How could you do this? Chris is a great guy. We want him reinstated, now!" When I refused to change my mind, they said, "We are flying back now!"

I arranged to meet them at the George V hotel in Paris; I booked us all a suite each. I reckoned that if I could just keep them away from London and Chris, I could sort it all out amicably and they would understand my position. George and Petros had been sympathetic, if concerned about the timing; with our assault on America imminent, who was going to replace him? I hadn't thought of that at the time.

When I arrived in Paris the boys were already ensconced in the hotel. The first day's communication was through Miggy, as I'd always got on with him the best. The others were apparently seething with anger towards me, for sacking Chris and having to interrupt their holiday. That I suspected there was a lot of coke going around didn't help matters.

We were all going to meet the next afternoon. But I was determined not to take Chris back. I couldn't believe this had now happened twice. Friends told me it happens all the time; you discover a band, they're a big success, somebody whispers in their ear and they're gone.

"What about the management agreement? Doesn't that mean anything?" I'd asked John.

"You cannot force them to stay. You can sue them, but it gets very messy, and expensive. It's just like a divorce. A messy one."

The morning of the meeting, I got a call from Petros. They were flying over in George's private jet and bringing Chris with them. "It's only fair he should be able to put his side of the story. Don't worry, we will support you." This made me even more determined. Chris had gone behind my back to my partners? 'He made a mistake there,' I thought to myself.

At the meeting, the band were definitely all high and very hyped up. I explained the reasons behind my firing Chris. Then all hell broke loose. I was attacked from all sides.

"You can't do this Peter!" Ben shouted. He was usually the quietest, rarely saying anything.

Nick weighed in: "Chris has done everything for us the last six months and he's done a good job! Why fire him now? Are you crazy?"

"You can't do this without our agreeing," said Julian.

Miggy agreed with him. "Look, I started this band, Pete, and we appreciate everything you and Petros and George have done. But Chris knows what he is doing and you don't! We have got very close with him; he understands what we are all about. He has to come back!"

I soaked it all up, but kept fighting back. "Listen to me for a second... Chris, do you admit telling the boys they should go off with you? Yes or no?"

He shrugged. "I might have said you don't know what you are doing once or twice."

"No Chris, you did more than that and you know it!"

They all weighed in again. I felt like I was Kitchener at Khartoum. In the middle of the pandemonium which had descended in this grand Rococo-gilt suite, the door flew open and Paula Yates, the TV celebrity married to Bob Geldof, strode in, went up to Ben, kissed him and left again without a word. Was I paying for a suite for her too, I wondered? I was sure Ben had taken someone else to the Seychelles.

The shouting moved on to threats; "If you don't take him back, we will go!"

Petros, silent until now, said, "I think we should hear from Chris now, please calm down everyone."

Chris spoke very calmly about the situation as he saw it. He was prepared to put things behind him and work with us, and me.

Petros spoke. "Look Peter, we are not taking sides here. You discovered the band, and without you we wouldn't be here today. And you shouldn't forget that," he said, turning to the boys. "Peter, we will support whatever you decide."

I stuck to my guns. I looked at Chris. "I am sorry but I'm not changing my mind. What you did was unacceptable. We were bringing you in anyway as a partner. But that wasn't enough for you, was it?"

The meeting broke up, with the boys muttering threats. I left them with Petros and George. Chris was still hanging around.

The next day we checked out; the bill for two nights came to over £10,000.

A week went by and things quietened down. They hadn't followed through with their threats, and when we met up the atmosphere was strained, but at least we were talking. They wanted to know about the upcoming American visit. Ben said that Siobhan Barron could do Chris's job. Siobhan had her own successful video promos company and was a close friend of Ben's. The idea didn't thrill me with delight.

The others agreed with Ben; clearly he had already sounded them out. I talked it over with George and Petros. They felt we had no choice after the Chris affair but to go along with the boys. We could always review her role when they got back from the US.

They were due to leave in less than a week. The record company was releasing their first US single, 'Down to Earth', to coincide with the visit, and were going to do a lot of promotion and gigs in LA and New York. An awful lot was hanging on the trip.

The first inkling that things were not going as planned was when I heard from the record company that the boys were running round LA in a chauffeured white Rolls convertible, and had cabled for more money to be sent out. This was crazy; they had left London with over £10,000 cash for living expenses.

News came in every day. I heard that some of the boys were doing a lot of coke; maybe not unique in the music business, but at this particular time key players in the American record business were appearing before a Congressional committee examining pay-offs to radio stations and the use of cocaine as a currency. Any mention of cocaine sent the executives into a frenzy. The head of promotions was due to appear before the committee imminently, and the more news came in about the boys' behaviour, the more nervous they got.

The single was released and was climbing the Billboard Top 100. After a couple of weeks, it entered the Top 40 at No. 37. Things were looking good.

Then it stayed there. And then, it started dropping.

"What happened?" I asked the record company. "It had momentum!"

"These things happen, Peter," they said.

Later one of their top execs took me aside and told me they pulled the plug on the band because of their behaviour. They had simply stopped promoting the record as they couldn't afford any bad publicity around their man's appearance before the investigating committee.

The trip ended prematurely. They flew back to London.

Siobhan didn't last long, and I realised it was time to bring in a professional manager. It was only a matter of time before they left anyway. So better to choose someone ourselves, do a good deal and retain a stake in their future. This was the advice when I had bumped into Laurence Myers, an industry veteran who once managed David Bowie. "Do yourself a favour, get out now and keep 10% for doing nothing. No aggravation. Trust me, you have to do it, before it's too late."

I was recommended two managers. Tony Gordon, Culture Club's manager, and Jazz Summers, who had discovered Wham. I knew Jazz from the 1970s when I sold him life insurance. He'd been a radiographer at the time, who as a hobby managed punk bands and put them on at the Green Man pub in Great Portland Street.

They were both very interested and wanted to do a deal. I told them the boys would have the final decision.

I preferred Jazz Summers, as I knew him and trusted him to do a good job. Tony Gordon was all over me with charm and compliments, telling me I'd be kept in the loop and could play an advisory role. And he would always be available to me.

I told the guys about my decision and suggested they talk to Jazz and Tony and decide who they wanted. They chose Tony. He was delighted. Jazz not so delighted. We signed an agreement with Tony and kept a share of their future income.

That was to be the last time I ever heard from Tony Gordon.

The band recorded another album and released a single called 'Name and Number', which became a hit and a top choice for kids to put on their answer phones; 'Hey, what's your name and number and I'll get right back to you!' And then, with a new deal with a guy called Simon Cowell who was running a label at BMG, a cover version of 'Hang on in there, baby'.

There were to be no more hits.

How to get a car with your name on the bonnet
Early 1988

I was walking past a car showroom in Wandsworth, South London. They had some classic sports cars in the window, so I went in and introduced myself to one of the salesman. "Hi, I'm Peter Rosengard."

"Like the car?" he asked me.

"What do you mean, like the car?" I asked, looking around.

"Your name... like the car? There's a French car called a Rosengart."

"You're kidding me! My name's Rosengard." I spelt it out; R-O-S-E-N-G-A-R-D. "There can't really be a car called a Rosengard!? Do you also have a Goldberg in stock? Or any Cohen sports coupés, by any chance?"

"I promise you there is a Rosengart... Only it's got a 'T' on the end, not a 'D'. It was designed by Lucien Rosengart, who left Citroen in 1927 to set up his own car company in France."

I had visions of a beautiful sports car like a Bugatti or perhaps a vintage version of the old pre-war Bentleys.

"It was the French version of the Austin 7," he continued. "It was made from the 1930s until the early 1950s. There are quite a lot of different models."

So what if it was one letter out? Clearly we must be related; obviously I had to have one.

"You haven't got one, have you?" I asked. "I'll buy it right away if you do. I'm the only Rosengard in the country, and I like the idea, when people ask what car I drive, of saying 'a Rosengart, of course... what else would I drive?'"

He said they were very rare in France, let alone England (they'd stopped making them in 1955, when Lucien had gone bust) and he'd never even seen one, but he promised to keep an eye out.

A month or two later he rang me up. "I thought you'd like to know, I've found a 1936 Rosengart for sale, in a village near Lyons."

The next morning, Shirley and I were on a plane to Paris, and then a train to Lyons.

We rented a car and drove out into the countryside. We were heading for a small hamlet an hour from the city. When we got there it was like scene from the movie *Jean de Florette* with Gerard Depardieu. This was a real French village with real French peasants, and one of them was the owner of my Rosengart.

We knocked on the door of a run-down farmhouse. Eventually a very old man slowly opened the door. Naturally, he was wearing a smock and black beret.

"Bonjour monsieur," I said. "Je suis ici pour acheter le Rosengart voiture." He looked at me uncomprehendingly.

"Je suis de Londres. Je m'appelle Monsieur Rosengard! Pour acheter le Rosengart!" I repeated.

At the mention of my name his eyes came alive. "Vous êtes un Rosengart!?"

"Oui! Peter Rosengart... c'est moi. Le même comme votre voiture, oui?"

"Vous êtes vraiment Monsieur Rosengart?" he asked. I nodded. "C'est vraiment incroyable," he said.

"I think he thinks you are the Mr Rosengart who made the car," Shirley said.

"I must be his ghost then; he must have been dead for years!"

He ushered us in like honoured guests. We sat down in his ancient kitchen at a large wooden table. He brought in a young man; his nephew, a pharmacist in Lyons, who had come out that day to interpret for us.

"I am very sorry but my uncle speaks no English," he said, smiling at us. "He is very sad today to sell this car. He loves him very much... the car."

The old man looked very sad, nodding occasionally at me while his nephew translated. He'd bought it in 1936; it was new, and his first and only car.

"It is very difficult for him. But my aunt, his wife, died some years ago, and he hasn't used it since. It has been in the barn for a long time. Come, let's go and see it."

We walked across the farmyard. With some difficulty, he and his uncle managed to open the barn doors a little; it was surrounded by weeds. The old man gestured for us to go inside.

The sunlight was streaming in, and inside I could see something very, very rusty... the Rosengart. It wasn't quite what I'd imagined. I felt more than a little disappointed, with no feeling of family at all! It looked like something you'd find in your local scrap yard; but as the old man was so upset – I thought at any moment he was going to cry – I decided I had to act like it was the most beautiful car I'd ever seen. It was the least I could do.

I looked inside; there were two ducks fast asleep on the half-eaten back seat. Cobwebs hung from the windscreen. I decided not to ask him to open the bonnet.

He turned to me. "Elle est très belle, oui?"

"She is très belle," I said. "Fantastic! C'est une très belle voiture! Just as I imagined!"

As his nephew translated what I'd said, he took my hand in both of his. "C'est ma vie, Monsieur," and he started to cry. We left him inside, communing silently with the Rosengart, and went back to the farmhouse.

The nephew offered us a glass of wine, then pulled out of a tattered cardboard box the original registration papers, manual and log book, dated 1936.

We looked through the kitchen window and could see the old man standing with his head down, as if in prayer, in front of the little rusty car that had meant so much to him for so long. He had both hands on the bonnet.

He was saying goodbye to a very old and dear friend.

I suddenly felt guilty. "Are you sure he really wants to sell it?" I asked his nephew. "Please tell your uncle, it's okay if he wants to change his mind, of course I'd understand. It wouldn't be a problem at all for me."

"No, thank you, but he cannot look after it anymore, he is 86 now and he wants someone who will restore it to how it was when he first bought it as a young man. I know it would make him very happy and of course, you will do this, because you yourself are a Rosengart! You are already part of the family!"

Later his uncle told me the story of how, during the war, he'd gone up into the hills to join the Resistance. Soon afterwards, hearing of this, German soldiers stationed nearby came and took the wheels off his car for the rest of the war.

I liked the idea that my car was a Jewish war hero! A car called Rosengart had to be Jewish.

The price was £1,000.

"When I saw him saying goodbye to it, I felt I was going to cry," Shirley said on the way back.

"Me too," I said.

Chapter 8

Two weeks later, it arrived by boat in Dover. I'd contacted a restorer in Essex who, after inspecting it, told me he should be able to restore it within six months to its original condition for about £3,000.

Two years and £20,000 later, it was finally delivered on a trailer, outside Claridge's. It was great timing as it was the day before Shirley and I got married. I was having my stag breakfast party with a few friends.

"Mr Rosengard, your Rosengart is waiting outside to see you, sir," Nobby said.

We all went outside to see it. I'd been receiving monthly photos, accompanying the monthly bills, but nothing prepared me for the real thing. The little rusty, ancient wreck I'd seen in the barn had gone, and in its place stood a beautiful, gleaming, dark-blue car that looked as if it had just left the showroom. Its flared wings were highly polished and the two enormous headlamps made it look like the aristocratic continental relative of the humble Austin 7, to which it was distantly related. It now definitely had French élan... real style. The original badge gleamed on the bonnet; it simply said 'Rosengart'.

On the back of the boot was the spare tyre. It looked like a car from a 1940s 'film noir'.

I got in, put the key in and turned the ignition.

Nothing happened.

I tried again... still nothing. I got out and looked at it.

"Don't worry, it probably just needs a little push, sir," Roman the commissionaire said.

I got back in and everyone pushed it along Brook Street; after 20 yards I let the clutch out and the tiny 750cc engine spluttered into life. Three of my friends piled in, and I took a right down Bond Street. We drove round Grosvenor Square half a dozen times, at a steady 20mph.

It's now over 20 years later, and I've still got my Rosengart.

And since that morning, I must have driven a total of three miles in it. It's been living happily at various friends' houses in the country, in their spare garages. To date, its only passengers have been a family of mice, who moved in.

I'm keeping it for Lily. But I told her recently, "If I buy a big house one day, maybe we'll keep it in the living room. After all, it's more than just a car, isn't it? It's a piece of our family history... an objet d'art." I had discovered there is a Rosengart museum in Germany.

Lily looked at me as if I was mad. "Thanks Dad, that's lovely, but if you don't mind I'd prefer a Mini."

How to create the world's largest charity in a day
Life Aid – 1990

I was in Barbados in March 2010, working on this book, when I read that Bob Geldof was angry. Make that "fuckin' furious with the fuckin' BBC!" as he was quoted, by the BBC, as saying, after they'd reported that up to three-quarters of the Live Aid millions had been stolen by rebels in Eritrea to buy guns and ammunition for their civil war with Ethiopia (the accusation was later retracted by the BBC, who apologised to Geldof).

He was upset because he felt it might put people off donating to charities in the future.

Er, yes... it just might, Bob.

Geldof was the inspiration for a real Eureka moment I had, when relaxing in a hot bath one night in 1990. I suddenly came up with the idea to create the world's largest charitable foundation, in one day!

The idea? A combination of one huge global media event... and life insurance! 'Life Aid'.

It was very simple. I'd get all the life insurance salesmen in the world to go out on one day, Life Aid Day, and sell a million-plus policies, and all the proceeds on the eventual deaths of the people who'd bought the policies would go, not as is usual to their families, but to a new charity called 'Life Aid'. The buyers would be able to split the proceeds of their policy between medical research, children's charities, old peoples' charities and so on.

At the end of Life Aid Day we'd have a bucketful of policies, worth billions of pounds. I had to admit to myself (and very soon, to anyone else prepared to listen) that it was a brilliant idea! Possibly the only original idea I'd ever had in my life.

Of course, all the insurance companies would have to agree to give up their profits on these policies, as would the salesmen their commissions.

Not only would it solve the biggest problem facing all charities, medium- and long-term funding, but it would also be great PR for the insurance companies, who'd always had a terrible image with the public and media.

I rang a few friends who ran insurance companies and they agreed it was a great idea. In particular, an old pal from the Million Dollar Round Table, a super-salesman called Ron Barbaro who was now president of Prudential of America, thought it was terrific, but advised me to try it out in the UK before going global. "It's a lot easier, a lot more doable, and you're there on the ground," he said on the phone from New York.

My next move was to form a committee of the heads of Life companies. I approached the leading half dozen, including Standard Life, Eagle Star, Allied Dunbar and my own Abbey Life. Everyone was enthusiastic, especially Keith Carby, who was running Allied Dunbar; only the Prudential weren't interested. I'd never even been on a committee before, let alone chaired one of chief executives. I'm definitely not a committee person.

This was a new world for me, one of consensus and politics, and I made a couple of big mistakes. I let myself, early on, be persuaded that the project could only go ahead if all the major UK insurance companies unanimously agreed, and there were 60-plus of them. The second big mistake, in retrospect, was in not going public with the idea right away.

All the companies contributed seed money for a feasibility study, and we brought in Price Waterhouse and Mercers, the actuarial consultants, to work out how it would all work in practice and to project the flow of funds to the proposed new foundation, 'Life Aid', over the next five, ten, 15... even 50 years.

Over the course of 1990, meeting followed meeting. It had received an amazingly enthusiastic reception in the industry press, but my committee didn't want to go public until we had everything ready and had the whole industry's okay.

I had my first foretaste of the trouble that lay ahead when I met with Joe Palmer, the chief executive of Legal and General and also president of the ABI (Association of British Insurers).

"You do realise you'll be shooting the industry in the foot, don't you?" he said.

"How do you mean?" I asked, surprised. "It'll give the industry the best

159

PR they've ever had, to be seen to use our unique product, life insurance, to create enormous funds for charity."

"You'll be telling people what we earn, what the salesmen's commissions are."

This was incredible to me. We knew we couldn't be seen to profit from Life Aid, so we'd devised the 'Life Aid Margin' (LAM) which was basically all the profit the companies would normally make on the policies, including salesmen's commissions, and this alone was some millions of pounds that on day one would be paid into the fund. But it was only a tiny fraction of the funds that would be generated over the years. The salesmen themselves had greeted the plan with enthusiasm and excitement. It had been unanimous. The editorials in the industry press were all in favour, without reservation. I left the meeting realising we had major opposition coming, but I didn't know where from at that time.

The old Scottish life companies were, I discovered, a very different breed to the new index-linked companies of the south, like Abbey Life and Allied Dunbar. Their whole culture and way of thinking was quite different, as if on a different planet. Although I did have the support of one of my committee members, the general sales director of Standard Life, the biggest Scottish company, we soon heard we had strong opposition from most of the others.

But importantly, I'd got the support of Mark Weinberg, who had revolutionised the UK industry when he founded Abbey Life in the early 1960s, gone on to start Hambro Life (later Allied Dunbar) in 1970 and then, in the late 1990s, a third, very successful company with Jacob Rothschild, called J Rothschild Assurance Group (now St James's Place).

We needed trustees for Life Aid of worldwide renown, and among many other potential trustees I met Lech Walesa, who was on an official visit to London. I gave him a gift of a statue of Winston Churchill, but never heard from him again, let alone received a thank you note.

Towards the end of 1990, we were ready to launch and I called a meeting of all the UK companies. Sixty-seven chief executives turned up; I was told this was the largest-ever gathering of insurance chiefs in one room. I got Michael Heseltine, the maverick former Tory minister, to open the meeting with a hearty endorsement of Life Aid – this was two months before he ran for the Tory leadership against prime minister Margaret Thatcher.

After Heseltine came Mark Weinberg, offering his support, then it was my turn to speak. I made an impassioned, emotional call for us to move forward with Life Aid.

We then took questions from the floor, and this was the opportunity for the Scottish representatives who, one after the other, told the meeting it was a terrible idea. Basically, they felt we would be ruining the industry by telling the public the money we made. They couldn't have cared less about the billions of pounds we could create for charity; it was pure self-interest. A vote wasn't necessary; clearly, we had no unanimity. Life Aid was finished.

It was all over in an hour, after a year spent thinking of virtually nothing else; as always, it had become an obsession and totally taken over my life. I felt shell-shocked. It was like I'd run into a brick wall at 100mph.

But I let go. I'd given it my best shot.

I knew I'd made a big mistake by agreeing (make that, being railroaded) not to go public with it early on, because then the industry couldn't have backed out. They'd have been shamed into it. Also, the idea of needing unanimous support was clearly never realistic. We should have gone with the 30 or more companies who wanted to participate and left the others out.

The next morning, I got out of bed, got dressed and went out the door.

"Next!"

Postscript:

Within two years of the demise of Life Aid, all life insurance companies in the UK were required to disclose the commission they paid to their salesmen.

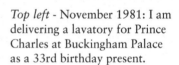

Top left - November 1981: I am delivering a lavatory for Prince Charles at Buckingham Palace as a 33rd birthday present.

Top right - 10th December 1976: My first wedding reception: From *left*, Dad, Stu, Tabetha, Irkku, me and Mum.

Bottom right - November 1981 London: In expansive mood at opening night of The Last Laugh.

Centre left - March 1984: Curiosity Killed the Cat sitting on a wall in the King's Road.

Bottom left - 1987 London: Curiosity Killed the Cat party to celebrate the album going straight to No. 1. *Left*, Maurice Oberstein, Chairman Phonogram UK, *right*, Dick Asher, President Polygram USA. I am at *centre*.

Top left - 1988 Claridge's: Across the breakfast table (*left*, Mariano Viva takes our order)...fresh squeezed orange juice, scrambled eggs and crispy bacon.

Top right - 1985 Marylebone: Dad at lunch at the Hellenic.

Bottom left - 4th May 1990: Marriage to Shirley. Chelsea Registry Office, King's Road.

Centre - 1991: 'Rosengard meets Rosengart.' Shirley and I finally welcome the restored Rosengart to Claridge's.

Centre right - 28th December 1991 Bombay, India: I gave a speech to Life Insurance Round Table of India.

Bottom right - 1990 London: Author meeting President Lech Walesa of Poland to discuss Life Aid.

CHAPTER 9

How to get married for the second time
4th May 1990

Shirley and I had been living together since she finished college and came back to London to be with me in 1985. She was definitely the most wonderful, uncomplicated, honest and loving girl I'd ever met. And amazingly, she loved me. How lucky could a man get?

Many times, people would come over to us and say, to her great embarrassment, "Excuse me for interrupting… but I've got to say you're the most beautiful girl I've ever seen." The funny thing is she spent no time in front of a mirror at all. She had to be taken at gunpoint to go shopping for clothes.

After six years of living together, whenever we were out for dinner we still talked all the time and laughed a lot. (Okay… she still laughed at my jokes.) Most old married couples you see are sitting there in silence. I was sure this would never happen to us.

She was 27 and I was 43 but luckily I was a very young 43! ("When I shave I look two days younger," I told people.) The age gap was never a problem; I didn't think it mattered that she was far more mature than me.

For the wedding, my friend Harry Leventis lent us, from his wonderful car collection, the Rolls specially built for the Queen's 1958 visit for Nigeria's Independence. Probably it was more appropriate for the occasion than the Ferrari that won Le Mans, which I was tempted to ask for. The huge maroon drop-head Silver Wraith Rolls came with its own chauffeur, Matt.

Chapter 9

Naturally, we stood up and waved regally to the shoppers on the King's Road – where we'd first met – on the journey to the reception after the Chelsea registry office ceremony. I later discovered the car had had a less than grand post-independence life in Nigeria and in 1979 had been found in a field, used as a chicken coop. Harry had shipped it back for a total restoration job.

I was enjoying the ride so much that I asked Matt to turn around and drive up and down the road again, so we could wave to the people over again. "It's good to be the king!" I said to Shirley.

I was a non-Chinese Jewish divorced man 16 years older than Shirley, so I probably wasn't exactly the dream husband her family had expected. But even so, they warmly welcomed me into the Dong family. It was more like marrying into a dynasty than a family.

Shirley's great-grandfather, Yip Sang, had been a founder of Chinatown in Vancouver in the 1890s. Now it was the fourth biggest in the world outside China, after Hong Kong, San Francisco and New York. On his death, he left a fortune of over $1m. Unfortunately his sons were all gamblers and it was soon all gone.

The year before I met Shirley, they'd had a Yip family reunion and over 500 family members had attended. It had made the front page of the *Vancouver Sun*.

Her immediate Dong family had flown over from Canada and the US for our wedding. Her parents, Eunice and Jim, her sisters, Barbara and Kathy, and the eldest children, identical twin boys Ed and Darryl, who I knew would definitely be doing their five-minute cabaret mime act as the Two Amigos.

We had the reception at 30 Pavilion Road, a large antique-filled private house in Knightsbridge, owned by a functions company.

I started my speech by saying, "Thank you for coming from all over the world. Canada... America... France... Italy. It's a big day in a man's life... as he only gets married five or six times in his life." For some inexplicable reason her parents did not find that funny. (Shirley wasn't exactly crazy about it either.)

We had 100 guests. Mum and Dad were there, although Dad was still in the grip of the clinical depression that had come on slowly over the previous two years.

It became so bad that a few months later he was hospitalised. Another battle for my remarkable mother Sally to fight. But she never once wavered in her love for my father, through all the years of gambling and drinking, and now she had to deal with the depression, which slowly and silently had taken away the charismatic, smiling, kind man we'd rediscovered in the 26 years since he stopped gambling.

After a year in hospital, another miracle happened when they finally got the combination of drugs right and we got our father, the man we knew and loved, back again.

I threw a 'Jack is Back!' party at our flat in Cranley Gardens.

The reception was a great party, and my comedian friend Arnold Brown gave a speech. "It's true, I am a friend of Peter's... to some extent," he began. "What can I say about Peter... that he hasn't already said about himself?" And so on.

Afterwards, Shirley and I took the Rolls to Claridge's where we were given as a wedding present the Scottish castle suite, complete with wood-panelled living room and moose head, for our wedding night, before leaving next day for a three-week honeymoon in Prague, Budapest and Vienna.

How to surprise your parents
April 1994, Jerusalem, Israel

I was finishing breakfast at Claridge's one day when I decided to surprise my parents, who were on holiday in Israel, by flying over to Jerusalem for the weekend.

To achieve the maximum element of surprise, I thought I'd hire a big black beard, moustache and a large black hat and disguise myself as a Hasidic Jew.

I leapt into action. I called El Al, booked tickets for my wife and myself and then looked in *Yellow Pages* for a 'rabbi beards to rent' section. Nothing. So I tried 'fancy dress'.

I dialled Caribbean Carnival Costumes of Portobello Road. A happy West Indian voice said, "We are all out of rabbi beards this morning, but we have got a Rasta beard?"

"No, thank you. It really is a rabbi's beard that I'm after."

"It's got good locks... dreads man, very reggae, you know, Bob Marley?" he persisted.

I tried a shop in Hayes, Middlesex, not exactly famed as a centre of Talmudic learning.

"Oh yeah, we've got loads of those," the girl said, as if it was the 100th request for a rabbi's beard that morning. They cost £2.95 – to buy, not rent. They were made of crepe.

"Crepe?" I exclaimed. "Nobody's going to be fooled by that!"

"Well, they will be if you don't get too close."

"Yes, like two miles!" I put the phone down.

I finally tracked one down in Covent Garden. I picked up a black Homburg hat at Simpson's in Piccadilly and we took a taxi to the airport. The famed El Al security interrogation at Heathrow would make even the Chief Rabbi break down and confess to being Yasser Arafat.

"Did anyone give you anything before you left the house?"

"Are you kidding? No one's given me anything since my Barmitzvah." The situation was not eased when they opened my bag and found my beard and moustache.

"It's an emergency," I explained. "For a big wedding; the rabbi's got alopecia."

They looked at me intently. "Do you have any Jewish friends, Mr Rosengard?!"

I had been waiting all my life for someone to ask me this. "Actually, some of my best friends are Jewish."

In the taxi into Jerusalem, I started to glue on my beard. In Shirley's hand mirror I looked like a cross between Moses and ZZ Top.

I sat self-consciously in the Sheraton lobby with a newspaper held high around my head, while Shirley checked us in. She came over. "You are okay; nobody would recognise you in a million years. But what about me?" I looked at her. She had a point. As possibly the only five feet ten inches Chinese woman in Israel, my parents might just spot their daughter-in-law.

"You can wear the moustache," I suggested.

I borrowed a jacket from a waiter and a tray with a couple of cups and we took the lift up. It was packed full of men with big black beards.

Somehow, I still felt different. The lift seemed to stop at every floor for five minutes at a time. It got very hot. I started to sweat. I felt the other passengers were staring at me. My beard began to melt.

A little blonde girl looked up at me. I felt the glue running down my cheek. She watched silently as half of my beard peeled away from my face. I gave her my 'It's a funny old world' shrug, pressed my face against my shoulder and, when the doors opened on the 12th floor, pushed my way out like the Hunchback of Notre Dame, all the while carrying the tray in front of me.

I knocked on my parents' door. "Room service," I shouted in my best Israeli accent.

My father opened the door. "Hello Peter," he said.

When I asked later how he had recognised me, he said, "A father always knows his son."

How to spend a night on the town with a Mafia boss
April 1994, St Petersburg, Russia

Lev, the son of Alec Bukhman, an old friend of mine who was the top life insurance salesman in Canada, called me one morning.

The family were from Kiev, but emigrated to Canada because of the endemic anti-Semitism. Lev was studying for two years at the LSE. Although he was almost 25 years younger than me, we'd become great friends. He is a bright, curly-headed, energetic guy with an ever-present quizzical half smile, whose words tumble in cascades from his lips. He'd been taught to be careful with money, but in London I introduced him to the concept that money was for spending and having fun with, which involved staying in the best hotels and eating in great restaurants. He was getting to like it... especially the latter. Lev loved to eat.

"Do you want to come with me to St Petersburg for a week?" he asked.

I'd never been to Russia before. "Sure... why not? Let's go!"

Two days later, we flew out. His college friend Scott, also from Montreal, was working in Moscow and he was going to meet us in St Petersburg the next day.

We checked into our hotel, the Europa, off the main street, Nevsky Prospect. It was a great-looking five-star hotel and my spacious room was luxurious, furnished with Louis XV-style furniture.

I unpacked and turned the taps on in the marble bathroom to have a wash. There wasn't any water, not even a dribble. I tried the toilet... it didn't flush.

I called down to reception.

"How is everything sir?" a girl asked.

"Everything is fine... except there's no water in my bathroom and the toilet doesn't flush."

"Yes, we know this already, thank you, sir," she said.

"Okay, good, but when's it being fixed?"

"We don't know exactly... it's hard to know."

"So move me to another room, please."

"All the rooms have no water."

"Are you kidding me!? All the rooms? When did this happen?"

"Yesterday morning."

"Wait a minute! You've had no water in your hotel for 24 hours!? I'm paying $350 a night for a hotel with no water!? I'm checking out!"

I rang Lev. "Have you got any water in your bathroom!?" he asked.

"Don't worry about it... we're getting out of here!"

'Welcome to Russia,' I thought.

Fifteen minutes later, I was waiting outside for Lev when a shiny top-of-the-range BMW limo pulled up with a squeal of brakes. A 4x4 jeep immediately pulled in behind it, and six tough-looking guys jumped out and stood around the BMW, facing outwards. It had a sunroof but the driver was so big that his shaven head and massive shoulders stuck out through the roof. The giant got out and opened the passenger door.

A guy in his early thirties got out, casually but very expensively dressed in Italian designer clothes, with a large gold Rolex on his wrist. A man immediately came out of the hotel and walked up to him. Saying nothing I could hear, he just handed him a huge wad of notes.

It was more money than I'd ever seen; a cube of money, a foot tall, in brand new notes. The Rolex man handed the block of money to the giant driver, who held a leather briefcase at the ready. Still nobody had spoken, just a nod of acknowledgement from the man who now held the money. 'He's definitely not going to count it,' I thought. It would take hours.

The other man went back in the hotel, and a minute later another guy came out and also gave him another similar block of money. About 15 feet away, I watched all this in amazement.

Then I had an idea... this guy would probably know a hotel to recommend.

I walked over. "Excuse me, I'm Peter Rosengard from London. I've just arrived in Russia for the first time... and there's no water in this hotel! Can you believe it?"

His guards, who definitely had guns under their bulging jackets, tensed up and moved toward me as one as I'd approached. "It's okay," he said to them with a gesture of his hand. "You have no water... this is very bad. I'm sorry. You are from London? I like London. Please, come. I can help you," he said in slow, heavily-accented English. He gestured to his car.

At that moment, Lev appeared with his bag. "Hey... What's going on?"

"Lev, let me introduce you. This is, err...?"

"Sergei," my new Russian friend said, smiling and putting out his hand.

"We're going for a ride with Sergei," I said. Lev gave me a quizzical look. "Don't worry, we've got a new friend."

Lev got in the back with two of the bodyguards, and I sat next to Sergei in the front next to the driver. Off we went down Nevsky Prospect, the jeep of bodyguards behind.

"So... first time in Russia? Welcome to my city," Sergei said. "You like beautiful Russian girls?"

"Yes, I like girls very much, Sergei," I said. "Lev, we like beautiful Russian girls, don't we?" I turned, smiling at Lev, who is a big guy but looked like a midget squashed between the two unsmiling, leather-jacketed goons in wrap-around Ray-Bans.

"Yes, Sergei, we very much like the girls," Lev said.

"Good, tonight I take you with me. We go for dinner and then to my clubs. You will like!"

The driver pulled up outside another plush hotel. We all followed Sergei into the lobby. The uniformed doormen almost prostrated themselves when they saw Sergei.

"I think he's a mafia boss," Lev whispered as we followed him in.

"Really? What was your first clue?" I asked.

"Do you think we're safe?"

"Safe as houses," I said.

The manager and five assistants rushed out to greet Sergei warmly. It was as if the president of Russia had just turned up out of the blue. "These are my new best friends," he said. "They will be staying with you for...?" He looked at me for an answer.

"A week will be fine," I said. "Seven nights."

Sergei looked at the manager. "Please make sure my friends from England have everything they need." The manager nodded furiously and spoke a lot of words quickly in Russian to his assistants. I got the distinct feeling that if we ordered 20 baby elephants to be brought to our room immediately, they'd have been there before us.

We thanked and said goodbye to Sergei. He'd said he'd pick us up for our night on the town at 7pm.

In the lift with the manager, who'd of course insisted on personally showing us to our rooms, Lev turned to me. "You are truly incredible Peter!"

Our room was one enormous three-bedroom penthouse suite with a view over the whole city towards the Hermitage Museum.

"Unbelievable!" Lev said.

"It's good to be the king," I said. "But if you can't be the king, then it's good to be a friend of the king!"

Before seven, we were waiting in the lobby. By 7.15pm, Sergei still hadn't arrived.

"Maybe he's not coming," Lev said at 7.30pm.

"No, he's just running late... he liked us, remember? Probably just got some business to attend to. Being a mafia boss can't be a nine to five job."

At 8pm, he still hadn't arrived. Lev looked at me. "He gave you his number, didn't he?"

I looked in my pocket; I'd scribbled it down on a bit of paper. I rang him from the lobby; it went straight onto voice mail. I left a message and we went to the bar for a drink.

At 9pm, the receptionist said there was call for me. It was Sergei.

"Peter, I'm sorry my friend, but I'm stuck here in the dentist. I shouldn't be long. I will call you when it's finished."

"At the dentist!? At nine at night!?" Lev said when I told him.

"Yes, he's probably using the drill on someone who's being held down by the giant," I said.

We never heard from Sergei again.

Two days later, the police stopped a taxi at 4am in one of the main squares. It was towing a Mercedes saloon behind it. They asked the driver to open the boot.

Inside were the bodies of five men, riddled with AK-47 bullets. The newspapers said they were victims of a gangland hit.

The driver said he didn't know they were in the boot. He'd just had a call, he said, to tow it to a garage. The papers said a Chechnyan hit man had been paid $50,000 by a local mafia boss to wipe out an entire rival gang, but he'd missed two who had escaped. The word was he wasn't going to get paid until he finished the job.

At the end of our week, when we'd gone to settle our bill at the hotel, it had all been taken care of. "Please... with our compliments," the manager beamed. "Always for Mr Sergei."

Three months later, I read in the newspaper that the Chechnyan had returned to St Petersburg and killed the two men who'd got away the first time.

Clearly, the man was a professional. One way or another, he was going to get paid for the job.

It's difficult to find a reliable hit man these days.

How to talk to strangers (3)
September 2008, London

I'd just crossed Conduit Street when I saw a warden was about to write me a parking ticket.

I ran over. "Stop! Don't give me a ticket! I'm a great friend of the Yoruba people! I love Lagos! Nigeria is my favourite country!"

He stopped and looked up, his ticket writing arm suspended in mid-air.

"How did you know I am a Yoruba man!?" he asked, with a huge smile of amazement.

"I was a friend of M.K.O."

"You knew the chief!?"

"Did I know the chief!?" I said. "We were like that!" I held my crossed fingers up. "I was his personal life insurance salesman. He was a great man, M.K.O. Abiola... God rest his soul."

"Yes. He was a very great man."

"What's your name?" I asked.

"John Abidimbolou."

"You're from Abeokuta?"

"Oh, you really know Nigeria!" He laughed and put his arm round my shoulder.

Somehow I sensed I wasn't going to get a ticket.

"Do you know, John, that three years later the family's own head of security killed M.K.O's No. 1 wife? I read in the paper he got sentenced to death after a special fast-track trial... that had lasted only 13 years!"

"The wheels of justice go slowly in Nigeria," he said sadly.

His very attractive female colleague joined us. "You could go on safari in that car of yours!" she said, pointing to my giant Land Rover Defender with the big headlights on the roof – invaluable for spotting hippos at midnight at the local watering hole, Tesco, in Maida Vale.

"What is this?" She pointed at the three-foot-high chimney on the bonnet.

"It's my snorkel! I can drive underwater with it. I never go over Westminster Bridge anymore, I just drive straight through the Thames!"

"We could go round the world in it!" she said.

"Let's go!" I said. "Jump in! What's your name by the way?"

"Comfort," she said

"You're kidding!? Comfort? This is your lucky day! This car's built for Comfort!"

"I cannot come with you around the world," she said. "I have to work!"

"What do you do?" I asked.

She pointed at her uniform. "I am a parking warden!"

"Of course you are! I forgot. Are you a Yoruba lady by any chance?"

"How do you know that!?"

As I drove off my two new parking warden friends waved goodbye.

You don't need a PhD in Nigerian politics to avoid a parking ticket. "Are you a Yoruba?" usually does the trick.

How to buy a machine gun
November 1994, Dallas, Texas

The taxi I took from Dallas airport had eight-foot-wide cow horns tied to the roof. Curtis, an Afro-American in white Stetson and cowboy boots and the owner of the Cowhorn Cab Company, told me about his battles with City Hall to get permission. "I know how you feel," I said. "I had the same problem when I wanted to put a conservatory on my patio in Shepherds Bush."

He nodded sympathetically. "So in the end, we dropped the application to put the whole cow on the roof and just went with the horns." Despite being invaded by 5,000 life insurance salesmen – I was in Dallas for the annual Million Dollar Round Table sales convention – I couldn't discern any panic in the streets. Actually there were no people in the streets. It was way too quiet.

On the way to my hotel – The Mansion on Turtle Creek – I stopped off at the Dallas Convention Centre where the meeting was due to start next morning.

The Dallas Gun Show was in full swing in an adjoining hall. There were counters full of Smith & Wessons, Berettas, Glocks and Uzis. A Blake Carrington lookalike approached. "What kind of gun are you looking for, sir? Will you be shooting quail, pigeon, duck or boar?"

"Actually, it's to settle a family vendetta," I said.

"Sir, if you will follow me, I believe we can assist your requirements." I followed him to another room. It was empty except for a jeep with a silver machine gun mounted on the back. "This is on sale, sir. Reduced from $125,000 to $50,000." I said I would have to discuss it with my accountant.

The brochure said the rusty-pink Mansion – 'Where grace, taste and manner are the mode' – was built in 1925 for Sheppard W King, a Texas oil and cattle baron. Oil heiress Caroline Hunt had bought it as a ruin ten years previously. Tens of millions of dollars later it was voted the Best Hotel in America.

Throughout the hotel Mrs Hunt had casually scattered pieces of art and antiques 'found in the homes of internationally travelled collectors'. I assume she asked them first. 'We want our guests to feel they are in their own homes.' It wasn't quite like my home.

Half a dozen young staff greeted me with "Good morning, Mr Rosengard" before I'd even got to the desk to check in. During the week, I kept trying to catch them out by wandering the corridors until I met one of them. Without missing a step they all said, "How are you today, Mr Rosengard?" It was uncanny; even my mother forgets my name now and then.

"Good morning, Mr Rosengard, how are you today?" K-Jo, my blonde waitress asked at breakfast. I ordered a waffle. "Would you like a raspberry waffle, a strawberry waffle, a blueberry waffle or a fruit salsa waffle?" I chose blueberry. "With maple blue mountain syrup, Texas honey or cream?" I said cream would be fine. "Double cream, single cream, semi-skimmed cream, 97% fat-free cream or non-dairy creamer?"

I couldn't bring myself to order an egg.

The next morning, I registered at the convention centre and collected my name badge. They'd asked me what name I'd like to be known by. I suggested Mad Dog, but reluctantly settled for Peter as there were apparently a dozen Mad Dogs already. In the huge auditorium I was welcomed with bear hugs by at least 20 total strangers.

The opening ceremony, as always, had a cast of hundreds of singers and dancers, choirs and cowboys, and so many racial minorities that I felt I was at the UN General Assembly. This was not like the Pru's annual sales convention.

The climax came when the 1994 chairman rode on to the stage on his white horse. Billy Jo Bob Darnton was huge and could have lifted the horse with one hand. (Who wouldn't buy a policy from Billy Jo Bob?) Even the horse got a standing ovation; it was too much for him and men in blue overalls had to clean up afterwards.

The rest of the week was spent going between the air-conditioned hotel and the air-conditioned convention centre in the air-conditioned courtesy hotel limo. I didn't know how I'd managed up to then without my own limo and driver. I knew I was getting addicted when I started taking little limo drives round and round the circular drive.

One evening I was invited to join a group of fellow salesmen for dinner at the Mansion's restaurant. Just because you are staying in the Mansion, don't assume this automatically entitles you to a table in the 'most distinguished restaurant in America'.

My host, Micky Rosensweig from Manhattan, had been faxing me across the Atlantic for weeks to remind me that he had miraculously secured us a reservation, not to forget to bring a suit and tie, and furthermore if I didn't show up he would be personally liable for a $25 forfeit.

From one of the 'small, intimate dining areas', surrounded by leaded glass windows and carved ceilings and fireplaces, we watched the 'food cognoscenti and other well-heeled travellers' sample the south-western cuisine. Chef Dean Fearing moved among the guests in a chef's hat and cowboy boots with his 'non-stop down-home charm'. I couldn't imagine finer surroundings for a discussion on the latest techniques for selling split-dollar variable life annuities.

On my last night, I was at reception, ordering my breakfast for the next morning, when a well-dressed man with trimmed goatee appeared by my side in the otherwise deserted lobby. He waited patiently for a few minutes, then said to the clerk, "Excuse me, sir. I apologise for interrupting you, but I am suffering from a gunshot wound in the neck and I wonder if you would be kind enough to call an ambulance? Thank you, sir."

"I will be with you momentarily, sir," the clerk replied. "Now, Mr Rosengard, the courtesy limo will be at your service at 7.30am." He picked up a phone and spoke softly into it. He turned to the man next to me. "Sir, regarding your gunshot wound to the neck, your ambulance will be here momentarily."

I braced myself (I'd just seen *Reservoir Dogs*) and turned very slowly to the man next to me. He was staring straight ahead. Nothing. Not even a spot of blood, let alone the spurting carotid nightmare I'd prepared myself for.

"Are you quite sure you've been shot through the neck?" I asked him.

"Quite sure," he said.

I walked round him and looked at the other side of his neck. "I've got some good news for you... He missed."

On the plane home, I read a self-help book called *Get Out of My Way You Bastard!* (subtitled 'How to Get Everything You Want Out of Life... By the Use of Small Firearms'). I'd bought it at the gun show. Or was it the life insurance convention?

When I unpacked I found a note from the hotel. 'Dear Mr Rosengard, The Mansion on Turtle Creek hopes you enjoyed your stay and looks forward to welcoming you again soon.'

It was signed by the managing director, Jeff Trigger. Believe me.

How to get barricaded in the Ivy
1995, London

It was already 1.30pm and I was half an hour late for lunch.

An IRA bomb had gone off in a telephone box on Charing Cross Road, just a hundred yards from the Ivy, an hour before. Someone was dead and the whole area was cordoned off... but more importantly, nobody was being allowed in or out of the Ivy.

I was taking Tanvi, a young Indian friend of mine who wanted to be a TV presenter, to meet my friend Clive Anderson and I was determined to get in to the restaurant. I parked in the nearest street to the police barriers.

"Follow me!" I said. "We will dodge the police."

"You are crazy!" she said, running behind me.

I ran into the alley between two theatres across the road. I knew it came out opposite the Ivy's front door.

"Stay here while I see if the coast is clear," I said.

I edged my head round the corner; there was a policeman at both ends of the street. I waited until one walked round the corner and the other turned away.

"Okay... let's go!"

We ran across the road. I banged on the door. "Let me in! It's Peter Rosengard, I have a reservation for lunch," I shouted. One of the policemen now spotted me and was waving at me to go back. He started towards us. I banged on the door with both fists.

"Open the door! I have a guest waiting for me," I shouted loudly.

The door suddenly opened and we rushed in. "That was close!" I said.

"You are unbelievable!" Tanvi said as she got her breath back.

"I suppose I am rather."

"You are not a normal person Peter, you do know that?"

"Is Clive Anderson here yet?" I asked the receptionist.

"He is at the table waiting for you," she replied.

The room was packed, as always. I walked over to where Clive was sitting.

"Hi Clive, sorry to be a little late. This is Tanvi."

"Hello Tanvi. How did you manage to get in?" he asked. "Nobody has been able to get in or out since 1 o'clock."

"No one has endurance like the man who sells insurance! A small matter of a bomb in a phone box is not going to interrupt my lunch plans. What kind of a man do you think I am!? Let's get a bottle of champagne."

The police wouldn't let the doors be opened and so everyone was a prisoner in the Ivy. A kind of Blitz spirit broke out. People at neighbouring tables started talking to each other. I saw several clients and went over to them, and brought them over to introduce them to Clive and Tanvi. It was one big party; the foie gras and duck salads were eaten, the steaks washed down with bottles of red, and afterwards I suggested to the manager that everyone should be given free champagne. We were finally allowed to leave just after 5pm.

If you are going to be held prisoner somewhere while a bomb disposal squad works away outside, the Ivy isn't too bad a place.

CHAPTER 10

How you know when the carnival is over
23rd February 1996

We'd brought Lily home to Lansdowne Road from the hospital six months before.

She'd been born on 23rd August, the first day of the Notting Hill Carnival and we were incredibly happy.

But Shirley had become terribly upset as I'd been ignoring her for months while I worked compulsively on a new TV project.

She had finally had enough. She simply didn't want to be married to me anymore and she asked me to leave the house.

I moved into the Portobello Hotel, only a couple of hundred yards away, for a month, and then rented a flat in Warrington Crescent in Maida Vale.

The enormity of what was happening to us and what I was losing didn't hit me at the time.

I loved Shirley and Lily so much.

How to take up smoking at 50
1995, London

When I became a father for the first time, naturally I rushed out to buy a box of cigars. At moments like this, you don't stop to think that you have never smoked a cigarette, let alone a cigar in your entire life. Or that when we had dinner parties, my wife would routinely answer the polite request, "Do you mind if I smoke?" with, "Don't even think of lighting up one of your filthy death sticks in my house."

I had always wanted to smoke, but I'd never had the willpower to start... I lit up my first cigar (a Montecristo No. 3) in the euphoria of witnessing the birth of my beautiful daughter Lily, without having passed out in the delivery room. Five minutes after I lit up my first Havana, I knew I'd found true happiness. It was love at first puff.

A week later, I was smoking four a day and had managed to develop my own cigar-smoker's cough. Actually, I discovered that cigar smokers don't cough because of the smoke: it's because we remember how much each cigar costs. A Cohiba Esplendido works out at £19 plus, even in boxes of 25. As Gene Hackman said to Denzel Washington in *Crimson Tide*, "Once you get hooked on cigars, it's more expensive than drugs."

Even though I adhered to my wife's edict about not smoking in the house, I was still thrown out a couple of times – "You stink! Get out!" – allowing me to observe the effects my new-found passion had on others. For example, I found my elderly neighbour enthusiastically pooper-scooping my discarded cigar butts from the gutter. "My poor little dog is terribly constipated," she said. I nodded sympathetically.

More dramatically, I was driving home one night and, waiting for the lights to change, I opened the sunroof to look at the moon. So much cigar smoke billowed out that it was totally eclipsed, and a man crossing the road pulled open my door and attempted to drag me out, screaming incoherently about fire. I clung onto the wheel gamely, shouting, "Leave me alone, you idiot – it's only a Montecristo No. 3!"

One of the great things about entering the world of Dunhills and Davidoffs is that you meet a very friendly crowd. I found myself one night at 2am in that cigar-friendly establishment, Madame JoJo's in Soho, talking to a six feet four inches transvestite waitress about the respective merits of the Cohiba Robusto over the Bolivar Belicoso. All was going well until my cigar allegedly set fire to the plastic breastbones worn by a fellow dancer and I was asked to leave. This would never have happened in the humidor room at Dunhill's.

Still, it's definitely healthier to be a cigar smoker in England than America. My friend was having a quiet puff in a Manhattan bar when a well-dressed middle-aged man came over: "Excuse me, sir, but I have to inform you that unless you desist immediately from your cigar smoking, I will be forced to rip your kidneys out." What do you do when confronted by a man who plans to enrol you involuntarily in a major organ-transplant programme? I am pleased to report my cigar-smoking friend didn't hesitate: he laid the non-smoker out cold with one punch.

I had a similar experience at the Gay Hussar restaurant in Soho. I was halfway through my Cohiba Siglo, seated next to a table of four goatee-sporting black-clad non-smokers. The weaselly-looking specimen next to me announced loudly to his friends, "They really shouldn't let people smoke cigars in restaurants, should they?"

Leaning over their Perriers, I exhaled a blue cloud of smoke, scoring a direct hit on their mushroom risottos. "I'm celebrating," I said.

"Celebrating what?" my neighbour asked.

I paused between puffs. "I woke up this morning. You don't have a problem with that, do you?"

"Oh... cool. No, it's quite okay. Please carry on."

I invested in three humidors to keep my leaf-wrapped bundles of joy indefinitely. I quickly moved from mere dalliance to aficionado status. I opened London's first cigar club, the Havana Room. Ironically, while looking for a venue, I called the Groucho Club in Soho. They rang back: "Unfortunately, cigar smoking isn't really our image."

I am not making this up.

To quote another Gene Hackman line, "Never trust air you can't see."

A few years later, I finally managed to start smoking cigarettes, and when Lily was six I asked her what she wanted for her birthday.

"Just one thing, Daddy. I want you to stop smoking! I don't want you to die!"

I threw the pack in the bin and I've never had another cigarette. I want to walk her down the aisle one day!

Becoming a father is without question the best thing I've ever done. Nobody could wish for a better daughter; Lily is beautiful, caring and generous, a great student and sports player. My love for Lily is the greatest love I've ever known. Shirley has also been the best mother there could be and I'm so lucky she didn't go back to Vancouver and has always let me spend so much time with Lily. I can't begin to imagine what my life would be like without being able to watch her growing up into the remarkable young woman she has become.

How to discover you are a life insurance sex symbol
August 1997, Tokyo

I was about to go on stage to give a speech to 10,000 Japanese life insurance saleswomen ("there were no men left at end of the war, so it was a job
only women could do"). Aoki and Mayoki, my two simultaneous transla-
tors, ran up to me.

"Mr Losengardo! Please lemember, Japanese people do not laugh
outwardly, only laugh inwardly!"

This wasn't good news. My speech wasn't called 'The Actuarial Principles
of Life Insurance (Japanese mortality tables since 1945)'. It was entitled
'A Rock Star in the Life Insurance Business: The Confessions of a Life
Insurance Salesman... Sex, Drugs, Rate Books and Rock and Roll'.

I thought it was hilarious. Audiences loved it.

I walked on to the enormous stage to be greeted by a tumultuous silence,
which lasted the entire 45 minutes of my speech. I kept moving from one
silent punch line to another, like a World War One soldier ordered out
of the trenches into a hail of machine-gun fire. After what seemed like a
week, I finally approached my big finale.

"In closing: Thoreau once said, 'Most men live lives of quiet desperation!' But that's not how I want to live *my* life! OH NO!! When I die I
want to be totally burnt out! Running on full tilt and empty! Thank you!
Goodbye Tokyo, you have been great."

I walked towards the side of the stage, and that's when it happened.

The place exploded. Huge, wild applause... and suddenly all 10,000
were on their feet, stamping and clapping. I got a five-minute standing
ovation.

Outside in the corridor I was mobbed by hundreds of beautiful young
women, waving cameras and programmes for me to sign. It was a stam-
pede. I felt like Elvis in Vegas. They all wanted their photos taken with me.

"We love you, Peter!"

"You are great!"

"You are a funny man!"

"You make us laugh so much!"

Japan is the only place in the world where life insurance salesmen are
treated as sex symbols.

I might have to go and live there one day.

Chapter 10

How to manage a genius
Jerry Sadowitz – 1998, London

"Nelson Mandela, what a cunt! Terry Waite... the bastard. I dunno, you lend some people a fiver, you never see them again."
Jerry Sadowitz, 1989

The guy toppled backwards under the blow and straight through the plate glass door. 'I'm sure it's unusual for fights to break out in a West End theatre,' I thought, as two policemen jumped on the audience member who had just punched the man sitting next to him in the face. This was almost becoming a nightly occurrence during Jerry's show, which I was producing.

I should have been warned when I'd asked Jerry what he wanted the advertising to say. "Just say it's the most disgusting, offensive show ever to hit the West End," he said.

Jerry said everything sadly and angrily. It didn't matter what you asked him, from "How are you feeling today, Jerry?" ("Fucking terrible!") to "How was the show last night?" ("Fucking terrible!") to "How did your date go with the lesbian pole dancer?"... the answer was always the same. "Fucking terrible!"

The show was a disaster. The reviews were fantastic, but we were still playing most nights to half-empty houses at the Criterion on Piccadilly Circus, and the only good thing as far as I was concerned was it was only a two-week run. The bad thing was, we still had one week to go.

Jerry Sadowitz, in the mid to late 1980s, had been one of the biggest comedians in the country and sold out big venues across the UK. A 1989 tour had culminated at the Dominion Theatre on Tottenham Court Road in London. Every student loved him; he was totally non-PC while everybody else was in it up to their armpits. Nothing, and I mean absolutely nothing, was taboo for Jerry. Almost every comedian of his generation regarded him as a comedy god. "Genius" was one word everybody used to describe him. "Self-destructive" was the other one.

I'd had the idea of putting him on in the West End. He wanted to do a double act with his actor friend, Logan Murray. I was doubtful but he told me he'd done shows with Logan before, called 'Bib and Bob', and they would be brilliant. Who was I to argue with a genius?

Someone told me Matthew Freud would be a great guy to do the publicity; he knew everyone in show business. So I had breakfast with him at Claridge's. He wanted me to meet Sally Greene, who owned the Criterion theatre. It would, he thought, be perfect for Jerry. Sally let us rent the theatre for a fee and share of the box office. I was to be responsible for all the marketing and publicity. Naturally, I hired Freuds to do the PR.

The team at Freuds didn't get us as much publicity in the build-up to opening night as I felt we should be getting. Okay, I know some people can't deal with me – when I'm on a project I become totally committed, especially, as in this case, if I thought I was about to lose ten or twenty thousand pounds. Their team were a couple of nice middle-class English girls and they'd probably never met anyone as demanding as me in their lives, so I probably made things difficult for them.

When I bumped into Matthew Freud some months later at the Pharmacy restaurant in Notting Hill, he said, "I hear working with you was a nightmare." I, of course, disagreed. As far as I was concerned I'd been charming... and demanding.

"This show is insane, sick and shambolic but sometimes extraordinarily, wildly funny..."
Daily Telegraph (review of Bib and Bob, 2nd May 1998)

"The word 'dangerous' clings to Jerry Sadowitz like a limpet to a rock... Their act comprises an hour of material that taste forgot. No subject is beyond the pale. You find yourself guiltily laughing at such topics as paedophilia, homelessness and disease."
James Rampton (The Independent)

"Sadowitz is worth a 100 Harry Enfields, a 1,000 Bremners, 10,000 Frank Skinners or half a million Baddiels (and we're off the scale altogether with Jo Brand), and he's undoubtedly one of our finest talents, both as comedian and magician."
Victor Lewis-Smith (The Daily Mail)

Scottish and Jewish, Jerry had been brought up in New Jersey after his

Glaswegian mother married an American after the war. One day when he was nine, without warning, his mother had picked him up at the school gates, taken a taxi to the airport and flown back to Glasgow.

He never saw his father again until he was well into his thirties.

He was now 37 and, as critic James Rampton once remarked, looked like "the love child of Stephen Fry and Frank Zappa", with a head of wild, thick black hair. And still living in the same tiny Kentish Town bedsitter for over ten years. He'd never married, and he told me he had huge problems with the opposite sex, his constant bone of contention; "Why can't I get beautiful young women!? I want a girlfriend!" I would try and explain that shouting, "Hi! Do you fancy me?" at girls as they passed him in the street was possibly not the best way to meet your future soul mate. But he didn't understand why this was unlikely to end in a relationship.

Somehow I'd let myself be talked into it. Two months before, I'd agreed to manage Jerry. Okay, everybody said he was a genius, but he'd already had, at the last count, about 12 managers. And if 13 is a lucky number somewhere... I don't know where.

Arnold Brown, a huge fan of Jerry's, had heard he'd just fired the latest victim, and told me I should do it. And oddly, Clive Anderson also encouraged me to have a go: "He's a genius... you'd be great for each other."

Everybody had heard about his appearance at the Montreal Comedy Festival, when he'd strode on stage with his opening line, "Hello Moosefuckers!" This also turned out to be his last line, as a guy then climbed on stage and knocked him out with a single punch.

I'd never wanted to manage any of the comedians I'd discovered at the Comedy Store. I think if I'd wanted to, I could have managed all of them... Dawn and Jennifer, Ben Elton, Rik Mayall, Ade Edmondson and all the other stars who'd come out of the club in those first, explosive couple of years. But it always seemed like it would be really hard work. Comedians were nearly always pretty neurotic people, and often depressives. I didn't need any more people like that in my life; I already had me!

When we'd met up to discuss the possibility, Jerry, who in person turned out to be a very gentle, sweet and shy guy, was very keen on the idea. He told me he'd always come to the Comedy Store when first down in London in his early twenties and hung around the comedians, even done the odd open-mike spot.

Not only was he recognised as a great comedian, but amazingly was also one of the top five close-up card magicians in the world! He told me that in his spare time he worked two or three days a week at the International House of Magic shop in Leather Lane.

The idea that one guy could be a genius in two different worlds fascinated me. He regularly did magic shows mixed with comedy and every year still performed at the Edinburgh Fringe.

"So what happened, Jerry?" I'd asked him that first night, over a Chinese meal in Camden. He'd insisted on somewhere where his share of the bill would be no more than £5, something I would become used to over the year ahead. "You were at the very top... what went wrong?"

"Fucking Alan Yentob! I hate the fucker!" he said.

"What did Alan Yentob do to you?" I said in astonishment.

"He fucking commissioned my TV series, that's what he fucking did!" he said, attempting to suck up a whole bowl of noodles in one go.

Yentob ran BBC TV at the time and was a big fan of Jerry. He'd commissioned Jerry's first (and at this point, only) foray onto TV: a series called *The Pallbearers Review*. Clearly things hadn't worked out; something to do with censorship, Jerry felt. Some weeks later I bumped into Yentob, a near neighbour in Holland Park, at Osteria Basilico in Kensington Park Road and mentioned I was managing Jerry.

"Good luck," he said, smiling.

"He's really very fond of you," I said.

"Whose phone was that!?" the furious producer, Humphrey Barclay, shouted at the audience.

It was mine, of course. It was the live recording of *The People Versus Jerry Sadowitz*, a late-night TV series starring Jerry as a sadistic talk show host with (clearly masochistic) members of the public as guests, plus the occasional celebrity, obviously selected on the basis they knew nothing about Jerry's reputation. A first series had been commissioned by the new Channel 5 before I came on board, and they already had a hit on their hands. So this was Jerry's second chance to establish himself as a TV star, and win new fans for his live shows.

"So who the fuck are you?" is an unusual opening remark to your first guest for a TV talk show host. You watch a thousand Letterman shows; somehow I don't think it has featured as an introductory remark even once.

It was the first show for the second series and the day before, I'd come up with a publicity stunt to promote it.

I'd gone to Bermans in Shaftesbury Avenue and bought 20 Sadowitz wigs – long, black hippy-style things – and also 20 cardboard top hats, Jerry's usual on-stage head gear. And huge foot-long fake cigars; he smoked a massive Havana during every show.

Jerry met me at Claridge's. There were lots of paparazzi by the front entrance. "Who are you waiting for?" I asked one.

"Madonna, mate. She's due out any minute." She'd been living at the hotel for a few months.

I ran round the corner to Bond Street tube, with an armful of the wigs, hats and cigars. Five minutes later, I came back with a dozen Japanese tourists, all wearing Jerry wigs and hats. I'd asked them if they'd like to meet Madonna! "Remember, you must all shout 'Sadowitz! We love you Jerry!' when you see her... it's an old English idiom for 'Welcome to England'," I'd shouted as, Pied Piper-like, they followed at a trot as I ran back to the hotel.

I got Jerry and we all gathered round the limo waiting for her. I'd had placards made up: 'JERRY SADOWITZ AGAINST CLONING!' I handed them to the Japanese, who had no idea why they had to wear all this weird stuff. "Madonna likes everyone to wear these clothes!" I said.

Madonna came out surrounded by her three minders and they made a dive for the car but not before Jerry, myself – also now wearing a Jerry wig and hat, much to the amusement of Roman the doorman – and my Japanese Sadowitz clones had all surged round her, screaming, "Sadowitz! Jelly, we love you! Jelly, we love you!"

Madonna looked a little confused. It must have been the first time in 20 years she'd been mistaken for somebody else. She probably kept asking everyone all day long, "Who the fuck is Sadowitz!? Does she look like me?"

The paparazzi snapped away and it was an impromptu rehearsal for the real thing, outside No. 10 Downing Street. My friend Maya, also wearing all the gear, came along to film the whole thing. We did the same again, got a load of Aussie and Japanese tourists and, until the police moved us on, caused quite a disturbance. I'd got the TV news and Press Association there and it would definitely have been on *News at Ten*, if the Pope hadn't granted an historic audience to Yasser Arafat that day. "The fucking Catholics!" was Jerry's response.

Jerry and I got on very well. He was, most of the time, very easy to manage and I really liked him – particularly as he laughed at my jokes. "You're very funny, Peter," he'd say, much to my friend Arnold Brown's chagrin.

I'd lost a few thousand pounds putting him on in the West End, and though I too was now convinced Jerry was a genius, I didn't see how his humour could ever get onto mainstream TV. It was just too offensive: and importantly I was also finding that I didn't even like it myself some of the time, which was a big problem for me. And as he'd repeatedly made it clear that he'd never tone it down, after about ten months I decided I'd rather stay friends with him than manage him. Once again I told Jerry the news over a Chinese meal, just as we'd started off the year before. He wanted me to continue, but I said, "No, let's stay friends. I just can't give you the intensive care you need, Jerry."

I think I had the distinction of being the only manager who quit before Jerry fired him.

How to set fire to your flat
February 1999, Maida Vale, London

I had been out clubbing.

Okay, so I was 52, but I knew my rights. I can go clubbing if I want to. The fact is, I still go clubbing pretty regularly. Okay, once a year... but always on the first Saturday night in any month beginning with the letter 'F'.

My friend Maya, who had been painting earlier in my flat on my easel (when I'm not out clubbing, I'm in painting), had gone out to a party before I left. I got back around 4am with six of my closest friends, none of whom I'd met before that night. As I got to the front door someone said, "Man, your flat is on fire."

I put my key in the lock.

"Don't open the door!"

I opened the door.

Have you ever seen *The Towering Inferno*? I mean, in your own living room?

I closed the door.

Five fire engines arrived inside five minutes, and 20 firemen (I counted them) raced up the stairs to the third floor. I couldn't see who won.

They then came down again. I live on the second floor.

They put on their breathing equipment and hoods. Their leader said, "Blaa blaa blab lavble, sir?" I knew they were firemen.

"My friend Maya could be in there!" I shouted. They opened the living room door and plunged into the pitch-black smoke. They disappeared instantly.

I thought Maya had come back before us and fallen asleep watching TV, cigarette in mouth.

If she was in there, she was dead.

It took the firemen ten minutes – it felt like ten years – to tell me she wasn't in the room. I stood in the middle of what, only hours earlier, had been a white, minimalist art-gallery-style living room in Maida Vale and now resembled the ruins of Hitler's Berlin bunker in the last days of World War Two. Only without Adolf and Eva Braun.

Incredibly, the rest of the flat was unscathed, as Maya had kicked away the wooden jam that had kept the door to the living room permanently open ever since I'd moved in.

The fire investigations officer from Kilburn turned up at 6am, after the firemen had left – once they had located the windows and smashed them. They could have just opened them the usual way, of course... but they are firemen.

We looked down at the charred remains of my telephone, next to the charred remains of my Psion pocket organiser (it had 2,376 names and numbers in it... and I hadn't backed it up).

"Do you use your phone a lot, sir?" the investigator asked.

"I suppose I do," I replied. "I've been known to make as many as three calls in a single day. Why do you ask?"

"Cos your phone caught fire, sir. A sudden surge of power down your line, sir, and... whoosh!" He told me it happens all the time.

The fact that the fire might just have been caused by the large candle, wrapped in tissue paper with a raffia bow round it, that I left burning away as I'd gone out, escaped him – or was it just too simple? With the 'flat destroyed by burning candle' exclusions to my home insurance policy downloading in my brain, I decided not to draw his attention to the large pool of molten candle wax on the floor next to the epicentre of the fire, formerly known as my lacquer coffee table.

The next morning ten painters, who didn't, I noticed, own an easel between them, arrived and within 48 hours my flat was restored from Berlin 1945 back to London-cool 1999.

So, did I learn anything from the night my phone caught fire?

Next time you are having a heart attack and dial 999, when they finally take you off 'hold' and ask, "Do you require fire, ambulance or police?", always answer "Fire!"

I've read the ambulance response times in central London: they average 12 minutes, unless it's raining, in which case they can take up to three months to arrive. By which time, if you are having a heart attack, you are almost certainly dead, buried and the memorial service already held; or at the very least, you have suffered the kind of permanent brain damage that would end most careers, except clubbing. But my five fire engines got there in two minutes! And they all carried defibrillators to start your heart up again, if by sheer bad luck it has stopped ticking. So remember that, next time you feel even a mild heart attack coming on.

Yes, reading this could one day save your life! Don't thank me; thank your local fire station.

I found out that Maya had gone home to her family in Wimbledon.

"I thought you were dead!" I told her, when we met up a couple of days later.

"Yeah, well I'm not, am I?" she said.

"No, I can see that now. But at the time, Maya, I didn't know that, did I?"

"I don't know what you were worried about. I was fine."

Sometimes, I had a problem communicating with Maya.

Postscript:

A few years later Maya, who had never had a job in the four years I had known her, or any money at all, transformed herself into M.I.A., the multi-million record-selling rap star and nominee at the Brits, Grammies and Oscars in 2009.

Chapter 10

I always knew she was very creative and always had loads of ideas, which told me she would make a talented artist and video-maker, but I can't believe I didn't spot that she could also sing or write hit songs. She moved to New York and *Rolling Stone* magazine voted her album the best of the year for 2007, ahead of records by U2 and Springsteen.

And she was sleeping in my flat! I should have managed her. Better still, I should have married her! But I don't think that was ever an option.

CHAPTER 11

How to get thrown out of Disneyland
2000, Paris

Shirley had suggested that Lily was old enough to enjoy Disneyland, so I booked up for us to go to the new one outside Paris.

We stayed at one of the hotels inside the park, and because I refused to wait an hour to get on a ride, I bought a special pass so we would avoid the queues. Lily loved it as we spent our day on *It's a Small World*, *Dumbo* and *Pirates of the Caribbean*.

On our second night, we were in the restaurant and there was an autograph night with Goofy, Donald Duck and Mickey and Minnie Mouse. Lily asked if she could go down to get Mickey's autograph; they were doing it right next to where the lift opened.

"Just go straight down in the lift, Lily, get Mickey's autograph and come straight back up, okay?" We gave her the card that opened the lift doors and she ran off. It was the first time we'd let her go off by herself.

After Lily had been gone 15 minutes, we got slightly concerned. Okay, we panicked. "Don't worry Shirley, I'm sure she's fine... I'll be back with her in one minute."

I stood up to go and at that moment, the lift opened and there was little Lily, crying her eyes out.

"What happened darling!?" I asked.

"I got Mickey's autograph!" she said, sobbing. "Look Daddy, I really did get it." She held a sheet of paper up with an indecipherable squiggle on it, presumably the mouse's signature.

"That's wonderful! But why were you so long, darling? We were really worried."

"I lost the lift card, so I couldn't get back in!"

"So how did you finally get in?" I asked, picking her up in my arms.

"Minnie Mouse saw me crying and put her card in so I could come back up." I made a mental note to slip Minnie €50 when I next saw her.

Next afternoon, we were strolling along the main street when we saw another autograph signing.

"Look Daddy! Please! Can you get me Goofy's?" Lily asked.

"No problem darling, just leave it to me. Shirley, hang on here with Lily... go and get some candyfloss over there." I pointed at a nearby kiosk.

There were about 50 children and some parents in a long line. I went straight up to the front of the queue where Goofy was standing.

"Excusez moi, mon enfant, pour just un moment," I said to a small boy.

I pushed a sheet of paper towards Goofy and picked up one of his floppy ears. "Do me a favour Goofy, I'm in a petit rush... make it out to Lily. That's L-I-L-Y, please."

"Can't you see zer is a beeg queue?" Goofy said from somewhere inside his big doggy head.

"I know, but I have un special fast-track pass."

"Eet doesn't apply for autographs. Only for zee rides. You must go to zee back, I'm sorry."

I reached into my pocket and, picking up his paw, tried to stick a €20 note in it.

"This is for you Goofy, Lily's a personal friend of Minnie's."

I must have stood on his foot because the next moment, Goofy totally flipped and pushed me in the chest.

"Non. You 'ave to go back," he shouted.

"You can't push me, Goofy!" I shouted, giving him a shove back. Some of the kids started screaming and Mickey and Pluto ran over; Mickey tried to grab me and Goofy hit me on the nose. In self-defence I landed a pretty good blow, I thought, to the dog's stomach. Goofy bent over in pain, tripped over his tail and fell over, pulling me down on top of him.

"Goofy, give me back my €20!" I shouted (it had fallen on the ground), as two security guys appeared and pulled me off him. "The dog's on the take!"

"He started it! Goofy started it!" I shouted as they frogmarched me towards the exit, passing Shirley and Lily who just stood staring, two big candyflosses in their mouths.

"It's all right Lily... all a big mistake. Daddy got into a little disagreement with Goofy. Nothing to worry about, darling..."

"You hit him, Daddy!"

"He started it!"

They told me I had to leave the park. "But I'm staying in the park!"

It didn't seem to make any difference. I had to hang around for two hours before I was allowed back in.

Lily didn't talk to me for a whole day. "Daddy, I can't believe you hit Goofy!"

How to pretend to be a policeman
2000, London

I had left the Aston Martin with the engine running for thirty seconds while I bought a paper in the local newsagent. When I came out of the shop, I saw a car exactly like mine coming down the road towards me.

Actually, it was my car! There were two young guys in it; they must have been 18 years old.

At moments like this, the words 'don't do anything stupid' have no meaning. I immediately ran after the car. They were driving it like they had just won the lottery. I caught up with them as they were still looking right, left, then right again before crossing the junction into the main road.

"I'm a police officer! Get out of the fucking car!" I shouted at the top of my voice. I've watched television.

Guess what happened next? They jumped out of the car!

I couldn't believe it! One push on the accelerator and they could've been heading down the M1 at 150mph, en route to dying young in a blazing inferno, embedded in a bridge.

They ran off, but the car continued on its own, both doors wide open. I ran after it, like a cowboy running after his horse. I caught up with it before it hit anything and jumped in. I managed to stop it; I knew where the brakes were. That's the kind of driver I am.

I rang 999. And was put on hold for 12 minutes. They should play soothing 'muzak' and have voicemail. "Thank you for calling 999, your life or death call is very important to us. Our operators are very busy at the moment, but if you are being stabbed, please press '1'. If you are being shot, press '2'. If your car has been stolen... HA! HA! HA!"

The next day, Scotland Yard's only comment was, "It's a criminal offence to impersonate a police officer."

I am not making this up.

Somehow, "Stop! I'm a life insurance salesman! Get out of the car, or I'll sell you life insurance," doesn't have quite the same ring of authority.

I sold my car. I thought it was jinxed. I started driving a Mini.

Some nights later, someone broke into the Mini and tried to take it to bits, from the inside.

He didn't succeed. The police thought he was disturbed.

How do they think I felt?

How to realise you cannot hate them as they hate you
15th September 2001, London

I was visiting the US embassy with Lily and my ex-wife. We had gone there to place a bouquet of flowers to honour the thousands of innocent people who died in the attacks that week and to offer our support for their families and the American people.

As we joined the long, silent line stretching round Grosvenor Square in the mid-afternoon sun, I pointed out to my daughter the plaque on the building opposite, recording that General Eisenhower was based there during World War Two. It was from here that he had built up the force of millions of US soldiers that led to D-Day, the invasion of occupied Europe in 1944 and the ultimate defeat of Hitler and the Nazis.

It was the greatest military force the world has ever seen.

As we moved slowly closer to the entrance to the square, where the embassy had erected a marquee housing the books of condolence for the public to sign, I reflected that in the weeks ahead, once again the world could likely be required to assemble a huge military force.

As we came under the gaze of the huge bronze eagle on the embassy roof across the street, on the pavement opposite a group of Arabic-looking men had gathered near the statue of Eisenhower and were looking towards the queue.

As I looked at these strangers – middle-aged men and men in their twenties, some people's fathers, some people's sons – I experienced an emotion I'd never felt before; so unfamiliar, so unsettling, that it was a few seconds before I identified it. But then I knew what it was.

It was hate. I hated them. In four days I had become what I'd spent my whole life fighting; I had become a racist.

I immediately loathed myself for feeling this most horrible of all emotions. I felt dirty, unclean. In that split second of revulsion, and self-revulsion, I felt as if my lungs too were full of that same huge, choking cloud of dust that I had watched, mesmerised, as thousands in the streets around the collapsed towers fled before it.

I looked down as my daughter flipped a coin into the air. "Heads or tails, Daddy?"

"Tails."

She looked, very slowly, under her clasped hand. "Heads, Daddy! You lose!"

I realised that, after the events of the previous days, I was no longer capable of seeing these people as the ordinary people in the street we all pass every day. Instead, I was now seeing them, automatically, as part of the evil; as if, because they were Arabs, they naturally supported the monsters that perpetrated the horrors of the World Trade Center, the Pentagon and that which left the passengers and crew of United 93 dead in a field in Pennsylvania.

There had been thousands of losses suffered by fathers and mothers, wives and husbands, sons and daughters in those few terrible days. But, after the tears I'd shed during the 16 hours a day I had been watching this unbearable tragedy unfold on television, I came this day to realise that I too had suffered a loss – albeit one of infinitesimally smaller magnitude than that experienced by many thousands across America, here in the UK and in dozens of countries across the world since 8.48am the previous Tuesday morning.

After a lifetime as a liberal 'baby boomer', I too had finally learned to hate.

Later that day, I was once more looking at my TV and the 19 pictures of the hijackers that the FBI had just released. As I stared at their photographs, I realised one other thing: I hate them for making me hate.

I hope and pray I never again experience the feelings I felt that afternoon, because, if I do, I will have become like them.

And only then will they have won.

How to talk to strangers (4)
10th January 2012, Marylebone High Street, London

My friend Arnold was waiting for me at Providores as I pulled up on my scooter.

"Let's sit outside," I said, pulling up a chair. I ordered a glass of red wine.

"A diet coke with a slice of lemon, please," Arnold said to the waiter.

A street cleaner stopped his cart next to us and started sweeping away.

"Hi. Where are you from?" I asked.

"Algeria," he said.

"I love Algeria!"

"You have been to my country!?"

"Yes, many times."

"Where have you been? I am from Algiers!"

"I love Algiers! I love your city!"

He gave me a big smile and leaned on his broom.

"By the way, did they arrest you last year for plotting to kill the Pope?" I asked. "Were you one of the Westminster Dust Cart Six?"

"No, that was not me!" he said. "That was the *day* team! I am the *night* team!"

"What did they think you guys were going to do? Shout 'Okay men! Up brooms!' and charge the Pope mobile with your cart? It was ridiculous!"

"They let them go the next day!" he said. "It was all a big mistake, someone heard them joking about the Pope, and the next minute all these policemen with machine guns came and made them all lie on the ground. They even took their brooms away."

"What's your name?" I asked my sweeper friend.

"I am Mustafa."

"Mustafa," I said, getting up to shake hands. "My name's Peter

Rosengard. I'm a life insurance salesman. Salaam alaikum, Mustafa...
shalom!"

"Salaam alaikum, Peter." He picked up his broom and carried on
sweeping.

"What a very nice man," I said.

CHAPTER 12

How you never stop loving someone
May 2002

I got a call from Juan, my parents' Spanish friend who lived in Marbella.

"Peter, I'm so sorry but I have some very sad news; Irkku is dead."

My ex-wife Irkku had been living in Spain for over 20 years; she'd never remarried or had children, and now she was dead. She was 51.

She'd rung me a few months previously, which was the first time I'd heard from her for a couple of years. She was broke and had been sleeping on friends' sofas for months. She had no job... she'd never had a job. She had gone from one bad relationship to another, always with much younger Spanish guys.

I hadn't seen her for over ten years, but every now and then she'd call and ask how I was. I'd insisted on giving her money to go home to Helsinki when we'd spoken, and she finally agreed to go. Her mother died when she was 12 and her father some years previously, but her sister and brother still lived there. But after a few months over the winter, she'd had enough.

"Who's going to give me a job here?" she asked me. "I haven't got a social security number, and as I've got no place of my own, I'm sleeping on my sister's couch. I'm going back to Spain... at least it's warm. It's freezing here."

I thought she had a drink problem, although she swore she didn't. I sent her more money, just enough to rent a small flat somewhere, to get her back on her feet. "Irkku, you have to get some kind of job. In a boutique or hotel... anything, Irkku."

She promised she'd start looking. I'd asked Juan if he could find her somewhere to live and she'd been staying at an apartment owned by some elderly English friends of his.

She'd been found dead that morning. "It seems she had a heart attack," he told me.

I was numb. "You were very detached," someone told me years later.

She had so much life in her, it seemed impossible it had gone. She was one of those special people who, when she walked into a crowded room, lit the whole room up. She had a wonderful smile and was very beautiful, your classic Scandinavian blonde beauty, when she was younger. But more than that, she just had an effect on people. She was a crazy Finn who, like so many of her countrymen, could be very quiet normally but after a couple of vodkas became a different person, who never stopped talking and laughing... and drinking and chain-smoking and laughing. But always the laughter... and her throaty cigarette voice.

She'd stood by me all through my gambling. She had a big heart and was very loyal. Though we'd split up more than 20 years before I would still always help her if I could. I think when you had loved someone very much, you'll always love them and it doesn't matter how long ago it was. She never abused it, and in all those years really never asked me for anything.

She'd long ago used up the money she got when she'd sold the flat I'd bought her in Battersea, when she'd moved to Marbella in the mid-1980s.

I rang Annie, her old Finnish friend in New York. I hadn't spoken to her for over 20 years.

"I've got some very bad news, Annie... Irkku's dead."

She couldn't believe it, either. "I only talked to her a week ago. She sounded fine. What happened?"

"They think she had a heart attack," I said.

"I don't understand; she never had heart problems. She was just 51... how is that possible?"

It upset me to think of her dying alone in a small flat in Marbella. I kept asking Juan when the post-mortem would be; in England, any sudden death of a previously healthy 50-year-old would automatically require one to establish cause of death. He finally told me that the undertakers, in preparation for her being sent back to Finland (which I'd decided to do, so that she could be buried at home with her mother and father), had embalmed her and that made a post-mortem impossible. He sent me a police doctor's report giving cause of death as a heart attack.

I flew to Helsinki to arrange the funeral. With the help of her old friends, I had already managed to find her older sister and brother – he was living in an alcohol rehab centre – and other family members and friends.

On a warm September afternoon, the sun high in the sky, we buried Irkku in a beautiful pine forest cemetery outside Helsinki, close to the graves of her father and mother. There were about 30 people there. Afterwards we held a reception back in the city to celebrate the life of Iris Irmeli Syrjaaho... Irkku.

Back in London, I threw another party at my flat and invited all her old London-based friends. Another 30 or 40 people came; many I hadn't seen for over 20 years. We had a good time and there was a lot of laughter when I made a speech about all the crazy things she'd done, how wonderful and loving she was, how she had an incredible temper and how much fun she'd been and what she'd brought to all who'd known her. And how much I'd loved her and would always miss her.

Annie, who'd flown over from New York for the funeral, also came back to London for the party and stayed with me for a few days. We sat up late over a drink or two, talking about the early 1970s when Irkku and I had first met at Samantha's club. I told her about the time we'd gone to Munich for Christmas and looked up a friend, Heinz Herman – Herman the German – who'd always said, "You must come and stay, Peter." When we turned up in the middle of a blizzard, Heinz was smoking dope on the floor, wearing a long Afghan coat, fez and dark glasses. He'd said nothing for a minute then said, "Bad vibes, man..." and that was it. We never even got to sit down. So we went back out into the snow, with just a Diners Club card, as I'd been gambling and had no cash. So we had to book into an incredibly expensive hotel as, like the time I'd been to Stockholm, only the top Munich hotels took Diners.

And we tried to remember why I called her 'Winkle'... but mostly we remembered her beauty, that huge, amazing smile, her big laugh. And the way she always made everything and everyone come alive when she walked through the door.

How to get your glasses smashed by a famous friend
21st August 2002, Regents Park, London

I was playing with Lily and her cousin Tarka, my sister's son who was visiting from Bali. They had gone off on skateboards and I was dozing under a tree. I could hear some American voices; they were playing a game of baseball.

Suddenly, I heard the sound of a ball bouncing near my head and feet running. I opened my eyes to see Chandler from *Friends* standing almost on top of my head.

He had a baseball in his hands.

"I'm really sorry to disturb you, sir," he said.

"Don't worry," I said. "I am a big fan."

He ran back to his game.

I sat up and reached for my glasses, which I had put next to me at the foot of the tree.

Both lenses were smashed. Chandler had been standing on my glasses.

Lily and Tarka ran over, very excited.

"Daddy! Did you see who that was?" Lily asked.

"Yes, I know. Chandler from *Friends* has just stood on Daddy's glasses."

How to be a film producer in Cannes
May 2004, Cannes, France

I'd always felt that I'd make a good film producer. An old friend, Bill Dale, who I'd first met when I'd sold him a policy in 1991 when he was a young investment analyst at Warburgs, had recently retired aged 32 from the City and was going to write and produce films. He was the last person I would think of as being in the film business; he is a dour, serious and extremely intelligent Scot. I thought he was mad and told him so.

I should have known better. Another client of mine called David Ross, a young accountant at Arthur Anderson 20 years ago, told me he was leaving to open a shop on the Marylebone Road.

"What are you going to sell?" I'd said.

"Phones," he said.

"You are crazy. It'll never work... you could be a partner at Arthur Anderson one day!"

Chapter 12

Well, Carphone Warehouse turned out quite well. I'd read in the *Sunday Times* Rich List that David was now worth over £500m.

That's the kind of advice I give people!

Bill made his first film, a psychological thriller set on a North Sea oil rig, called *The Devil's Tattoo* (later changed to *Ghost Rig*). It was terrific. It had only cost £400,000 but looked like a movie costing 150 times that amount. I'd told him, whatever his next project was, I wanted to be part of it.

A year later, he and his writing partner, a former pub owner called Graeme Clapperton, had written a script called *Onward Christian Soldiers*. It was about the Knights Templar, and what if they still existed today? (And they hadn't even read *The Da Vinci Code* when they'd written it.) A contemporary thriller with a historical legacy... a *Name of the Rose* meets *The Bourne Supremacy*.

I thought the title would be a great first movie for a Jewish boy to produce, and sold them on the idea I'd get it made for them. All I had to do now was get someone to give us $100m to make it. That's why I was in Cannes with Bill and Graeme.

I hadn't even got a contract with them yet. I met an American lawyer, Harris, in the hotel, again over breakfast. He was an independent legal gun-for-hire from LA, a grizzled industry veteran who'd clearly been around the block a few times but seemed to know what he was talking about. I certainly didn't, but that had never stopped me in the past.

I explained that I needed a contract giving me exclusive rights as their executive producer for *Onward Christian Soldiers*. Over coffee I negotiated a fee of $1,000 for his services and Harris went up to his room to type an agreement out. He promised me he'd have it by that evening, when I was meeting Bill and Graeme at a restaurant in the Old Port for the celebratory dinner.

You only have to know one head concierge at the best hotel in any town and it can transform your stay. It opens all doors... especially if he is a member of Les Clefs d'Or, as he is almost certain to be.

If it hadn't been for a Clefs d'Or member, I would never have got into the *Guinness Book of Records*. The ones I've known were all wealthy men. You only have to know one Aga Khan!

So I'd already made a point of stopping by and introducing myself to Rogere, Head Concierge at the Majestic Hotel on the Croisette. We found we had mutual friends in the Clefs d'Or; John Spahr at Claridge's had once been their international president. I explained I was staying with friends down the coast, but would be in Cannes every day. I didn't want to admit I was really staying in a small three-star up the road. Image is everything at Cannes, but all the five-star rooms were booked months previously and going for £1,000 a night or more.

"What's the hottest ticket in town, Rogere?" I asked.

"Well it's tonight, for the biggest film of the festival, *Troy* with Brad Pitt."

"Rogere, can you help me get a ticket?"

"Well, I must make some calls. It's totally full, but why not? It should be possible."

I gave him my number and he promised to call in an hour. He was true to his word, and my mobile rang exactly one hour later.

"Mr Rosengard, I have one ticket for you but you must be on the red carpet by 7pm, when they will close the doors." It was 5pm already and I had to get back to the hotel to change. I didn't have a dinner jacket but my dark blue suit would do; Rogere could lend me a bow tie.

I hailed a taxi on the Croisette. The traffic was solid, so I said to the driver, "Monsieur, si vous aller très vite, je vous donnerai un grande tip!" This had the desired effect; I did a five-minute change of clothes, then back to the Majestic, where Rogere tied the black bow tie on for me. It was five minutes to 7pm.

"You must hurry! Run... they close the doors in five minutes!" Rogere said.

Clutching my ticket, I shot out the door at full tilt and somehow got across both lanes of the Croisette without being hit by a speeding taxi. There were thousands of people behind crush barriers outside the Palais (where the big premieres take place), and there must have been another thousand photographers and TV crews. Out of the corner of my eye, I saw that the riot police were sitting in vans on a side road.

Two policemen stopped me. They'd already closed off access to the red carpet. The only chance was to run along by the beach and hurdle a barrier further along. I was badly out of breath by now, and sweating heavily ('Man drops dead on red carpet at Cannes'... 'If only I could get onto it,' I thought).

Remembering my Bentworth Primary career as a hurdler (I came fifth, out of six, in the Hammersmith schools' final at White City in 1956), I zigzagged through the crowds, shouting, "Excusez moi! Je suis un American acteur! Je suis dans le movie!" and threw myself over the barrier.

Staggering to my feet, I managed to get onto the stairs and was striding up the legendary and now empty red carpet, when I heard the crowd screaming, "Brad! Brad!" I was a little surprised, but I thought, with my shades and healthy glow, the sweat dripping down my face, I probably did look a little like him. But I decided not to risk stopping for any autographs. Halfway up the stairs, I glanced back to see Brad Pitt four steps behind, arm in arm with Jennifer Aniston and Orlando Bloom.

The film was terrible and I walked out of my first Cannes premiere after 40 minutes.

I don't think Brad noticed.

The crowds were still there, and once again I was the only person on the red carpet.

The next evening I met up with Alki David, the young movie producer son of an old friend. I'd heard he was in town.

"Meet me at Hugh Hefner's Playboy party on his boat," he said. Or rather he was saying, 'Meet me by the boat after the cocktail party that I'm invited to.' I stood on the quay and could see dozens of young, busty blondes in bikinis cuddling up to elderly bald, fat men, one of whom had to be 'Hef'. I'd read that he was slowing down at 82 and so was now living with 18-year-old twins. Or was it triplets?

Alki walked over to a yellow Ferrari. "I've rented it while I'm here," he said and jumped in.

"Where we going?" I asked.

"The Majestic, for a drink," he said, roaring off. The Majestic was 100 yards away at most. After crawling through the traffic, we roared into the driveway and smashed straight into the back of a Mercedes limo that had just pulled up.

Three tall, broad-shouldered, handsome men in dinner jackets jumped out, followed by three shaken pneumatic blondes in black mini-evening dresses. "What the hell was that about, buddy?" one said to me.

"Don't ask me, I'm just the passenger." I pointed at Alki, and for good measure added, "I'm English... from London."

"Well, jolly good for you," an impossibly good-looking man said.

"What movie are you here for?" I asked. 'Bond with him before he hits you,' I thought.

"The porn awards," he said, as casually as one might say 'the children's muscular dystrophy ball'. He ran a hand through his gleaming, gelled black hair. "We've flown 8,000 miles from LA and we could've been killed by your jackass friend before we even made the porn podium," he said, taking one of the porn starlets by the arm and heading into the hotel.

On the third day, my total festival film viewing to date was 40 minutes of *Troy* and the first half of a three-minute short (did you have to watch films to be a producer, I wondered?) I was sitting on the Carlton terrace (along with the Majestic, the place to be seen for early evening drinks, I'd been told by Rogere), when I noticed at the next table a young pony-tailed, flamboyant English guy. He seemed to think he was Errol Flynn in *Captain Blood*, wearing the whole pirate number... flowing embroidered shirt, slashed open to his midriff, and big piratey sleeves.

All he needed was an eye patch and sword to be ready for the big 'boarding the enemy ship' take, I thought, as he was courted by a succession of middle-aged fat producers with ponytails. 'He must be important,' I thought, as an elegant Italian woman approached him. "Michael, eez possible we meet tomorrow when you 'av a moment, yes?" This was about the fifth person to come up as he talked continuously into one of his two mobile phones and ask the same question in the few minutes I'd been watching. Clearly, he was hot stuff.

In this business, when you're hot, you're hot... and when you're not, you're not.

He seemed like the kind of guy I should talk to about *Onward Christian Soldiers*. I had an idea. I waited until he was alone and in between calls.

I picked up my phone, pretended to dial and said loudly, "Duncan Heath, please."

Duncan was a very successful London film agent and I'd got on nodding terms with him when he was a regular at Claridge's in the 1990s. For some reason, he always wore white tennis shoes at breakfast. I knew this guy would know Duncan.

"Okay, just tell Duncan Peter called, and ask him to call me when he's off the line. Thanks." I hung up.

Sure enough, the guy looked over. "Hi, I'm Michael Cowan... you're a friend of Duncan's too?"

"For years... Hi Michael, I'm Peter Rosengard."

"Do you mind if join you for a moment?" he said. He came over and sat down.

In less than a minute, he'd told me he had a £100m film fund and was producing half a dozen films. One was *The Merchant of Venice* with Al Pacino, the others all had big stars and, to my surprise, he did all this from Brighton.

"What are you doing in Cannes, Peter?"

I told him about *Onward Christian Soldiers.*

"The *Name of the Rose* meets *Indiana Jones,*" I enthused. "It's going to be massive; I want John Cusack or Brad Pitt for the lead. It opens in Beirut, where John Lewin is blindfolded, surrounded by Hamas-type terrorists. They drive him away, you think to be shot, but they dump him outside a five-star hotel, where the commissionaire says, 'Welcome home, Professor Lewin.' The next scene is St Andrews University in Scotland, where Lewin is taking a class... his father is dying, he's an Oxford don and turns out he's the grand master of the Knights Templar, who everyone thought were liquidated 1,000 years ago, but NO!..."

He stopped me in full swing. "It sounds great. I'm in! I want to make this. You got a script?"

"I certainly have," I said.

We shook hands. I'd made the sale!

"Peter, let's meet up in London as soon as I get back." We exchanged cards. His said 'film producer'; mine said 'life insurance salesman'.

"Great, Michael! I've just got to talk to Brian," I said, spotting Brian Cox, one of the stars of *Troy,* sitting down at a table.

Two years later, the option with Cowan expired, his company went into mothballs with the general decline in the film finance market and the nearest we got to making it was when Sidney Pollack, the director, read the script; unfortunately, he then went and died soon afterwards.

I've kept meaning to go out to LA to get a studio interested ever since.

I wasn't ready to give up the dream of being a film producer just yet. In 2009 I'd called Sid Sheinberg, who I'd sold the $100m policy to.

"Sid! It's Peter Rosengard! I don't know if you remember me...?"

"I remember you, Peter... how could I ever forget?"

He was now retired but running his own production company. I told him about my idea for a movie about the Great War poet Isaac Rosenberg, who died in the trenches on 1st April 1918.

Rosenberg was not just a "poet of genius" (T.S. Eliot) but also a wonderful painter; his self-portrait hangs in the National Portrait Gallery and there is plaque in his memory in Westminster Cathedral. He was obscured for a long time by the public-school officer poets, Brooke, Owen and Sassoon, and only with the unflagging efforts of his sister Annie Wynick is he now regarded as one of the greatest poets from that period. Annie died in 1969 in a freak accident; when walking along the promenade in Brighton, a sudden gust of wind picked her up and blew her into a cement mixer.

I've always had a personal interest in Rosenberg, as his younger brother was married to my grandmother's sister, my Auntie Ray. Okay, maybe not a blood relative exactly, but as far as I was concerned he was my great-uncle, and I'd recently bought the film rights to an acclaimed new biography by Jean Moorcroft-Wilson.

Sid asked to read it. After a few months I emailed him, asking if he'd like to pass it on to his protégé, a young director who in the 1970s Sid had given a film to make about a shark.

He emailed me back in block capitals: 'PETER, I HAVE A LONG-STANDING POLICY NEVER TO PASS STEVEN ANY PROJECTS.' That's Steven... as in Spielberg.

A friend explained that block capitals in an email meant he was shouting when he wrote it.

A few months later, I looked up from my breakfast to see Spielberg at the next table.

"Hi, Steven, I'm a huge fan of Sid Sheinberg," I said when I bumped into him an hour later... in the Gents cloakroom.

"Me too!" he said.

"I sold him a $100m dollar life policy, on David Geffen, from a cold call!"

"You're kidding me!?" he said.

"No, really! I'm a life insurance salesman." He didn't look thrilled at this news.

I pitched him the Rosenberg project.

"Steven, it's a big movie... a poor Jewish Cockney boy, dreamer, poet and most unlikely soldier... events leading to and during the Great War... the 100th anniversary is coming up, Steven! It's a war story and a love story! His best friend is an American officer... I thought Johnny Depp? Brad Pitt plays Rosenberg... how tall is Brad by the way? Rosenberg was five feet tall... maybe Brad could always be in the trenches, anyway, they both fall in love with the same girl, a 'femme fatale' actress called Martha Vane... Angelina Jolie... what do you think Steven?"

He gave me a look that I think said, 'I don't believe this is happening. I'm being pitched by a life insurance salesman in the Gentlemen's cloakroom.' I sent a copy of the Rosenberg book – I just happened to have one on me – up to his suite. Later, I sent Sheinberg an email: 'I've just bumped into a good friend of yours here in London.'

I'm still waiting to hear back from Steven.

How to talk to strangers (5)
31st May 2011, London

"Tim says I'm wasting my time going to the Biennale. He says none of the artists go, just dealers and collectors... How often is the Biennale held?" I asked Simon Schama as we sat outside Raoul's café in Maida Vale. I'd ambushed him on his way to collect his dry cleaning.

"Every two years, Peter," he said.

Well, how would I have known that? I'd stopped Latin when I was 14.

I hadn't been to Venice for 25 years. I flew there two days later to find artists to donate works to my 9/11 charity art auction.

I couldn't get a room at the great hotel I'd stayed at in the 1980s, the Gritti Palace on the Grand Canal. In fact, it seemed like every room in the city was full, booked months before. I kept hearing laughter down the phone when I called to ask for a room. Finally, I managed to get one at a small hotel in the Canareggio district, the aptly named Casa Pissani. When I arrived at midnight, the clerk was asleep at the desk, stank of whisky, unsteadily climbed three flights of stairs and finally, after trying two already-occupied rooms, found mine but then discovered he'd left the key downstairs.

I moved my breakfast table from Claridge's to the Gritti for the week. I took a motor boat taxi for the 15-minute trip over. The first morning, I overheard someone say that Julian Schnabel, the famous American artist, was staying there. I had a word with Umberto, the head concierge (and of course, a member of Les Clefs d'Or). The next morning, I was sitting at the corner table I had commandeered, having my fifth espresso, when Umberto approached me, followed by a sleepy-looking, burly, grey-bearded man in his fifties, wearing sunglasses. I noticed he was still in his pyjamas.

"This is Mr Schnabel," he whispered to me as he departed.

"Hi, Julian, good morning, I'm Peter Rosengard. I'm a life insurance salesman from London, but it's okay, I'm sold out, I'm out of stock... Look, I've got an idea for you. Sit down." He sat down. "I'm the chairman of the 9/11 London project. I've flown out just to talk to you."

He gave me a sideways look. I think it said, 'Why am I here with this guy?'

"I've got a breakfast meeting in a minute," he said.

"That's great! I'm a big breakfaster myself, every day... sometimes I have two or three of them. I'm a serial breakfaster."

Silence. I thought of US president Calvin Coolidge: "He don't say much... but when he does... he don't say much."

"Don't worry, this won't take more than 60 seconds, Julian. Where were you on 9/11?"

"I was surfing in Hawaii."

"Hawaii!? Great! Look, I'm holding the world's first 9/11 art auction in London in September to raise money for our 9/11 education project. We've got all the top artists in the UK giving us work. Tracey, Tyson, Davenport, Raqib Shaw... we need one great American artist! Will you give us a painting?"

He didn't say anything; he just sat there. "So what do you think, can we have a painting?" I finally asked again.

At that moment he waved over to his guest. "Got to go," he said.

"So is that a yes, Julian?"

"It sounds interesting; let me think about it." He stood up.

"What's your email?" I handed him a pen. He wrote it on a paper napkin.

Chapter 12

Two months and ten emails later (and I think, a very helpful call from Tim Marlowe), he gave us a painting. If you don't ask, you don't get.

Postscript:

Later, someone in the art world told me that Julian Schnabel always wears pyjamas.

I'm a life insurance salesman; I didn't know that.

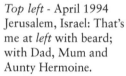

Top left - April 1994 Jerusalem, Israel: That's me at *left* with beard; with Dad, Mum and Aunty Hermoine.

Centre left - 1993 Claridge's: Role reversal - I serve Nobby breakfast on his retirement.

Left - 1999 Outside No. 10 Downing Street: Publicity stunt to launch Jerry Sadowitz's new TV series. I got 20 tourists in the street to dress up as Jerry. I am at *right*.

Top right - 1996: Rosengard family at home in Holland Park.

Bottom right - August 1997 Tokyo, Japan: Surrounded by Japanese life insurance saleswomen. I might have to go and live there one day.

Below - 1999 My party for Jerry Sadowitz's new TV series: Maya, *centre*, now rap star M.I.A. who has been nominated for an Academy Award, two Grammy Awards and the Mercury Prize!

Above - 1999 Notting Hill: Lily showing early signs of potential.

Right - 2005: Lily Rosengard, age 9. She really is a Rock Star.

Top left - August 2007 No. 10 Downing Street: John Smeaton, the baggage-handler hero of Glasgow Airport terror attack. 'Smeato' meets Prime Minister Gordon Brown.

Left - 12th September 2007 City Hall, New York: 'Smeato' meets Mayor Bloomberg.

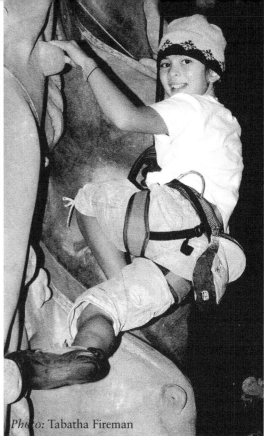

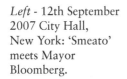
Photo: Tabatha Fireman

Above - May 1999 The Ivy: My party celebrating the 20th anniversary of the Comedy Store. From *left to right*, Comedy Store veterans Malcolm Hardy, Clive Anderson, Tony Allen, Alexei Sayle, Tom Tickell, Nick Revell, Phil Munnoch. That's me, *centre front*.

Left - 21st March 2009 London: Proud dad with daughter Lily at her Batmitzvah.

CHAPTER 13

How to give people a lift
After the bombings – 7th July 2005, London

The paper said Lee was 31 when he died. He had been in a coma ever since a British-born terrorist got on his Piccadilly line tube carriage, over two weeks previously, and self-detonated his bomb in the morning rush hour at King's Cross station.

Sam, his girlfriend of 14 years, died instantly in the blast. Of the 55 tube and bus passengers murdered in four separate bombings that day, they were the only 'couple' to die.

Lee died without knowing that Sam had been killed.

Holland Park Avenue is a leafy neighbourhood, west of Notting Hill. Lily, then nine, went to Norland Place School in one of the white stucco Victorian houses that line the street. Between 1951 and 1954, I had gone to the same school.

Almost four years before, I'd been sitting outside the school in my car waiting to pick her up after the planes had just flown into the World Trade Center.

Shortly before 10am on the 7th July 2005, I had just parked my car by the school.

I had cut short a breakfast meeting at Claridge's because it was the last day of the summer term, the annual prize-giving day, and Lily was playing her cello in the string quartet. As I drove there, the usual radio programme had been interrupted by reports of smoke and possibly explosions at two London tube stations, Edgware Road and King's Cross. A Transport for London spokesman had just announced it was caused by 'power surges'.

It sounded strange to me, and when eyewitnesses spoke of hundreds staggering out of the stations with bloodied and blackened faces, it definitely didn't sound like power surges.

What it did sound like was a terrorist attack. The attack we had been expecting in London, ever since that day I was sitting outside the school in September 2001.

I sat and listened to the news flooding in. A report came in that a double-decker bus had just exploded in Russell Square, a five-minute walk from the British Museum. Any lingering doubt about what was happening was gone. We were being attacked.

I got out of the car and walked up to the Ukrainian Hall a few doors from the school, where all the big events were held. There were some parents chatting, waiting for the doors to open. Most of them hadn't heard what was happening. People started getting calls on their mobiles.

When the old Ukrainian caretaker opened the door, I asked him if he had a radio. He went off and eventually reappeared with a large battered transistor set. It must have been 30 years old. He led me through to an empty room with a green baize table and a few chairs.

I tuned in to the BBC. We listened to the stories of badly injured people being loaded onto buses and taken to hospitals, and of the lucky, unhurt survivors streaming from the tube stations. Nobody knew if more bombs were on the way in the minutes and hours ahead.

The children arrived from next door and I went down into the hall. The headmaster, Mr Mattar, welcomed us and the prize giving commenced. It seemed that just about everybody in the school was getting a prize for something. Perhaps they were running out of prizes, because at one point a beautiful watercolour of the school was shared by two girls.

Lily played the cello with the quartet, we all sang some hymns and then there were more prizes. Lily won the fifth year 'best progress' prize and, caught by surprise, I tried to get a photo of her receiving it with my mobile phone, but failed to capture anything apart from the back of the head of the mother in front of me.

In a break between prizes, I went up to the front room and listened to the radio.

There were no casualty figures yet but reports and rumours were coming in continuously. The whole tube system had been evacuated, and all buses stopped. I went outside. A crowded bus went by; didn't they know all services were suspended? I looked at the passengers; normal people on their way to work. I expected the bus to blow up in front of me. I went back inside. Everybody was standing and singing 'Onward Christian Soldiers'.

Lily had a sleepover with a friend arranged for immediately afterwards so I just had time to congratulate her. I attempted a kiss... which she dodged.

Her mum had just remarried and was in Tahiti on honeymoon, so Lily was staying with me for two weeks and I'd booked tickets for a classical concert that evening at the Wigmore Hall for Lily, her friend Tessa and myself. It was going to be Lily's first time at a concert.

Tessa's mum came over. "I'm sorry, but I don't want Tessa away from home tonight because of everything that's going on."

I said I understood, but that I still planned to take Lily and we would talk later.

We drove into town. The buses were now off the road and there was hardly any other traffic. It was a beautiful sunny day.

Twenty-four hours earlier, it had been the happiest day I'd known in London. Against the odds we had beaten Paris in the bid to stage the Olympics in 2012. I had been on the tube at Baker Street and listened to my radio as the announcement was made. "And the 30th Olympiad will be held in the city of... London." All the passengers were talking to each other; there was great excitement at the news.

I went for lunch at the Hellenic in Marylebone High Street; the street was almost completely empty of traffic, more like a Sunday than a Thursday. The radio was telling people not to drive into London. I parked right outside the restaurant on a yellow line. The manager told me all the parking wardens had been called back to base and the daily £8 congestion charge was suspended for the day. Peter took me to the door. "Look, all the others, they have closed. It is not right." He pointed to the shops across the street. "I will not close, that is what they want me to do. I will stay open."

I turned up the radio and, leaving the car door open, stood on the pavement listening to the news. Still no casualty figures were being given. Much of central London was cordoned off to all but the emergency services.

Around 5pm I went over to Claridge's. Brook Street, normally bustling, was empty. "How are people going to get home tonight?" I asked Roman, the commissionaire.

He shrugged. "They are going to have to walk, Mr Rosengard. There are no buses or tubes."

I looked at my car; actually, it was a huge Land Rover Defender truck that I'd found for my Canadian friend Helen five years before. I'd asked her what her favourite car was, thinking she would say a Porsche or a Ferrari.

"A Defender Tomb Raider." I had no idea what that was; I had just about heard of Land Rovers. But I tracked one down for her; they only made 300 of them, for the movie *Tomb Raider* starring Angelina Jolie. I had asked a Claridge's doorman to drive it up the mews behind the hotel as we were driving towards it. He blocked the way and turned on the four huge spotlights on the roof. He'd walked round to her door and handed her the keys. "I believe these are yours, madam."

A year or two later, she'd gone back home to Vancouver and I inherited the truck. Sometimes I'd been as far as my local Tesco in it.

It looked like a tank about to fight its way into Baghdad. It had a chimney for driving underwater; very useful if Chelsea Bridge was jammed with traffic.

But this evening I had an idea. "Roman, where would you go to if you wanted to give people lifts home?"

"The bus stops outside Selfridge's."

Five minutes later I pulled up at Selfridge's.

There must have been a hundred people standing at each bus stop.

I wound down the window. "Hi... Where you all heading to?" I shouted.

"Where are you going?" a girl with a German accent shouted back.

"I'm going wherever you want to go." I jumped down and opened the back door. There were three seats on each side, facing each other. About 30 or 40 people gathered round. They climbed up and down, and when I counted ten in the back I said, "Okay, we're full up now... but I can get another three in the front if you don't mind squeezing in."

I headed east. Thousands of people were walking calmly along; if you hadn't heard about the bombs, you would never have guessed what terror had happened just hours before. It was a surreally beautiful drive through the heart of the city.

And there was something else, but I didn't know what it was. Then I got it... the silence.

The streets had no buses, no taxis, no cars on them. We were driving along one of the busiest streets in Europe, Oxford Street, and we only saw three or four other cars. The whole city was empty of traffic. Not even many police cars; they must have been at the stations.

I turned round and looked at my passengers, crammed in next to each other. They were very quiet, some talking quietly to their neighbours.

"Hi, I'm Peter Rosengard! So where are you all from?"

They were from everywhere: Zimbabwe, Poland, Lithuania, Ghana, Spain, Slovenia, Germany. I think there were ten different nationalities in my car that evening. And that's when it hit me for the first time; what an amazing international city London had become. There was only one born and bred Londoner and that was me!

The German girl in the seat right behind me told me she worked in an architect's office and that one of her co-workers was missing; he was due to fly out from Heathrow on a business trip that morning, but they hadn't heard from him.

We got as far as Liverpool Street and ran into a police barrier. We couldn't go any further, a policewoman told me.

"Sorry, but this is the end of the line," I said. I helped my passengers out.

I turned around and did the same thing all over again, this time ending up in Ealing. In all I dropped 25 people off. I felt I'd done just one little thing to help out.

The next day, driving around, I kept hearing a phone ringing somewhere in the back of the truck. Later I stopped to search and finally found a mobile wedged behind my seat. I looked in the address book and found an entry for 'Home'. I rang it; it was on answer phone. I was sure it must be the German girl's phone. I left a message.

When she called me back, I invited her to Claridge's for tea with Lily and myself. She brought me a cake to thank me for the ride. Her friend, the missing colleague, had been found. He was in a coma in hospital.

His name was Lee.

How to deal with death at breakfast
Across the breakfast table – 1983, Claridge's

Nobby put down the silver marmalade pot and poured me a glass of iced water.

I glanced up from behind the *Times*, where I'd been reading of the latest Mafia killing in New York. "Nobby, have you had a lot of people killed at Claridge's during breakfast?"

"If you mean murdered… no sir, not that I recall. Of course, we've had the occasional stabbing in the kitchens. You know what chefs are like, it gets very hot in there, someone spoils the soufflé and next thing you know, it's kitchen knives out and all hell breaks loose. But murders at the breakfast table? No, it's too early in the morning for that kind of thing, isn't it? I think murder's more of an after-dinner occurrence. But now you mention it, about 30 years ago I did have a regular who died during breakfast. He fell head first into his bacon and eggs… One minute he was eating them and the next, he was face down in them."

He smiled fondly at the memory.

"What did you do, Nobby?"

"I carried on serving, sir, of course. I put a tablecloth over him, a fresh plate and knife and fork setting on one side, a vase of flowers on top… and carried on as normal."

"Are you serious? A vase of flowers on top of a dead body and nobody said anything?"

"Well sir, the flowers were a mark of respect really, but no, none of the other guests noticed a thing. Too busy doing their business deals, I should imagine, or reading the papers. If they did, they probably thought it was a new floral arrangement."

"Amazing! You are a real professional, Nobby."

"Thank you, sir, we try our best. Of course, later in the morning when things had quietened down, I did erect a screen around the gentleman. And when the last breakfast customer had gone, me and Mario and couple of the boys carried him out."

How to tell if your daughter is a genius
September 2004, Sunderland

She was halfway up the 22-metre wall when she stopped. The crowd that had been cheering her on stopped shouting. After 30 seconds, she let go and made a leap, away from the wall and upwards. For a second I thought she hadn't made it, but her outstretched arm grabbed the hold and she held on, 80 feet in the air. The crowd roared: "Come on, Lily! You can do it!"

It was the finals in Sunderland of the 2004 UK national rock climbing competition and, with 665 points, she was just two points behind the leader, a girl from Cornwall. Lily, my 9-year-old daughter, is a rock star... a rock-climbing star. Everybody asks me the same thing – where does she get this urge to climb? Why isn't she afraid of heights, like me, her mum... in fact, my entire family?

I asked her one day why she liked it. "I just do," she replied.

"Does it feel great to get to the top?"

"Yes."

"Do you ever look down?"

"Sometimes... mostly when I'm coming down, that's the fun bit."

I was 48 years old when Lily was born. I had always thought I would wait until I grew up before having kids, but then I thought, '80 is too old to be a dad, so I'll have one while I'm still a kid, too.' She was born in the Portland Hospital in the West End, which is really a luxury hotel where guest amenities include a baby delivery service. We took a two-bedroom suite; it was so luxurious I wanted to stay for a few days after mother and baby checked out.

When we took Lily home to Lansdowne Road in a laundry basket, the Notting Hill carnival was in full blast. I have always told Lily we threw a big party to celebrate her birth. Until she was 11, she believed me. It was her carnival.

Like every Jewish father, I think my daughter is a genius. One afternoon, we were in the children's playground in Holland Park, playing in the sandpit. She didn't want to, but I insisted. I had brought my bucket.

Lily sat down heavily on my castle and said, "Daddy, I have a philosophical question to ask you." Infinity had started to fascinate her, stimulated by that well-known physicist, Ali G. We had been watching one of his TV interviews: "So professor, dis infinity ting... what is it exactly? Is it bigger than a billion billion trillion trillion?"

"Oh yes! It's much bigger than that," replied Professor Heinz Wolff. For months afterwards, Lily insisted all her bedtime stories started, "Once upon a time, there was dis really big ting called infinity..."

She had begun putting on her imaginary thinking cap whenever I asked her any question. Even when asked, "Do you want a McDonald's?" she would tie it up under her chin and, with head tilted slightly, she would stroke her chin whilst gazing upwards. I told her it was not a good idea to do it when riding her bicycle. Einstein had become her hero a couple of years previously, when she saw him in an Apple computer advertisement. Now, it was, "Daddy, but Einstein said this!" or "Einstein said that!" when all you've said is, "Lily, it's time to go to bed," before you know it you've got the 20th century's greatest genius backing up your five-year-old's argument on why she should stay up to watch *Willie Wonka and the Chocolate Factory* for the 56th time.

One day, we were walking through Regents Park, discussing global warming – she was explaining it to *me* – and as we fed the pigeons, I turned to her: "You know darling, Daddy's not happy all the time... sometimes he is sad. What should he do to be happy again?"

She put on her thinking cap, stroked her chin and said, "Eat more ice cream, Daddy."

She is not only the youngest in her class, but also the only Scottish-Jewish-Chinese-Canadian girl in the school. I once told a woman, on a first date, about Lily being four racial stereotypes in one. She looked at me. "That's funny. You don't look Chinese."

"No..." I said slowly. "I am the Scottish-Jewish part." I knew, at that moment, this was not the woman of my dreams. My family should be in the *Guinness Book of Records* as the world's only Jewish family where all three children have half-Chinese kids.

Two weeks after Lily started kindergarten, her headmistress came up to my ex-wife and myself. "I really do think Lily is St Paul's material, you know." I expected her to continue: "She's definitely a double first at

Oxford, and do you mind if she does her PhD next term?"

When she was five, Lily woke up in her mummy's bed at 4am. Holding her in her arms, Shirley said, "Lily, darling, I love you more than anything in the world."

Lily looked up at her. "But Mummy, that's not possible."

"Why not, darling?"

"You can't love me more than anything in the world; you haven't been to Uzbekistan yet."

I had to admit, her logic was impeccable. But this Uzbekistan thing really puzzled me. Where had she got it from? Nine out of ten people haven't even heard of Uzbekistan.

I rang her school; her teacher said they currently didn't offer Uzbek as a language. "Frankly, there's not really a lot of demand for it. Even St Paul's doesn't require it. She didn't get it from us, Mr Rosengard, I can assure you... we don't even teach them Greek." That only left the nanny, who was Polish. During interrogation, she never cracked once, and denied ever having discussed the break-up of the former Soviet Union with Lily.

A couple of months later, Lily, Shirley and I were having lunch at 192 in Notting Hill. I'd just bought the *Who Wants to be a Millionaire?* quiz book, and for fun I asked Lily a £1m question I'd chosen at random; amazingly it was, 'What country is Tashkent the capital city of?' When she'd immediately replied, "Uzbekistan, Daddy," I wasn't surprised.

After Shirley and Lily had left, I was sitting having an espresso when a man at the next table leant across. "Sir, excuse me but I couldn't help overhearing just before, and I have to tell you that your daughter is a genius."

He turned out to be an American lawyer over here for the American Bar Association annual meeting, which was being held in London.

"What kind of law do you practise?" I asked him

"I'm a judge," he said.

"A judge? What kind? Criminal or civil?"

"Actually, he's on the Supreme Court," his wife said.

He was the Supreme Court Judge Stephen Breyer! He'd been appointed by President Clinton.

So my daughter's a "genius", and if anyone wants to argue the point with me... I'll see them in the Supreme Court.

Chapter 13

Postscript:

In 2010, Lily represented Great Britain in the World Youth Climbing Championships in Ratho, Scotland. It's the biggest climbing wall in the world and she came 35th! I was the proudest dad in the world. When she was just four, her mum had thrown her against a climbing wall and she had just stuck to it! And here she was at 15, representing her country.

Which is amazing, as the only climbing I've ever done has been social!

But I do think that in the interest of fairness, they should ban all countries from competing that have mountains in them, like Switzerland and Austria. Clearly they've got an unfair advantage. We should only have to compete against flat countries, like Belgium and Holland.

How to meet the Rosengards
2006, London

As I walked into Bernard's bookshop, his right-hand lady said, "Congratulations, Professor Rosengard!"

"What are you talking about, Lucinda?" I asked.

"Take a look at this!" She pointed at the front page of the *Times*.

The headline read: 'Heart Transplant breakthrough... a first for the UK'. A new record-breaking transplant technique had been performed the day before at Papworth hospital in Cambridge... by Professor Bruce Rosengard.

I sent him a congratulatory email. 'Congratulations! Well done Bruce Rosengard, from Peter Rosengard, clearly no relation.' I enclosed my phone number.

Now, all my life I'd been told there were no other Rosengards anywhere.

As far as I knew, apart from Lily, my father's youngest brother, Ernest, and his son, Tim (Rebecca, his daughter, joined an Indian cult and changed her name to something unpronounceable), I was the only Rosengard in the UK. And only because I changed my name back from Rose in my mid-twenties.

That night, the phone rang around 10.30pm.

"Is that Peter Rosengard?" a deep American voice said. "It's Bruce

Rosengard here. Thanks for your email... sorry to call so late, but it's been a long day."

When I put the phone down two hours later, I had discovered I wasn't alone anymore.

Bruce and I, after ten minutes on the phone, were sounding like we'd known each other all our lives; he'd asked me my father and grandfather's names, and the names of my grandfather's brothers and sisters back in Glasgow. I hung on while he looked up the Boston Rosengards' family tree; something I never knew about.

He came back on the line a couple of minutes later.

"Peter, I've got big news for you... you're my fourth cousin! We're both descended from Abraham Rosengard, who lived in northern Poland someplace, and you've got 400 other Rosengard relatives you never knew existed in Boston!"

This was amazing. He told me the Rosengard who'd put together the family tree had stopped around the time my father was born in 1915, but he could see his name and five of his six brothers and his two sisters, Mina and Sadie, on it.

We agreed to meet up as soon as possible. I'd asked him if there was a Rosengard family characteristic; any life insurance salesmen amongst them, for example?

He thought for a minute. "Well, all the men are well over six feet and a lot of them are six four." This was quite a surprise, as at five feet eight inches, I was thought to be the tallest Rosengard that had ever lived. ("He's so tall," my grandmother Diana would proudly tell everyone on the regular Sunday family gathering in the 1960s. She was five feet nothing, so I suppose I was tall to her.)

"But no super-salesmen among them?" I asked Bruce.

"No, I don't believe so. But you'll like this. My Uncle Julius, my grandfather's brother, was an accountant to the Mob."

"That's wonderful... you mean, like Meyer Lansky?"

"Well, not quite that involved, we don't think. He did their accounts. He was called Big Julie, but actually barely scraped five feet five." This was back in the 1940s. Big Julie was even a part-owner of the famous Riviera Hotel in Havana, when the Mob ran the city. Vito Genovese, the 'capo di capi' of the US Mafia, was his client.

"I can email you a letter we have," he said, "which Big Julie had written to the IRS, explaining that unfortunately his client couldn't provide them with any records for his businesses as Mr Genovese only ever dealt in cash!"

Bruce told me they couldn't wait for the collapse of Castro so they could make a claim for the Riviera, which was still there.

"It's a pity we didn't connect a month ago, as you've just missed the annual Rosengard picnic in Boston. You could have flown over and met the Rosengards!"

I rather liked the idea of being a great nephew of Big Julie, accountant to the mob. It certainly beat being the nephew of my Uncle Lomley, the cabinet maker from Manchester.

A few days later, I went down to Cambridge for the weekend and met Big Bruce and his family in their beautiful house. His wife, Ariella, was also a doctor (Bruce told me her father had invented something very important, like the world's first defibrillator that you could implant inside your body without having to be permanently connected to your car battery), while Bruce was a tall, athletic-looking, very relaxed man with a great sense of humour; well, he laughed at my jokes. He reminded me of a Jewish Dr Kildare. He immediately made me feel part of the wider Rosengard family. I'd Googled him and found out he was one of the world's leading heart transplant surgeons.

I told all my friends about my new American family. "Listen, if ever you need a new heart, just let me know and I'll get you one wholesale; I'm connected!"

How to learn not to stand up in a canoe
August 2006, Ontario, Canada

When your ten-year-old daughter shouts, "Don't stand up in the canoe!" it's probably a good idea to listen.

I didn't. A second later, we were both swimming in the Lake of the Two Rivers. We were in Algonquin Park in Ontario, a couple of hours from Toronto. Now, this is not a 'park' as in Hyde. This one is the size of England, with 2,300 rivers and lakes, bears, moose, wolves, billions of trees... and a population of three people. Yes... as in one, two, three.

As soon as you land in Canada, before you even collect your baggage, someone will invariably say, "You didn't know Canada is the second-larg-est country in the world, did you?"

But what they forget to tell you is that there is no one there. Apart from a little strip just north of the US border, it is basically empty. If everyone in Canada got drunk one night and fell over, half of them would probably wake up in America.

One of the three people who live in Algonquin was away that week, so we pretty much had the place to ourselves for our stay at Killarney Lodge, a group of log cabins by the lake.

"Good morning, I would like a room... with a canoe," I said to the woman at reception.

"All our cabins come with their own canoe, sir."

"Of course they do... I forgot, we are in Canada."

It had been my idea to paddle from our cabin to the breakfast room... the whole 25 yards. Lily had wanted to walk. "Daddy, do you even know how to canoe?"

"Of course I do, darling." I nonchalantly threw a paddle into the air, like I'd seen Hawkeye do in *The Last of the Mohicans*.

I almost caught it.

"Do you remember the time I took you out in a boat in Regents Park, when you were five?" I said.

"Yes," she said. "The time when we nearly sunk that boatful of Hasidic rabbis?"

"It was their fault. They were totally lacking in navigation skills."

Luckily, this time we were wearing life jackets, and I was confident at least one of our two cameras would have dried out by the next summer holiday.

After breakfast we met Don, our guide for a 24-hour trip into the wilder-ness the next day.

"Don knows this place as well as the bears and moose do," the Lodge manager said. Don certainly looked the part of the grizzled old timer; late sixties, six feet tall, 200lbs and with a salt and pepper beard and white Stetson.

"So Don, you must be, what... 55?" I hoped a little flattery might break the ice.

Chapter 13

"Actually, I'm only 42, but a lot of folks think I look older. Leave everything to me, I can carry the canoe and our supplies, it's six months now since I had the stroke... course, had to learn to walk and dress myself again, but reckon I'm almost good as new."

"Well, er... that's really great to hear, Don. Very reassuring."

That night, I looked for my Wilderness Survival Kit. At $8.95 in the Mountain Equipment Co-op in Ottawa, it seemed a bargain, especially compared with the $25,000 'Dream Canada' camper van, with two canoes on the rack, that the assistant tried to sell me.

"If you throw in a sledge and a team of Huskies, I could be tempted," I said.

I fell asleep trying to remember what the Ontario Rangers Guide Book said about the two types of bear you found in Canada. One type just wanted to play with you, but the other was going to kill you. And there was absolutely nothing you could do to stop him.

I just couldn't remember how to tell them apart. It also said you must not leave your food in the tent; you had to put it in a bag, attach it to a rope, climb up a tree, throw the rope to another tree and, somehow, hoist the bag between the two trees, high above the ground. Later, I read that seven people died in 2005 from bear attacks, and 27 from falling out of trees trying to hang the food.

Don collected us the next day in his battered pick-up, and two hours and two lakes later, we were fishing for lunch on the edge of Lake Bruce.

Lily caught 14 fish in 30 minutes, which could be a world record for a first-time fisher. I put it down to my newly-discovered expertise in putting the worm on the hook.

"Daddy! You do it!"

"No, I really can't darling... you do it."

"Are you scared of a little worm?"

"Okay, Lily, Daddy will do it." I reached into the carton of worms we'd bought at the store. They kept them in the soft drinks freezer.

Over the camp fire that night, Don cooked us a steak dinner. It was Friday, so Lily lit the candles and said Shabbat prayers.

As she did this, her steak slid off the plate on her lap and onto the ground.

"No problem, Lily, just wash it in the lake," Don said. "It's so clean, you can drink the water."

So Lily went down to the water's edge and gave her steak a good scrub. Just try that in the Thames at Tower Bridge.

After dinner, I opened my survival kit; or rather, I tried for 15 minutes to open the vacuum-sealed pack.

'Lucky I'm not about to be attacked by a bear,' I thought. "Excuse me, sir, but I wonder, could you possibly clarify exactly which type of bear you are?" I'd ask, while desperately attempting to open my survival kit.

Don took the smaller of the two huge knives from his belt and sliced it open. I looked at the contents: a needle, 100 metres of what looked like dental floss (was I meant to floss the bear to death?) and a magnifying glass. To make sure it really was a bear?

Don then told us about the time he had dinner at the White House with President Clinton and his fishing buddy, the head of the FBI. I think the Pope dropped by for drinks afterwards.

Finally, we crawled into our tents and fell asleep. In the morning, Don said, "Did you hear that bear growl around 4am?"

"That was Dad snoring," Lily said.

On the canoe trip back, I tuned my pocket radio into the BBC World Service in time to hear, "Police in London have arrested 23 people for plotting to blow up planes over the Atlantic..."

"What do you think about canoeing back to London?" I said to Lily.

Then I stood up again.

How to talk to strangers (6)
November 2008, Notting Hill, London

I've discovered I'm a member of the band of biker brothers. But I'd never have known this if I hadn't been knocked off my scooter in Ladbroke Grove one dark and stormy night by a young hit-and-run Porsche driver, who'd suddenly turned right without signalling.

As I picked myself up off the ground and pulled the scooter upright, out of the darkness and pouring rain a man suddenly appeared, dressed in black leathers with a full-face black helmet. He was dragging, by the scruff of the neck, a frightened, soaked guy who appeared about 14 years old.

"Who are you?" I asked the helmeted one.

"Vd mmj vvs brtrr," he replied.

"What!? I'm sorry... I can't understand you."

He lifted his visor up. "I see what happen. I chase. I catch. I bring him to you. We band of brothers: you know that?"

"Okay... band of bike brothers, very good. I like it. What's your name?"

"I Vassi."

After I'd got the kid's father's insurance details – he turned out to be the son of a well-known property tycoon – Vassi let go of him.

He told me he was a courier by day and pizza delivery driver by night.

"You are a busy guy," I said.

"Just work all the time, that's all. I work, I sleep, I work again, every day."

"Well Vassi, give me your number and I'll take you for a meal soon, to thank you."

"It is not necessary, but thank you. I am just a biker, like you. We have to look after for each other, no?"

"Yes, we have to look after each other, Vassi. Thank you. You are a good guy."

A week later I rang and invited him for dinner. As I waited in the restaurant, I realised I had no idea what he looked like without the helmet.

Vassi turned out to be a normal guy of about 25 with a big smile – that is, if a shaved head, tattoos, skull-and-crossbones rings dangling from each ear and a piercing through the nose is normal. I guess it is today.

I liked him immediately; he had a good sense of humour, and we had an enjoyable meal together.

Although he looked tough, he was actually a very gentle, nice man. His family lived on a small farm in Bulgaria and he was working hard here to save money to send home.

Over breakfast a few days later, I mentioned my Good Samaritan to my friend Nicky.

Nicky is also a nice young guy, who also happens to be rich and a talented racing driver.

"You know something, Peter? He sounds just like the kind of guy I need to assist me," he said.

"You'll like him, I'm sure; he's a good guy, honest and hard working."

They met up, and he gave Vassi a job.

So for the last three years, Vassi has travelled the world – only by plane, not bike any more – and has become an indispensable part of not just Nicky's life but his whole family's lives.

And the funny thing is, none of it would ever have happened if I hadn't been knocked off my scooter that dark, stormy November night.

How to manage a hero
'Smeato' – 30th June 2007

"It's lucky we're leaving London today," I said to Lily and Shirley at Heathrow.

Two nights earlier, two car bombs had been planted: one outside Tiger Tiger nightclub near Piccadilly with 2,000 people inside, and another at the bottom of the street to catch the people directed away from the first blast. The police managed to defuse the bombs before they were set off by mobile phones.

The terrorists were at large and London was on maximum alert for more attempts.

As we walked through the arrivals hall at Edinburgh Airport an hour later, a crowd was gathered round a huge TV screen: a jeep was engulfed in flames, stuck in the doors at Glasgow Airport, just 40 miles away. Two men had driven it, filled with explosives, into the terminal on the busiest day of the year, the first day of the school break; a burning man, one of the terrorists, was being hosed down. A young baggage handler called John Smeaton was being interviewed; apparently, he had run up and attacked the terrorists.

"Och, I just tried to give him a kicking! It wasn't just me, a lot of other guys had a go too," he said.

"What is your message to terrorists?" the reporter asked.

"Don't come to Glasgow, 'cos we'll set aboot ye!" he said, punching the air with his fist.

Everybody watching shouted "YES!" and applauded, me included. 'Good for him!' I thought.

That clip went around the world and John Smeaton became an instant phenomenon. Over the next week the 'Smeato' story, as everyone had started calling him, just got bigger and bigger. It became clear the terrorists

230

were the same guys who had tried to bomb the club in London – and incredibly, they were doctors! And at the centre of it all was John Smeaton and the sound bite of that summer, "Don't come to Glasgow 'cos we'll set aboot ye!" It made Scots the world over proud to be Scottish. Those words could only have come from a Glaswegian.

A website – johnsmeaton.com – was set up within 48 hours and 'Smeatomania' was launched. He was featured in profiles across the world. Americans in particular loved him and, as a clean-cut, good-looking guy, he got marriage proposals from all over. The 'Buy John Smeaton a pint!' campaign earned him 1,200 beers at the Glasgow Holiday Inn; he donated half the money to the Erskine Army Veterans Hospital outside Glasgow.

After ten days of reading about Smeato, I called to congratulate him.

"How did you get his number?" people asked me, incredulous.

"Directory enquiries," I said.

He was living with his parents, having recently split with his stewardess girlfriend.

"Hi, John. My name's Peter Rosengard and I'm just calling to say congratulations!"

"Oh thank you very much, Peter," he said in a friendly, very broad Glasgow accent.

"My father's from Glasgow actually, and we're all very proud of what you did."

"Och, I just tried to get a few kicks in." Again, he said others had done more than he had.

He sounded a likeable, modest and intelligent guy. I happened to say I lived in London and he replied that he'd never been to London and had always wanted to visit.

My response was to change the course of my life for the next two years.

"Well, John... On behalf of the British people, have a trip to London on me. In recognition of the great thing you did!" I loved the fact that somebody had at last done something!

I met him at King's Cross – he wouldn't fly, he was scared of planes! We took a taxi round the main sites on the way to lunch at the Ivy. He was the most enthusiastic tourist I'd ever shown round and it was all totally genuine; what you saw was what you got with John.

We stopped outside the gates to No. 10 Downing Street and I had a word with the policeman on duty. The security gates swung open and the policemen queued up to shake his hand. "Just go and knock on the door, John," one said. "They're expecting you."

So John pulled on the knocker and the black door swung open. A police officer stood there with a large book in his hands. "Hello, John," he said, shaking his hand. "Congratulations! You did the right thing! I'm from Glasgow myself, Maryhill."

"No!" said John incredulously. "What a coincidence!"

"The prime minister is abroad, but he'd have wanted to congratulate you himself if he'd been here." He presented John with the book; a history of No. 10.

As we got out the cab in Charing Cross road, Simon Callow the actor was coming towards us; I'd met him a couple of times. "Hi Simon, come and shake the hand of a British hero!"

Thirty yards on, Lord Bragg walked towards us. I greeted him like a long-lost friend (I'd met him once); "Melvyn! This is John Smeaton, who attacked the terrorists at Glasgow Airport!"

Melvyn stopped (he had to, I was barring his path) and smiled. "Well done! An honour to meet you," he said, as John vigorously shook his hand.

After lunch we went on the London Eye. Everywhere we went, I told people who John was and they congratulated him and slapped him on the back; he was unfailingly modest and charming.

I had the idea for a trip down the Thames, on one of the fast little orange SBS-type boats; their jetty was next to the Eye. They were fully booked but I had a word with the girl in the kiosk, who then radioed the boss.

"Johnny says you can have a special trip by yourselves. He's sending a boat over."

"Great!" I said. "How much is it?"

"Oh no, he wants you to be his guests, and says please congratulate Mr Smeaton for him!"

The boat took off like a rocket; it was basically an inflatable dinghy with a huge engine attached. We hit Canary Wharf in minutes. The pilot loved his tight turns; I've never been a great sailor and hung on like grim death, getting soaked, but John was loving it, whooping at the top of his voice. I copied him, only my whoops were whoops of fear.

Chapter 13

As I saw John off at King's Cross, he shook my hand. "Peter, thank you so much, it's been amazing. A 24 hours I'll never forget."

And that, I thought, was that. I hoped he'd had a good time; now he had to get back to work at the airport, as he'd taken a few weeks off after the attack.

The papers were still full of the attack. There was an online petition to change the name of Glasgow Airport to John Smeaton International Airport. He was voted the third most eligible bachelor in Scotland, was invited on radio and TV for his opinions on everything and his website had thousands of hits daily.

It suddenly dawned on me that he was an inspirational figure, who filled a universal need for someone to be seen to be doing something. And he was telegenic and likeable. So I naturally thought, 'Why don't I become his manager?' I'd take him to America, put him on the talk shows. I felt they'd love him there, where the blue-collar hero is king. The 9/11 anniversary was coming up; it was perfect timing.

I called John. "Fantastic! That'd be really great!" Smeato replied.

"I don't want any money for doing it," I said. "Unless you become a Hollywood star, then I'll take the usual 20%! I just think you can inspire millions of people... and it'll be a lot of fun."

Mark Borkowski, a top PR friend, recommended a veteran LA contact called Steve who he said was a top guy, with connections everywhere; he represented some big Hollywood stars. Steve sounded very professional and friendly as we agreed for him to represent John in the US.

"Think big, Peter," I told myself. "We'll do Letterman in NY, take a side trip to the White House so President Bush could shake the hand of a British hero, then fly to the West coast for the Leno and Craig Ferguson talk shows... How difficult could that be?"

Steve said it was short notice but definitely doable, and of course he had a connection at the White House.

We had only just under three weeks as I wanted Smeato to attend the 9/11 Ground Zero ceremony. I asked Steve to arrange an invitation for us, plus meetings with Mayor Bloomberg and NY fire commissioner Nicholas Scoppetta.

I was booked to go to Italy on holiday with Lily. But how was I going to maintain contact with Steve in LA from the medieval town of San Felice Circeo, south of Rome? So I finally did something I'd resisted for years; I knew I'd be addicted. I bought a BlackBerry.

This turned out to be a fantastic way not only to drive Steve crazy with a hundred emails a day but also to destroy totally my holiday with Lily. ("Dad! If you don't turn it off I'm going to throw it in the pool... Dad! Put it away!")

Before going to Italy, I got John on the *Richard and Judy* show, which went great. Whilst recalling why he'd gone to help the policeman, he said, "Because when the law falls, we all fall." Watching from the Green room, I thought you could lock a dozen Law Lords in a room for a month and they wouldn't come up with a better answer.

I had a surprise for him after the show. My TV producer pal Derek Guthrie had contacted the No. 10 Downing Street Press office and they'd said that Gordon Brown would be delighted to meet John.

This time the gates swung open for us and our car was waved through. John was ushered off to meet the prime minister, and after 30 minutes we were invited upstairs to join the press and TV.

The PM came in with John, who kept glancing shyly down at the ground. I made a mental note to tell him to look straight ahead.

The PM made a short speech, praising John's actions and calling him a true British hero. He then shook his hand as the cameras flashed away.

We were due to fly to NYC the day after I got back from Italy. Richard Branson had offered us free Virgin flights, which was great. I'd already figured this trip was going to cost me a lot of money. We were booked at the iconic Waldorf Astoria on Fifth Avenue. But I wanted John to have a great experience and as I was convinced he was going to become a star in the US, what did it matter if we spent a few dollars along the way?

My old school friend Guy Marriott, a retired chief general counsel for EMI, had drawn up a management contract between John and me. But after a week, Steve in LA still hadn't got us a single TV talk show or guaranteed press story.

"Peter, I'm working on it. Relax!" He'd been saying this for over a week now. I'd been calling him every day from the poolside in Italy.

"What about the pipe band at the airport? What about the White House? How about getting Schwarzenegger to meet him in LA? What about getting some of your big stars to hang out with him? I bet Tom

Cruise would love to meet him!"

He flipped. "Peter! You're the most demanding client I've had in my 40 years in Hollywood!"

By the time I met John at Heathrow, we still hadn't got a single TV talk show booking, not even a welcoming crowd of four tartan-clad pipers at the airport. "The Port Authority wouldn't allow it. Security," Steve told me. "But I have got some good news. I've got us an official invitation to a welcome reception by the Scottish American Association of New York."

"Terrific, Steve. But it's not exactly Letterman, is it?"

Clearly, I was going to have to take over the PR operation myself. Instead of giving Steve $20k, I might as well have stood in Fifth Avenue tearing up $100 bills.

At the airport, Smeato turned up with a cheerful guy in his thirties. "This is Matt, a *Scottish Sun* reporter; he's coming along to write about my trip. I forgot to tell you..."

We all flew Virgin upper class courtesy of Richard Branson. I spoke to the steward and the captain announced to the whole plane: "We are honoured to have with us today Mr John Smeaton, the hero of the recent Glasgow Airport terror attack." All the passengers and crew applauded John.

After a three-mile customs queue, we finally made it out to meet Steve, a balding guy with a grey goatee, along with Steve Dunleavy of the *New York Post*; a TV friend had given me an intro to Dunleavy before we'd left. My friend Lev was also there; he'd flown down from Montreal, bringing the banners which Steve had failed to organise.

As we walked to our stretch limo, I noticed a young cameraman filming us.

"Which network's he from?" I asked Steve.

"Network Rosengard. Remember, you asked me to hire a cameraman for the week?"

That small detail, I now remembered, was costing me another $10k minimum.

Some baggage handlers were hanging around outside. I grabbed a huge 'SMEATO' banner from Lev, got two of the handlers to take an end each, and the others to stand behind Smeato, holding 'NY LOVES SMEATO' placards. I shouted, "Come and meet the guy who punched the al-Qaeda terrorists! Meet a real-life hero!"

A crowd of curious bystanders gathered round. They shook John's hand

and took his photo. My cameraman filmed the whole time. In fact, I don't remember seeing him without the camera on his shoulder in the whole week. We could have made 20 *Titanics*.

The next day's *New York Post* double-page story was headlined: 'Baggage handler hero of Glasgow Airport attack arrives NY'.

We had the Scottish American Association 'official' welcome party that afternoon; John had brought his kilt especially. At least, there was a door with a piece of paper on which someone had scribbled 'Scottish American Reception', and inside, a room the size of my living room. There must have been 12 people there.

"Well they told me they'd sent out the invitations," Steve said to me.

"When? This morning!? I have more people for breakfast than this!"

John didn't seem to notice and was talking animatedly to a tiny girl wearing a tartan skirt. I joined them. "This is Christy," he said, introducing me to the girl.

Things picked up in the days that followed. Steve came good with a booking for Smeato on the Geraldo show on Fox, we met police commissioner Ray Kelly and fire commissioner Nick Scoppetta, and we got invited to the official Ground Zero ceremony.

That day is the one that remains most in my memory from that week.

Security was intense, with hundreds of police officers on every corner. It poured the whole time as thousands stood under umbrellas with a huge American flag as a backdrop, listening in silence as the names of all 2,976 World Trade Center victims were read out by family members and fire and police officers.

"It takes five hours," someone told me. "We do this every year."

On our last day, we met Mayor Bloomberg at City Hall. He remained standing in an outer office full of staff as he told John a long story about fly-fishing in Scotland, about his English first wife and how her father had been a squadron leader in the RAF. He didn't ask John a single thing about himself or what happened at the airport.

There was no point in going on to LA as we had nothing lined up, and the White House had finally said there was no possibility of the president meeting John... so much for Steve's contact.

So we flew back to London. John changed planes to Glasgow and as we shook hands, he said, "Thank you, Peter, so very much. It was amazing, really amazing."

Before we left New York, I had a call on my mobile.

It was No. 10 Downing Street, inviting John to the Labour Party Conference as the prime minister's personal guest. And so ten days later, we were on the train to Bournemouth. With us was Lev, who'd flown over for the occasion.

John was seated next to the PM's wife, Sarah. The auditorium was packed as Gordon Brown strode confidently to the podium to open his first conference as prime minister. Twenty seconds into his opening remarks, he adopted a serious tone. "Just a few weeks ago, terrorists attacked Glasgow Airport and attempted the mass murder of innocent children, men and women. They were prevented in their evil objective by the courageous actions of a few good men, and one of those, a young baggage handler, is here today as my guest. Ladies and gentlemen, please join me in welcoming a real British hero, John Smeaton."

Everybody leapt to their feet in a spontaneous standing ovation! The photographers flashed away as John, urged on by Sarah Brown, stood and waved to everybody. "I told him this would happen!" I said, high-fiving a beaming Lev.

We were invited to the private cocktail party the PM was throwing for a few of his financial backers. The waiters were all in their early twenties – I knew they weren't cabinet ministers because they wore white jackets and kept filling my glass. A 14-year-old boy, who turned out to be David Miliband, the foreign secretary, told me that Smeato's was the first spontaneous standing ovation in eight years, since Mo Mowlam's return following her recovery from brain cancer.

Lev was busy snapping away with his camera. He put his arm around a bemused Jack Straw. "Peter, can you get one of me and Jack?" he said, as if they'd been friends all their lives.

I introduced John to Sir Ronald Cohen and Lord Hollick: "Smeato, meet Ronnie and Clive."

I left them talking and wandered over to say "Hi" to Ed Balls, the education secretary, and Jacqui Smith, the home secretary. Everybody was very friendly and the champagne was flowing. They all agreed Smeato had been a huge success, and I said I thought the PM had done pretty well, too.

I got talking to a man with a white goatee, who turned out to be Sarah Brown's father. "Does the PM like champagne?" I asked him.

He said he did. The PM was surrounded by a group of ministers in one corner. I'd noticed he didn't have a glass.

I fetched a champagne from the bar and went over and patted him on the shoulder. He turned round and I was about to pass him the glass when a hand shot out from nowhere, grabbed my wrist in a vice-like grip and I felt myself being steered away. A grey-suited man took the glass. "I'm sorry sir, but you can't give the prime minister a drink."

"Oh, I'm sorry. I just saw that he hadn't got one."

I had just started talking to Sir Sigmund Sternberg, who must have been in his late eighties, when Lev came up, dragging David Miliband behind him. "Peter, can you get a shot of me and Dave together?" Clearly, Lev was out to bag the entire cabinet.

Miliband turned to me. "Your friend is quite a character, isn't he?"

"Yes, Smeato certainly is," I said.

"No, I mean Lev. He's invited me to stay with him in Montreal."

I spent the next few weeks calling dozens of companies – from Irn Bru to Scottish & Newcastle Brewery, from Cadbury's to Coca-Cola – to try to get Smeato to feature in their advertising. But to my amazement, I hit a total brick wall. Apparently, nobody wanted to use someone who kicked somebody, even if he was an international hero.

In the meantime, John signed up to write a column for the *Scottish Sun*: 'Smeato! The column that sets aboot ye!' You couldn't imagine anyone better to appeal to the typical *Sun* reader, though I was annoyed he'd signed without speaking to me, and for just £150 a week. I told him he was being taken for a ride, but he was fine with it.

He'd gone back to work at the airport, as I'd advised him. It was important he didn't let it all go to his head, and it was a big part of the blue-collar hero image. Interestingly, John wasn't quite your typical working-class Glaswegian. His father Iain was a retired health service accountant and his mother Kate was a pharmacist; by an amazing coincidence, she had worked for my cousin, Ralphie Steinberg, who had a chemist's shop in Newton Mearns. John's sisters both excelled academically but he couldn't get on with his studies and left school at 16. His parents hoped this sudden popularity would enable him to move up in the world. They were immensely proud and supportive of him.

Over the last weeks of 2007, John was honoured at a succession of awards ceremonies. The news came through that he'd been awarded the Queen's Gallantry Medal, one of the highest civilian awards, and he made the finals in the new CNN Heroes awards, a kind of Oscars for Heroes.

We flew to New York again for the star-studded televised ceremony. I didn't know who any of the stars were but everyone said they were famous. Before the show, we were told that John had won one of three Global Everyman awards. I had guessed he'd won and had given him a few ideas for his speech, which I knew he'd not bothered with. Nothing seemed to faze him, which was remarkable when I reminded myself that only weeks before, his day was lifting bags for 12 hours then back home to play his Xbox.

As he went up to collect the award, a huge screen played the famous news clip; he got a standing ovation. Speaking without notes, he concluded: "I'm no hero. The real heroes were your brave firemen and police officers on 9/11; what I did was nothing compared with them." Another thunderous ovation followed him back to his seat.

John had invited Christy, the tiny wee girl from the Bronx who'd been at the NY welcome party, as his guest. On the plane back, John told me they were engaged! It seemed a bit quick, but he said with a smile, "You know, Peter, when you meet the right one, you just know she's the one!"

John himself had the knack of getting on with everybody he met. He definitely had Kipling's 'If...'; whether chatting over a pint with Glasgow dustmen or a glass of champagne with the prime minister, he treated them all exactly the same.

In the new year, John came down for the palace ceremony and the Queen herself presented him with her Gallantry Medal. As he posed afterwards with his family for pictures, John proudly showed me his medal and told me the Queen asked if he'd been afraid. He told her it all happened too quickly to be frightened, and if he hadn't popped outside for a "quick ciggie break", she wouldn't have been giving him his medal today.

Thank God for cigarettes! 'They save peoples' lives,' I thought.

A few weeks later, I got a call from Smeato. "Peter, we've got a wee problem."

The *Daily Express* headline that morning read: 'SMEATO'S A FRAUD!' Two other guys at the airport that day, a taxi driver called Alex McIlveen and a groundsman called Stephen Clarkson, were accusing John of having done nothing while they'd tackled the terrorists. The third man, Michael Kerr, who'd broken his leg and who John had dragged away from the burning jeep, was only saying he was grateful to John for helping him.

"I've always got on well with these guys and said they did just as much as me, if not more," John said, perplexed. "I know what I did, that's all there is to it, and the police know it too."

Clearly, they were jealous. They saw John meeting the prime minister and being hailed as a hero wherever he went. They also probably thought John was making a fortune. 'How wrong they are about that!' I thought.

The story was quickly carried by other media, though there were a couple of excellent pieces in Smeato's defence. Friends of the 'forgotten three' launched a Justice for Heroes website, in an attempt to get honours for them also. They missed the whole point of the Smeato phenomenon. It wasn't about what he did or didn't do. It was about what he'd said and what the media had eagerly built him up to be: the national hero we always want.

A month after the *Express* piece, their sister paper the *Sunday Express* ran a front-page story: 'Smeato's No Fake'. A senior police source had confirmed he did just what he said he did. But it didn't stop attacks from the other two.

The 'Smeatonator' craze was still going strong a year later. There were YouTube videos featuring Smeato as all kinds of super hero, Facebook fan sites and lots of sites selling Smeato memorabilia. John had quit his baggage-handling job and taken a job at double the money at an airport car park; it was basically publicity for the guy's business – 'Your car's safe with Smeato!' – while the job seemed to consist of John sitting in a hut by himself, all day long. I thought it a big mistake but he didn't see it that way.

I'd tried to secure a publishing deal, but English publishers said he wasn't well-enough known down south and the Scottish publishers felt everyone already knew the story. In mid-2008, I found a keen Edinburgh publisher, but with a tiny advance and no editorial control I advised Smeato not to take it.

The trial of the terrorist who'd attacked Glasgow airport opened in October 2008; the jeep driver who'd set himself on fire had died a month later. The same day, John had a massive asthma attack and was rushed to hospital – the Royal Alexandra in Paisley, the same hospital where Bilal the terrorist doctor had worked.

John had had asthma since childhood but hadn't had a serious attack for years. He was now in a coma in intensive care. It was the front-page story in all the Scottish papers, but not the kind we ever wanted. Christy was flying over from New York. I rang every few hours and it sounded like he was getting better.

Early next morning, Iain rang, close to tears. "They say he's only got hours to live... we're at his bedside now."

I rushed to Heathrow and managed to get on the next flight to Glasgow. I got to the hospital about midday, fearing the worst. I eventually tracked down Iain at the end of a corridor.

"Peter! He's still with us, thank God," he said.

In desperation, the doctors had tried something never done before: they'd put him on two ventilators at once. John was still in a coma but stable, and the immediate crisis had passed.

I sat drinking coffee for a few hours as Iain, Kate and Christy would come in from his bedside. They thanked me over and over for coming to be with them. I checked into a hotel and next morning, after another update that John was stable, flew back to London.

John was in a coma for 11 days, then finally came out of it and made a slow recovery. I rang him before he left hospital. He sounded weak. "I like you on the front page, but promise me you won't pull another stunt like this!"

"Oh right, I'll try not to. Don't you worry about that," he said.

By early 2009, with marriage to Christy looming, John was getting desperate. He'd enrolled in a fish farming course (fishing and Xbox being his main activities) and got a diploma, but there weren't many fish farms in Glasgow. He was broke, living at home; his only income was the weekly *Sun* column fee, which was itself under serious threat, as someone (suspected by some at the *Sun* to be his beloved wife-to-be) kept selling Smeato stories to rival papers to earn a few bob on the side.

I had an idea. I would put Smeato on at the Edinburgh Fringe in August, in his own show, *An Audience with John Smeaton*!

I thought it must be a big hit; he was so popular in Scotland, and he'd be a natural on stage. I called William Burdett Coutts, who ran the Assembly Rooms, a major venue; he thought Smeato would be great, and offered us the Edinburgh Suite for a two-week run. I was offered the 5.50pm slot but switched it to 11.30pm, as I thought his would be a younger audience, straight out the pubs.

When I told Arnold Brown about my plans, he said, "Why don't I introduce him?" His idea was he'd do five minutes of stand-up, related to John, bring him on stage to chat about his life before and after the incident that changed it, then throw the second half open to the audience.

I was convinced John could carry the whole show himself, but Arnold was a Fringe veteran – he'd been the first comedian to win the coveted Perrier Award in 1987 – and he would make sure John turned up at the theatre every night. I couldn't be there after the opening night as I was going to Italy again with Lily for our summer holiday. It wasn't great timing but I couldn't switch the dates.

"Okay, let's do it," I told Arnold. I was sure we'd have a sell out; the room only had 140 seats. I organised 500 posters and 10,000 flyers, and a two-night try-out in a Glasgow pub the week before. The *Sun* ran a competition offering free tickets. They'd definitely be the odd couple of the Fringe; the 73-year-old Scottish-Jewish comedy veteran and the world-famous baggage-handler hero.

In the Glasgow try-outs, Smeato proved a natural storyteller and got a lot of laughs. Arnold, though, was a little rusty and I had to take him aside and explain that it wasn't the greatest idea to slag off the *Sun*, as the editor and his top reporters were in the audience and paid Smeato's wages.

I'd been concerned there weren't queues of Smeato fans outside, as it had been well publicised in the *Sun* and through my posters. The Blackfriars pub, a well-known venue, only had 90 seats, but I'd had to go out and offer free tickets to fill the room the first night.

The day before the opening night, Rebecca at the Assembly Rooms rang and told me our advance ticket sales were 37... for the whole run! We now had a small technical problem: nobody wanted to see the show. "It is rather low," she said. "Peter, don't worry... a lot of shows build an audience by word of mouth and play to sell-out audiences in the second week."

"But we haven't got the mouths for the words to come from!" I said.

But I didn't panic; I just sat down and worked out how much money I was about to lose.

Chapter 13

I bought up 120 seats for the first night and, by running up and down queues going into earlier shows, I managed to paper the entire room. Arnold's stand-up went okay, though he was clearly uncomfortable with John. But once John got into the stories from the baggage hall, the evening took off. The questions from the audience came thick and fast and Smeato handled them brilliantly; self-deprecating and funny. He was besieged for autographs in the bar afterwards and everyone wanted to buy him a drink.

I flew out to Italy, telling Arnold only to call me in an emergency. The next afternoon I got the call. "Peter, we've got a small problem; John doesn't want to go on. Last night there were five people in the audience and two of them were his parents. He feels humiliated and blames it all on you."

"Put him on the phone!"

"He won't talk to you."

"This is ridiculous!" I shouted. "He's the Smeatonator! The baggage-handler hero who tackled al-Qaeda terrorists! He's frightened to talk to a life insurance salesman!? Arnold, you grab him by the scruff of his neck, drag him to the theatre and make sure he gets on stage tonight."

"I'll do my best, but I can't force him on stage."

"Just tell him that if he thinks he's humiliated now, wait till he sees the headlines if he walks off... 'Hero Smeato Quitto!'"

He went on stage. This time there were 15 people. I tried to speak to John during the week but he still wouldn't come to the phone. Someone had told him he was in the wrong venue at the wrong time; the Pleasance and Underbelly were the only places to be, and people only wanted comedians at 11.30pm. So it was all my fault. The fact was thousands were lining up every night for other Assembly Room shows, and nobody had previously suggested the late slot was wrong for Smeato.

The show struggled through the week, but at least John had gone on stage every night; some nights they had 35 in, and on the weekend 50 or so. But I couldn't keep giving away tickets; I had to buy them first. So on the Sunday I emailed Rebecca, saying I was closing the show. I rang Arnold, and finally got Smeato on the line.

He didn't exactly protest! I told him that as I saw it, for him it had been a success, he'd had great publicity. Okay, we had two stinker reviews but both targeted Arnold, with the *Sun* in particular getting their revenge. Smeato got two rave reviews, in the *Sun* (of course) and on the STV website, which called the show "A hilarious night out... a must see."

I'd done the best I could, and could now add Edinburgh Fringe show producer to my CV. You win some, you lose some.

When I got back to London, I told John I really felt we'd run our course and he needed a local full-time manager. I wished him all the best of luck for the future.

Postscript:

In November 2009, Smeato, strongly encouraged by the *Sun*, stood as an independent candidate in the Glasgow North East by-election, contesting the seat vacated by Speaker of the House Michael Martin, following the MPs' expenses scandal.

At a disastrous opening press conference he answered every question by staring blankly into space, before finally ending the silence with, "I'll have to get back to you on that one." (Ironically, as at the start of the Smeato phenomenon, this also became a YouTube classic.) He then spent the early weeks of the campaign being served tea by his mother in bed, citing health concerns.

In a TV interview he said his policies were "to clean dog shite off the streets," and to listen to his constituents' worries and whatever they were... well, they'd be his policies.

He refused to canvas more than six hours a day, clocking off at 4pm.

He polled 258 votes, and came eighth.

At the time of writing, John Smeaton is living with Christy in Queens, NY. He is looking for a job in fish farming.

CHAPTER 14

How to show people what terrorism does (part 2)
April 2010, London

On my return from visiting Hangar 17, I had tea at Claridge's with Maqsood Ahmed, who had been introduced to me by Neil Blair and was now our first Muslim committee member and also a trustee.

Neil is a literary agent and when I first met him for breakfast a year earlier to sell him life insurance, I asked him if he represented anyone well known. "Well, there's Joe," he said.

"What's he written?" I'd asked.

"Actually 'he' is a she," he'd replied.

You only need one JK Rowling.

Maqsood was then the senior faith advisor to the Communities Department and had been awarded the OBE for his work in prisons.

We discussed how everything we wanted to do was about the future, whereas the UK families' memorial was about the past. We wanted to educate future generations about 9/11, to try and stop it happening again. "Peter, they get almost all their information on 9/11 from the internet and get overwhelmed with conspiracy theories."

He said that nothing about 9/11 was being taught in schools! I thought this unbelievable until I remembered that at school from the late 1950s to the mid-1960s I'd never been taught anything about the Second World War.

"If we could develop and fund an education programme then that would be very important," Maqsood said. "And the steel would be its symbol...

kids need something physical, you can have all the books in the world and the internet, but only when they see with their own eyes what terrorism does will they believe it happened. And then they will understand."

That was it! Maqsood had come up with what we should be doing. Nobody would ever oppose education.

The next day, I went to a reunion dinner at my old school Latymer Upper in Hammersmith. I'd only been back a couple of times since I left in 1964; the first had been when Lily applied there in 2005. It was a boy's school for 300 years and had just become co-ed. They had 600 applicants for 150 places but she had got in and loved every minute of it.

When I arrived in the Great Hall, I saw headmaster Peter Winter. "I think I've aged pretty well don't you?" I said pointing to a group of very old-looking, bent and grey-haired old boys. "I don't remember any of them; they all look as if they're in their eighties!"

"They are in their eighties," he said. "They left the school in 1947."

At dinner, I was sitting next to one of the few there from my year. I recognised Geoff Whitty immediately. You just know what some boys, when they're 12, will look like when they're 65, and Geoff was one. The only difference was his hair was now grey and he had a goatee beard.

"So Geoff, what have you been doing for the last 50 years?" I asked over the soup.

"After Cambridge, I became a teacher," he said.

"Where are you teaching?"

"Actually, I'm the director of the Institute of Education at London University."

"Geoff, let me tell you about the 9/11 Project..."

He was very interested, and next morning came to breakfast with me. By the time he'd finished his eggs and bacon he was part of the team. The world-renowned Institute of Education was going to develop our education programme. And all because I went to my old school reunion!

We now formed yet another committee: the education committee, chaired by Professor Geoff Whitty. For the least likely committee man in the world, who'd never worked with anyone, never been a team player, I was now running, in my own inimitable style, four different ones! How many people do you know who continuously send texts to people sitting across the table? Finally, they confiscated my BlackBerry at the start of every meeting!

Sarah Matthews joined us as our project manager. In her early thirties, Cambridge-educated and very logical and organised, I felt sure she was the right person to get the project up and running, develop the education programme and make sure the steel went up. How she put up with me I have no idea. Maybe because we hardly met; she worked from Sussex. This is probably the key to working with me. (Currently I have a secretary I've never met. Well, she's only been with me three years! What's the rush?)

We started looking for UK architects to work with Miya and our structural engineers SOM were to make sure the WTC steel wouldn't fall down and kill someone; they told me a sculpture had once fallen through a US gallery floor and done just that. They explained that the steel had been through temperatures and stresses after the attacks that no steel had ever been subject to, so they would conduct thorough tests to ensure it would stand up for a thousand years. My planning-barrister friend Toby Davey had joined the working committee and he introduced me to Chelsea architects Michael Aukett. I chose them because I liked the partner we'd be dealing with; a big, burly guy with a shock of white hair and stubble, a superbike fanatic called Steve Baker, who had a very deadpan sense of humour.

Although Potters Fields next to City Hall had been our original first choice, we'd been advised to forget about it. Keith Lindblom, a top planning barrister (and now High Court Judge), told me that years earlier he'd attempted to get planning permission for a human rights sculpture on the site; it had gone all the way to the secretary of state but been refused on appeal. Naturally, we started looking elsewhere.

One evening in April, I had dinner at my favourite restaurant, the Hellenic in Marylebone; I'd been going there since I was 14. Peter the owner and Pepe the waiter had been there over 40 years. I was with an old pal Charles and he'd brought along his friend Alan, who, after hearing about the project, said, "You should meet my friend Annie. She's the chief executive of Southwark; she can help you find somewhere. I'll call her and arrange for you to meet up."

When I met Annie Shepperd, it was obvious she'd come to pitch me on why Southwark was the right place – as far as she was concerned, the only place – for our steel artwork in London. Southwark, she told me, was the "new heart of London" and had a great connection with the US: "John Harvard, who founded the university, came from Southwark!"

The location she had in mind, she said, was Potters Fields.

"Really!?"

"Look, we own the land. It's leased out for 30 years to the local Potters Fields Trust, but if we support it I'm sure that won't be a problem. I'll arrange for you to meet the new leader of the borough, Peter John. I'm sure he'll want to support this."

And he did.

Potters Fields, we all agreed, was the perfect location. It was alongside the Thames and looked across to the City skyline that increasingly reminded me of a mini New York. The South Bank was the only place you could really see the City; if you were inside the Square Mile, you couldn't see it, with its warren of higgledy-piggledy streets. To the right of Potters Fields was Tower Bridge and across the bridge was the Tower of London. It had everything: the historic old city and the new dynamic London and, most important of all, up to seven million people from all over the world walked past every year on their way from the Tate Modern to the Tower. Most Londoners knew it as the site where American magician David Blaine had lived in a glass box for 44 days in 2003.

Miya flew over and luckily also loved the location. Back in New York she was going to work on the steel with Milgo Bufkin, a 90-year-old family-run workshop in Brooklyn, run by a guy called Bruce Gitlin.

I arranged to meet the PF Trust board. We had decided we needed a PR firm to handle our media strategy in the months leading up to the tenth anniversary; we still had to plan for the possibility of the UK families opposing us, even though we were the only 9/11 education project in the UK.

I rang Lord Tim Bell, who ran top PR firm Bell Pottinger. "We will do this, and we'll do it for nothing, Peter," he said. Their team was headed by Simon Jones and David Hill. David, an Alf Garnett lookalike, had taken over from Alistair Campbell as head of communications in Tony Blair's No. 10 Downing Street and over the months ahead would prove a brilliant strategist and invaluable advisor to me.

Basically this meant he just said 'No' to all the crazy ideas I came up with.

Research for us by education consultancy Edcoms with schools across the UK showed that over 90% of teachers were interested in having a 9/11 programme. But it also clearly showed the tremendous level of ignorance about 9/11 among schoolchildren. Many thought it was retribution for Afghanistan! Or to do with trade, because it was the World Trade Center!

I kept telling people that in September 2012, children going to school aged 11 would not even have been born on 9/11. That's why this programme was so important.

When I presented our plans to the seven-member PF Trust board, they listened in silence as I enthused about the project and why we'd selected Potters Fields as the perfect location.

Afterwards, I went to a nearby cafe for an espresso. Half an hour later I saw their chairman at another table. I walked over. "Everything okay?"

"Well, nobody spoke against it," he said. "I think we'll want more details: designs, sizes, timetables, that kind of thing."

"Okay, we can do that." But I felt depressed; nobody had spoken for it apart from him. I was amazed; everybody I'd met before had thought it a great idea.

Minutes later, I saw Annie outside the Southwark offices as I shot by on my scooter.

"Well then, you've got it!" she said when I finished telling her what happened.

"How can you tell? They showed absolutely no enthusiasm at all."

"Look," Annie said. "They aren't like the people you normally meet, they're never enthusiastic about anything. But if they didn't object... then you've got it!"

A week later, they wrote asking for a detailed proposal. We got every-body round a table. Our new pro-bono project managers, Mace, produced a detailed timeline with the target date of 5th September 2011 to unveil the artwork, chosen so as not to clash with the UK families' ceremony in Grosvenor Square on the actual tenth anniversary.

We had decided to hold our fundraiser launch at Claridge's on 31st November. Two days before, we received a letter from Potters Fields. Having studied our proposal, they'd rejected our application, saying the WTC artwork was out of character with the park and overwhelmed it, ending by saying they might reconsider if we drastically cut it down in scale and submitted new designs!

"The WTC steel doesn't come in small, medium or large," I said to Steve. "Overwhelmed the park? Haven't they spotted that huge carbuncle, otherwise known as City Hall, right next to it!?"

At the Claridge's launch, the room was packed. I'd invited Lee Ielpi over as the keynote speaker, and my old Comedy Store friend Clive Anderson was master of ceremonies.

Lee gave a very moving presentation that left people with tears in their eyes when he spoke about how he'd found his son at Ground Zero. It was a successful evening and we raised enough money to keep going for another six months.

We had already arranged for our planning application to be heard by Southwark Planning Committee on 23rd December and despite Potters Fields' rejection, we were advised to go ahead with it.

At the meeting, a middle-aged woman – a PF Trust member – stood up and objected, saying how depressing it would be and a permanent reminder of "that terrible day".

'Well, yes,' I thought, 'that's the whole point.'

She called the park their little lung of fresh air... with its pristine grass.

"Pity they don't mention how they rented out their 'pristine little lung of air' dozens of times last year," I said to Steve Baker, "for everything from tapas festivals to giant cranes with Hugo Boss adverts and publicity stunts."

I made my presentation and the committee members asked some questions. Before they voted, one of our team next to me kept whispering, "We've lost it... we've lost it!"

They voted four to one... in our favour.

"You can put it up for a thousand years," Steve said. "Now you just have to get the PF Trust to change their minds!"

Winning planning permission was a great victory for us and a terrific Christmas present for me. The next morning, Lily and I drove to Blakeney in Norfolk for our Christmas holiday in our rented fisherman's cottage.

In January, Stanley was given a peerage for his philanthropic activities. As a gift, I bought him a book, *The Finkler Question*; what else could it be? I'd known the author Howard Jacobson for years and so the new Booker

Prize winner wrote a funny personal message to the wonderfully named Lord Fink for me. They were two nice Jewish boys from Manchester.

On 21st February, Simon Schama flew over to address a public consultation meeting we organised for invited Southwark residents. At the last minute, Peter John advised us to cancel as it could be a hostile crowd, but it was too late to do that.

Before the meeting, Simon, Annie and I went to meet Boris at City Hall. It was the first time I had seen him since we'd met at Lords over two and a half years earlier.

He was in expansive 'Boris' form, at one point asking, "You feel sure that people strolling down this riparian walkway, when suddenly confronted by this artwork, will think it fine?" I said I definitely did, although I had to ask Simon later what riparian meant ('by the river').

As we left his office, I glanced at a TV on the wall. A newsflash said William Hague had just announced that Colonel Gaddafi had fled to Venezuela. I went over and told Boris the news!

At the meeting later, Simon delivered a passionate, brilliantly argued speech which was met with stoney-faced silence from an audience comprising about 40 members of a 5,000-strong local residents' association, none of whom lived anywhere near the proposed site, other assorted Southwark residents and about 20 of our own team. I sat sandwiched between David and Simon from Bell Pottinger, who kept telling me to keep a low profile; "Just don't say anything!" David said.

Our supporter and former Lord Mayor of London Sir Michael Oliver was in the chair as things began to unravel. A long procession of elderly opponents walked up to the podium and delivered their prepared diatribes. When they finally finished, one young man got up and said how miserable they all were, how much he supported us and how he couldn't understand how anyone could think of opposing the artwork: "If it stopped just one terror attack it would be worthwhile."

During the questions session, a woman stood up and said, "I represent the UK Families Support Group," and took the podium to state that the UK families were totally united in opposing this.

When she'd finished, Simon Schama took the mike and said, "I'm really sorry but what you said about the families being totally united is simply not true." He reached into his jacket and pulled out a letter from a UK family member I'd met, who strongly supported what we were doing and clearly understood that the steel wasn't intended for the family members but for millions of other people. Simon read a few paragraphs from it.

"That was a bit of a show-stopper!" I said to my minders.

Then another family member made an emotional off-the-cuff speech, saying how dare we plan to put up bloodstained girders which had killed her sister and had "the remains of people all over them". I wanted to stand up and say that the girders didn't kill anyone, it was the terrorists, and that the girders had in fact saved another 15,000 lives, holding the buildings up long enough for them to escape. But David and Simon held me back by the arms.

As Michael was thanking everyone for coming, a man jumped on stage and demanded a vote. When Michael explained it was merely a meeting to exchange views, the man grabbed the mike and loudly repeated his demand. Simon walked over and grabbed the mike from his hand; there was uproar and for a moment I thought there was going to be a punch-up. I could see the headlines: 'World-famous historian floors 9/11 protester'.

Two days later, 'Schama clashes with 9/11 families' was the actual local paper headline.

A couple of weeks later, at the next trustees meeting I was told, "If you persist with the artwork you're going to lose your board's support."

I couldn't believe it. I thought to myself, 'Retreat is sometimes the best form of attack.'

"Okay, I'll go with the majority," I finally said. "I know you all realise how much the steel means to me and of course we wouldn't even be here today if it wasn't for it. But if that's what you want, how can I stop you?"

The majority clearly didn't want to go ahead with the steel. I was the minority.

Two days later, Jonathan Jones at the *Guardian* wrote a piece, backing the right of everyone to remember 9/11 with this artwork; the families didn't have the monopoly on memory, he argued, just as Schama had at Southwark. I pondered asking Simon if he ever wrote under the name of 'Jones'. Centuries before, Jones wrote, when Leonardo's David was dragged through the streets of Venice under cover of darkness, such was the opposition it aroused that it had been stoned.

A day later, Channel 5 daytime show *The Wright Stuff* debated the issue and also concluded we had every right to erect the steel despite the wishes of some family members. They too felt the right of the public to remember triumphed over private grief.

The steel was going up for the tenth anniversary... even if I had to put it up in Boris's back garden.

One day, I was told we needed to raise £300k by the end of September to pay the Institute of Education and everyone else.

We sent letters asking for donations to the chairmen of the top hundred City banks. The result? Precisely zero! I couldn't understand it. They all had colleagues who were in the towers or business relationships with people who'd died in the attacks. (With the exception of Rothschilds, no major financial institution donated to the 9/11 London Project.)

One morning in April, I was sitting in Claridge's, wondering how we were going to find £300k. If we didn't, the charity would go bust.

I waved across the room to Keith Tyson, another regular guest. He is a world-famous artist who had won the Turner Prize and we often chatted after breakfast.

I had an idea. "Keith, have you got a second?"

Over my seventh espresso, I told him about our education programme. "If we held an art auction to raise funds, do you think we would get some top artists to donate a work?"

"Well, I'll give you one for a start," he said.

"Are you serious?"

"Sure. I am asked all the time to give works to charities. All artists do."

And so that was it; we'd hold the world's first 9/11 art auction!

I called Harry Hampson, who chaired the fundraising committee. Stan called his friend Lord Dalmeny, a Sotheby's deputy chairman, who said of course they'd hold it for us and wouldn't charge their usual fees. In a few days I put together a committee of top names in the art world: Tim Marlowe at White Cube, who I asked to chair it; Simon Schama; Charles Saumarez Smith, director of the Royal Academy; Jenni Lomax, who runs the Camden Arts Centre; Matthew Slotover, who runs the Frieze Art Fair; and David Anderson, who had been director of education at the V&A.

Tim said we needed 20 artists offering art by the end of June to go ahead; 24 said 'Yes' by mid-June. Antony Gormley was one of the first to reply, followed by Raqib Shaw, Ian Davenport, Anthony Caro, Tracey Emin, Julian Schnabel in New York and many others.

We were ready to roll! I felt like a Martian who had landed on the summit of the art world.

Tim told me about an arts events company, Act IV, based in Soho above Ronnie Scott's club. I shot round on my Vespa to meet one of the partners, Rebecca King Lassman; she said they'd be happy to work on the project.

In early May, we went back once more to Potters Fields Trust, this time with a drastically changed proposal; the artwork footprint was now only eight feet by four feet instead of 18 by 18. It would take up less than 0.01% of the park... the size of a Mini. More importantly, we now only asked for a temporary site for just six months over the anniversary.

At 3am the night before the meeting (I'd been advised it was better if I didn't go along this time), I rang Bruce in Brooklyn and asked him if it was possible to cut it down by five feet to 22 feet tall. He said it was. I knew I should not be doing this. It was wrong!

Sarah reported back afterwards that she felt the meeting had gone all right. A week later, the Trust wrote to ask if we would consider a one-month-only location. One month!? We had planning permission for a million years!

I said yes.

Another week later, they wrote to say our proposal had again been rejected. We had another trustees meeting. We discussed the positive *Guardian* article and TV show and someone asked, what if we were offered a temporary site for the tenth anniversary? The board now agreed that if we were offered one, we should take it.

We were back in the steel business!

I got a call out of the blue from John Kay, the chief reporter at the *Sun*. He knew all about the WTC artwork and Potters Fields' rejection, and two days later we met for breakfast. "It's disgusting they won't put the 9/11 steel up! We'll do a massive front-page campaign, name and shame this Potters Fields lot and by the time we've finished, you'll have a choice of the Buckingham Palace courtyard or in front of the Houses of Parliament!"

"But," he stressed, "it's all or nothing! We'll go huge on it... a major *Sun* campaign: 'The ship's set sail... but no home for the WTC steel'. It's up to you."

I would've said, "Let's go for it!" in a second, but I knew I had to consult my trustees.

The Institute of Education was not happy about the naming and shaming and neither were my fellow trustees, so that was that. For three days I had my finger on the 'nuclear button' on the *Sun* missile deck. Not a lot of life insurance salesmen get to experience that!

I rang John with the news. "That's a shame," he said. "But good luck anyway."

The next morning I sent Boris a text message; the first since the one I'd sent, almost two years before, which had set me off on this incredible journey.

This one said that we now would accept a temporary site, just to have it up for the anniversary, adding that the media were all over the story, asking when and where the WTC steel was going up. Would he help?

Eddie Lister, his chief of cabinet and former long-time leader of Wandsworth, called me after my text to Boris. I explained that the steel was about to sail for London and we still had nowhere to put it. I repeated that UK and US TV networks were now calling every day, wanting to know what was happening. It would be seen as a huge snub to New York.

He rang again the next day to ask if we would be prepared to think of Battersea?

"Sure, why not?" I said. "Right now I'll take pretty much anywhere."

He introduced me to Ravi Govindia, his successor as Wandsworth leader and we met him and his team at the council offices. After rejecting their first suggestion – a large roundabout by a petrol station – we finally selected a great site in Battersea Park.

It was called the American Ground.

When the park was laid out in the late 19th century, they had brought over trees and shrubs from North America and planted them by the lake. This was to be our site for one month only, over the tenth anniversary.

I thought we'd get so much publicity when it was unveiled that we'd be fielding offers from all over the UK for a permanent site. I asked Eddie Lister to keep Boris's diary free for the morning of 5th September.

Finally, in the second week of July our WTC steel – still 27 feet tall – was covered in huge Stars and Stripes and Union Jack flags and taken to the New York docks to begin its journey. Seven days later, it arrived at Liverpool docks, where it cleared customs and set off by truck to a storage facility outside Cambridge.

At the end of August, work began to prepare the Battersea Park site and the steel was due to be hoisted by crane onto a concrete plinth on 1st September.

I was on holiday in Positano with Lily while this was all going on. It wasn't the greatest timing but it was the only dates we could go away before she went back to school, and I drove her mad, continually on my BlackBerry or calling London.

Just days before it had left Brooklyn we had a small confrontation with Miya. We discovered she had changed the title of the piece to 'Peace: After 9/11' rather than the title we'd all agreed on months earlier: 'After 9/11'.

She'd instructed Milgo Bufkin to weld on a plate with her new title. As there clearly had been no peace after 9/11, Schama and I were adamant it should remain as 'After 9/11'. Finally I had to remind her our contract gave us sole naming rights. Bruce replaced the plate with a new one with the correct title.

"Why did she do it?" I asked Sarah.

"I don't know, but she means well."

"I'd hate to see what she'd do if she didn't mean well," I replied.

I got back to London the day the steel was finally hoisted into a vertical position. But I decided to wait until it was unveiled to see it. I just hoped Miya had created something as remarkable as we'd all along hoped.

Monday 5th September 2011

The press release sent out by Bell Pottinger generated a great response and the launch and unveiling was going to be covered by all the major print, online and TV outlets in the UK and internationally, with crews coming from the US, Australia, Canada and Europe; Al Jazeera English channel was also coming.

Since early August, the media on both sides of the Atlantic had been full of 9/11 stories and it was increasing every day. I'd always been sure the tenth anniversary of 9/11 would be the world's biggest story and it proved to be the case.

The BBC weather forecast for the morning of Monday 5th wasn't good; rain and winds were predicted.

As I walked to the site opposite the lake, the sun suddenly burst through the clouds. It reminded me of the sky that day on 9/11; a beautiful blue, without a cloud.

I looked towards the steel, over 30 feet tall on its plinth, covered by an enormous white cloth. It stood alone in a half acre of green lawn; on each side were bushes and shrubs – American shrubs – with a backdrop of towering trees.

Tom Von Essen, the NY fire commissioner on 9/11, had already arrived. I'd invited him and his wife Rita as our special guests. Also there was a tall, blond all-American boy scout – Jeff Cox, whose story in the *International Herald Tribune* had given me the original idea over breakfast. I'd flown him and his family over. Mayor Gary Bruhn of Windermere, Florida was also there. Miya had flown in from New York and I saw her talking to Bruce Gitlin.

I went over to greet my mother, on Lily's arm. Sadly, my father was too frail to attend.

I saw all the hundred or more people who'd played a huge role in making this day possible. I greeted everyone. All the seats were taken and the sky was still a bright blue.

Now all we needed was Boris.

"He's definitely on his way," I was told. "He left City Hall half an hour ago... he's on his bike." Of course he was! Famously he cycled everywhere.

At 10.25am, just five minutes before we were due to start, Boris turned up! He was tucking his shirt in and running a hand through his trademark thatch of blond hair as he headed into the enclosure, surrounded by our PR people and his aides.

"Good morning, mayor!" I said, putting out my hand. "Thank you for coming!"

It was finally happening! Despite all the obstacles thrown in our path, the opposition, the setbacks... we'd really done it!

I walked over to the lectern. Over two dozen press photographers and TV crews were crammed into a small area to one side.

After taking a moment to look at the audience and wave to my mother and Lily, I began. "Good morning, everyone! Well, we finally got here... it's been an incredible journey!"

The rest of that morning, in fact the whole day, passed in a blur. I held my breath as the huge cloth covering 'After 9/11' fell smoothly to the ground, then came the silence... followed by a standing ovation!

Miya had done it! But until that last second, when Boris had tugged on the rope and I saw the steel again for the first time since that day 18 months earlier when it was lying in Hangar 17, I still hadn't known if it would be a success or disaster.

The three columns now stood tall once more for the first time since 9/11 and I shivered as a plane heading into Heathrow passed above it; it seemed only inches away.

The following evening we held the art auction at Claridge's. Clive Anderson hosted it and managed to strike the perfect balance between being funny and serious.

Every one of the 24 lots sold above their reserve estimates. A set of five monumental photographs donated by Wim Wenders, the German film director and photographer who had taken them at Ground Zero in November 2001, sold for £150k.

We raised the £300k we needed.

The launch featured in over 100 media outlets around the world from Sydney to New York, including the place where my journey had begun, the *International Herald Tribune*.

The education programme, 9/11educationprogramme.co.uk, is now being taught in schools throughout the UK.

One month after the tenth anniversary, in October 2011, the WTC artwork 'After 9/11' was taken down in Battersea Park and is once again lying on the ground, this time in its Cambridge storage facility.

In the month it was on display, it received an overwhelming welcome from the vast majority of the public who saw it. There wasn't a single piece of graffiti or vandalism.

Out of 150 comments written in the notebook I put out on the plinth over a two-day period just before it was taken down, 149 praised it highly and thought it was important it was there and wanted it to remain there. They regarded it as both a way to remember those who had died and as a powerful statement of hope for the future.

One person called it ugly. Which of course it is; but for me it's always been an ugly beauty.

Postscript:

On 16th October, the *Independent on Sunday* ran a story on the failure to find a permanent site, headlined 'London in row with NY over 9/11 memorial artwork', reporting that the row "threatened to put the special relationship under strain."

In January 2012, the leader of Hammersmith and Fulham said he wanted to put it up outside the Westfield shopping centre in Shepherds Bush. In February, I got a letter offering to site it in the Bahamas.

On 28th February, we launched the 9/11 National Schools Competition to increase awareness of the education programme: an essay/video-based competition, the theme 'How did 9/11 change the world?' The prize was a four-day trip to NY in September to visit the 9/11 memorial, for the six winners, runners-up and their teachers. The judges included Simon Schama, film producer David Puttnam and John Simpson, BBC World Affairs editor; I'd bumped into him in Bernard Shapero's bookshop in Mayfair.

I am still looking for a permanent home for the WTC steel artwork.

How to curb your enthusiasm at breakfast
Across the breakfast table – 22nd August 2008, New York

I was eating breakfast at the Regency ('Home of the Power Breakfast') Hotel. At the next table was a bald, middle-aged man in glasses, reading the *New York Times*.

"Larry!" I said.

He didn't look up.

"Larry!!"

He looked up.

I smiled and leant towards Larry David, my hand outstretched.

"Larry! Peter Rosengard! We met at Claridge's in London, about 18 months ago? It was at breakfast too. You were with your wife and children, your first time in London. I came up and introduced myself. The life insurance salesman?"

He gave me the 'I don't believe this, you bugged me at breakfast in London and now you're doing it to me again at breakfast in New York, I am being stalked internationally at breakfast by a life insurance salesman' look.

I didn't take it personally.

"Yes! Hah! I remember you now." He took my hand. "So what are you doing in New York?"

"I'm with my 12-year-old daughter, Lily, taking her to camp in Canada."

"Hah! Me too! I've got a 12-year-old. I just put her on a plane to camp too!"

"Larry, was that really your first time in London?"

"I don't like to travel... You know, my wife and I split up just after that trip."

"Oh, I'm sorry."

"No... you know. It's okay."

"Well, congratulations then. I know the feeling."

"How many times you been married?"

"Twice. Do you know what I said at my last wedding, Larry? I said, 'It's a very important day. A man only gets married five or six times in his life'. Her parents didn't find it funny."

"What did your wife think?"

"She wasn't crazy about it either. So, are your parents alive, Larry?"

"My father's 97, my mother's 93. They live in Florida."

"That's lovely! My Dad's 93, Mum's 86. We're lucky to have our parents alive, aren't we?"

"We certainly are."

"What did your father do, Larry?"

"He was in the garment business."

"How old are you, Larry?"

"61."

"I am 61 too!" I said. "11th December, 1946. When were you born?"

"1947... July."

"Let me be the last person to wish you happy birthday, Larry. I mean, for this year, not ever. What I mean is, I hope you have lots of birthdays in the future, for many years to come."

"Thank you."

I suddenly remembered I knew someone in LA. "Do you know Lee Kernis?"

"Lee Kernis? Sure I know Lee. Do you know Lee?"

"Yes, I know Lee. I met him through Morty."

"You know Morty?"

"Yes, I know Morty," I said.

"Hah!" He leant towards me. "Let me tell you a story about Lee. About 18 years ago, I invited Lee to play golf at my country club in LA. It was pretty, pretty strict. Formal, with the dress code. Anyway, Lee turns up wearing shorts. But I could see right away, they were too too-short shorts. You know what I mean?"

"The shorts were too short?"

"Exactly. They were too too-short shorts."

"Hah!" I said.

"So they said, he couldn't come in, his shorts were too short. They had a measure, and they were an inch too short. So Lee had to turn round and drive 20 miles home and change, and come back in longer shorts." He sat back in his chair. "What do think of that?"

"Incredible," I said. "So do you still see Lee?"

"Aaah! You know, not a lot. We run into each other now and then." Larry looked at his watch. "Well, got to catch my flight back to LA." He stood up.

I handed him my card. "Next time you're in London, Larry, give me a call. We can have breakfast. What's the best number to reach you at if ever I am in LA?"

"Call HBO," Larry said.

I didn't take it personally.

How to lose a nine-million-dollar napkin
October 2009

In 1999, at the height of the internet boom – six months before the bubble burst – I bumped into Bob Geldof at the Picasso cafe on the King's Road.

I'd known Bob from my Curiosity Killed the Cat days.

"Peter, come along tonight to Fabric," he said. "It's a new club in Clerkenwell. There's an internet networking party on; people with a lot of money meeting people with ideas."

A young friend of mine, Dan, had just wound up his first business. The idea had been to take on Blockbuster by putting automated video rental machines, like holes in the walls, all over the place, but people were beginning to be able to view films online and it hadn't worked out.

I and a few friends had all put in some money, and we had lost most of it. It was the first time I'd ever invested in anything, but something told me that Dan and his younger brother Geoff were going to make a fortune, whatever they did next, and I was determined to be in on it. "We should keep backing them," I said to the others.

Dan was a former investment banker and the extrovert front man; Geoff was the organisational and strategic brains. A week earlier they had told me about their new idea for a pop-up email advertising business. Over lunch in Notting Hill, they'd said they needed $4m to get it up and running. They asked me if I could help to raise it.

I told them I'd never done anything like this before, but if I did manage to get them the money, I wanted either a 5% fee or a 5% shareholding in the business. They happily agreed and we'd all signed the 'agreement' on a paper napkin there and then.

So I went along that night to Fabric, looking for a man with $4m to invest.

It was packed; there must have been more than 1,000 people there! The people with money were mostly in their forties and fifties and had red lapel badges. They were heavily outnumbered, by 20-1, by the people with yellow badges, who all appeared about 18. They were the ones with the ideas for making the odd billion or two.

It was like a new gold rush. The energy and enthusiasm in that room could have powered whole cities. As soon as I walked in I saw Geldof chatting to a man in the lobby; he waved me over. "Hi Peter, this is Simon." Bob then dived into the melee and left us to chat.

Simon, who was in his early thirties, told me he'd started an online book store 18 months before... and Amazon had just paid £20m for it! He was now running a $100m fund for Chase Manhattan.

I told him about Geoff and Dan and their new idea. "That sounds very interesting," he said.

"Come for breakfast at Claridge's tomorrow at 7.30am and I'll introduce you to them."

"Great! I'll be there."

He was the first person I met that night... in fact, he was the only person I met.

The next morning, Geoff and Dan came along for breakfast to meet

Simon. He liked them and their idea and, over bacon and eggs, agreed to invest $4m.

A couple of weeks later I called Dan. "I'll have my lawyer prepare a formal agreement, for my 5%."

"5% of what?" he asked.

"My 5% of the company."

"Are you crazy!? We're not giving you 5% for meeting someone; it's like you just made a phone call!"

"But we agreed it! We all signed the napkin! Remember!?"

"Look, Peter, you just met a guy at a party!"

"Dan, it took me my 30 years' experience to know Bob Geldof... to get invited to that party... to be introduced to Simon... to excite him about your idea... and to get him to meet you at Claridge's! It doesn't matter whether I met him once or had a thousand meetings! So are you going to keep to our agreement or not!?"

"Listen, don't worry, we'll give you something... but it's not going to be 5%."

I couldn't believe it! And this time, remembering the Comedy Store, I'd made sure I had it in writing. So what if it was on a napkin!? I'd once read you could legally write a cheque on an egg.

But what was I going to do now? Sue him? And lose a friend?

Months later, I finally received a share certificate saying I owned some shares in the company. It was less than 1%.

Later, as new investors came in, my share was diluted to a fraction of 1%.

The original company never made any money, only losses, and after about five years it reinvented itself as an internet security company.

In October 2009, almost exactly ten years after Geldof invited me to Fabric, I got a call from Dan. "I have some very good news for you, Peter."

"Like what?" I asked.

"We've just sold the company for $200m to a huge company in the US," he said. "Your shares are worth a lot of money."

I put the phone down and immediately started to look for the napkin.

A quick bit of mental arithmetic told me that if I could find the 'Napkin Agreement of 1999', I could be due as much as $9m!

I'm not a greedy guy, but if a napkin agreement's not a napkin agreement, what hope can we have for justice in this world?

Now, I never, ever throw anything away. It's a character flaw of mine... or maybe just laziness? But after 24 hours spent in non-stop searching of my flat, from top to bottom, I still couldn't find where I'd put the golden napkin.

I was absolutely sure I'd kept it. I remembered seeing it a couple of years before, when I was doing my annual 'going through my papers' routine.

Filing has never been my strong point; my 'system' is to pile everything into huge mountains of paper and leave it there. It's the same with my books. My flat is full of thousands of books, all kept the same way as my papers... on the floor. If I die suddenly in my sleep, it will be in an avalanche of books crashing down on me in bed. At least it would be both an adventurous and a literary death.

I was so determined to find it that the next morning, I recruited a private army of Filipino and Sri Lankan napkin hunters – Mabel my cleaner, her friend Roden, my father's carers Sharmani and Shanthi and their two nieces – to search for the $9m napkin.

"What does it look like?" Mabel asked.

"It looks like a white paper napkin," I said. "With some writing on it. The first one to find it gets a major cash prize. Get napkin hunting!"

I'd rung my lawyers, who said if I could find it, I might still have a good chance of challenging the shareholding I'd been given. But without it, I was sunk.

They turned the flat upside down, but we never found the napkin. After a week of searching, I reluctantly admitted defeat and disbanded my troops.

When, three months later, my bank emailed to inform me that a very large credit had arrived in my account, I didn't tell them to send it back.

I had to admit that it wasn't a bad payday for introducing someone I had met for two minutes in a club to a couple of friends over breakfast ten years before.

It had more than paid for the breakfast.

Chapter 14

How to meet a president at breakfast
Across the breakfast table – 16th November 2008, Claridge's

I was about to behead my fifth boiled egg of the morning, after saying goodbye to my second guest, when the entire Israeli secret service walked into the breakfast room.

A phalanx of around 24 extremely tough-looking, unsmiling young men with earpieces, mirrored sunglasses and shaved heads, moving as if on wheels... It was almost like watching a ballet, only these guys were definitely not the types to wear tutus.

Nobody spoke. In the middle of them, I could just see a dapper, slim, elderly man in a dark blue suit, with a high-domed, tanned forehead topped by swept-back white hair.

They were heading towards my table! Christophe, the waiter, was still kneeling beside me, trying to explain how they'd managed to get a four-minute boiled egg – "yellow runny, white hard", as I'd had it for over 25 years – as solid as a rock... and this elderly man was looking straight at me! "Don't make any sudden moves," I said to Christophe.

"Good morning, Mr President," I said, when he was two feet from me. He remained expressionless as he was propelled past my table. I don't think he heard me.

The convoy executed a right turn and headed off towards the table in the opposite corner, usually occupied by my friend, John Bartley.

The president of Israel sat down with his back to the wall, 15 feet across from me. A stoney-faced bodyguard stood next to him. Several attractive young women assistants joined the president's table. 'It's good to be the president,' I thought.

"Mr Rosengard, this time I promise you, your egg will be perfect," Christophe said from his kneeling position. He handed me a fresh knife, his head barely six inches from the egg cup. I raised the knife and brought it down very slowly... this was not a moment for sudden knife movements. It was a clean cut. The top fell onto the plate. A perfect egg.

"Congratulations, Christophe, fifth time lucky. Maybe tomorrow we will attempt the Everest of the breakfast table... the fried egg. Now, you'd better get up, or the president of Israel will assume I am a member of the Royal family."

All the other tables were now occupied by his people. I took out my sketch book and started to draw him surreptitiously. Should I go and introduce myself? I could tell him I was a volunteer in the Six-Day War.

A large gentleman in a dark grey suit suddenly appeared at my side. "Where are you from, sir?"

"Maida Vale," I said. "But I was born in Hammersmith, and then moved to..." He flashed an identity card: 'Special Branch'.

"No sir... I mean, who are you with?"

"I see. No, I'm not a journalist, if that's what you mean. I am a life insurance salesman. I have breakfasted here almost every day for 26 years. Have you eaten? Would you care to join me for scrambled eggs?"

"No, thank you, sir. Carry on." He sat down at the next table.

I decided I would like to meet the president. But how? It didn't seem a good idea to just walk up to his table; I'd probably be wrestled to the ground before I got within hand-shaking range.

I had an idea. I would give him a present. A book!

I had always admired Shimon Peres. He was a great statesman; a moderate in a world of extremists, the great survivor. In his eighties now, he'd been at the centre of Israeli politics since the founding of the state in 1948. He had held every high office, twice being prime minister, and had even won the Nobel Peace Prize. Unfortunately, he'd had to share it with that other well-known 'peace advocate', Yasser Arafat.

I got up from my table and shot off on my scooter to Daunts bookshop in Marylebone High Street. I stopped right outside and went in. What should I buy him? I had no idea.

Then it came to me... the new biography of Isaac Rosenberg. Okay, maybe he would never have heard of him, but he was definitely Jewish, and a soldier – even if he had been hopelessly unsuited to be one – and also a poet. It was the perfect gift.

More than that, I'd recently bought an option to make a film based on this very book. So it all fitted together very well.

At the porters' desk back at Claridge's, Tom, the head porter who I'd known since he started as a page boy over 25 years ago, greeted me.

I handed him the book. I had written an inscription inside the cover. Well, more of an autobiography actually; it was at least 200 words long.

"Can you run this up to President Peres' suite for me, Tom?"

Chapter 14

I went and read the *Times* in one of the big leather armchairs by the fire in the lobby. Tom reappeared five minutes later, the book still in his hand.

"They won't accept it. The security people wouldn't even touch it."

"You're joking!" I said. "What do they think it is, a bomb? It's a book on Isaac Rosenberg, the Great War poet. It's a present. I am big fan of his."

Tom looked around. "Well, they won't touch it sir, I'm sorry... Polonium, you know."

"Polonium!? Did you tell them who it was from? Peter Rosengard, the legendary breakfaster. I'm not an assassin working for the Kremlin! I'm a life insurance salesman."

"I did my best, sir."

I now decided there was no way the president wasn't going to get my present.

I saw a young, clean-cut guy in the lobby, who had been sitting at the next table to the president. "Hi, I'm Peter Rosengard," I said, extending my hand. "Welcome to London. What do you do with the presidential party?"

"I am an adviser to the president," he said in an Israeli-American accent. He handed me his card: 'Jonathan Avneri'.

"You, Jonathan, are just the man I want to see. I have bought the president a present." I showed him the book.

He looked at it. "I don't believe it! Isaac Rosenberg! That's amazing!"

"You've heard of him?"

"The president is going to address the Houses of Lords and Commons this afternoon, and he will be mentioning Rosenberg in his speech," Jonathan said.

"You're kidding me," I said. "How do you know?"

"I wrote the speech."

"Here, give him the book." I held it out to him.

He backed away. "I can't take it. Give it to security."

"They won't take it either, I've already tried." I had an idea. "Can I come to the speech?"

He turned to a guy who'd just walked up. "Do we have any tickets left?" he asked him.

"No way, it's impossible. I am sorry," the guy replied.

I went outside and dialled a number on my phone. 'Let's not mess around anymore!' I thought.

"Number Ten Downing Street," the operator answered.

"Good morning, the prime minister's office, please. It's Peter Rosengard."

A woman answered the phone.

"Good morning," I said. "I have met the prime minister recently on a couple of occasions, when I brought Glasgow Airport terror attack hero John Smeaton to meet him, and when John and I were his guests at the party conference. I wonder if you can help me..."

An hour later, the phone rang. It was No. 10. If I went over to Black Rod's office, an invitation was waiting for me.

I jumped on the scooter and headed over to the House of Lords.

I got fast-tracked past a very long queue of tourists through security by a helpful policeman and I got my invitation. A uniformed attendant escorted me to the Great Hall I'd seen so often on television. It led into the Royal Robing Room, where the president was giving his speech.

I had a pleasant chat with a Hindu gentleman, who turned out to be Lord someone; he told me what a great friend of Israel he was. "You know, Hindus and Jews have a lot in common."

The room was filled with rows of gilt chairs; I chose a chair on the aisle towards the back and sat down. It filled up quickly. I think I was possibly the only person there who wasn't a minister, lord or archbishop. I was pretty sure I was the only life insurance salesman.

I turned around to see Malcolm Rifkind sitting right behind me. Now that was a coincidence, because people always tell me we look and sound very alike. He was the Conservative foreign secretary and is also a Jewish Scot, with a deep, upper-class Scottish brogue. We had a brief chat and I told him how people said how alike we were. Perhaps we were related, as my grandmother was a Rifkin from Glasgow, without the 'd'? No, he thought not. Ken Clarke was now seated two down from me.

The president came in with his security team and walked to the platform. I saw the security guys scanning the audience. 'Unlikely to find a hit man in this lot,' I thought.

I was sure they'd recognised me, though; "It's the man who sat near the president at breakfast."

The speech went very well. He only mentioned three people: Ben Gurion, Churchill... and Isaac Rosenberg!

Chapter 14

Incredible! I felt a glow of pride. It was an historic occasion, the first time an Israeli president had the honour of addressing the House.

On the way out I bumped into Basil Feldman. After leaving dental school, I had worked for him and his partner, Richard Beecham, in 1966. They were young tycoons in the plastics business, and had just bought Marx, the world's largest toy manufacturer. I'd got the job by writing them a letter out of the blue; I had kept reading about them in the business sections of the papers, and I had just seen *The Graduate*, with the famous scene by the pool where Dustin Hoffman asks a successful businessman for advice, and the guy says just one word: "plastics".

"What are you doing here?" he asked.

"I came to listen to President Peres. What are you doing here, Basil?"

"I'm a lord," he said.

"You're a lord! Really Basil?"

"Yes, really," he said. Basil told me he was the former Conservative Party chairman of the constituency parties.

Next morning at Claridge's, I leant across to Jonathan, the adviser to the president, at the next table. "Congratulations! Great speech."

"You were there!?"

"The prime minister got me an invitation."

"Really? Is that so?" He now looked at me with new interest.

A few minutes later he came over to my table. "Okay, Peter, I have it arranged. You can meet the president and give him the book. The lady sitting on his right will give you a signal, as they get up after breakfast, to come over."

"Thank you, Jonathan, that will be great." I put a forkful of bacon into my mouth.

They don't call me Peter 'the impossible you can do at once, miracles take a little longer' Rosengard for nothing!

Half an hour later, I got the nod. I went over, holding Rosenberg in my hand.

He didn't seem to be expecting me. I put out my hand and smiled. Always a good move, I find; people will automatically put out their hand and smile back. They never say, "No, I am not going to shake your hand."

"Good morning, Mr President," I said. "Congratulations! A wonderful speech yesterday."

"Thank you. You were there?" he said, in a very deep baritone voice that almost equalled Kissinger's. I would love to see them talking together, like two men talking under water.

"Of course. I wouldn't have missed it for anything. Historic occasion."

"Thank you," he said again.

"Sir, I have a small gift for you, to mark your visit to London." I handed him the book. He looked at the title.

"He is translated into Hebrew, you know. I bought this before your speech," I said.

"That is incredible," he said.

"I know," I said. "Maybe you should make me minister of defence. I could see the enemy coming. What are the chances of me buying you a book about a man you were going to mention in your speech?"

He nodded. "I will say to you now his poem, 'Through These Pale Cold Days'. He died three days later, you know, in the trenches of Ypres."

"But Mr President," I interrupted him. "Look here." I took the book from him and opened it. I pointed to some of the lines I had inscribed the previous morning; the first four lines of 'Through These Pale Cold Days'.

He looked at me in astonishment. He then read them to me, out loud.

I suddenly realised I had forgotten to bring my camera, but I had my mobile phone. "Excuse me," I said to the woman who'd given me the wink. "Can you possibly take my photo with the president?"

She took the phone and took a quick picture of us, shaking hands.

I looked at it later; it showed two very blurred figures, one of whom might just have been the president. Christophe was standing behind him.

How to live to be (almost) 100
January 2012, London

My father, Dr Jack Rose (known by Gamblers Anonymous groups all over the world as 'Jack R'), died on 13th October 2012. He was just three months short of his 98th birthday. On 5th January 2012, Lily and I had gone over to my parents' flat to celebrate his 97th with them.

He was sitting in his chair as usual, his eyes closed and, as always, a smile on his face. Mum was sitting on the sofa next to his chair, holding his hand.

Chapter 14

If you have to get Alzheimer's, my advice is this: try to make sure you get the kind my father had, the 'happy, peaceful' version. He had it for about six years and was a very happy man. He still knew who everyone was and could remember people and events from many years ago, like Miss Totten, his primary school teacher in the Gorbals, who told the eight-year-old boy that he could become a doctor and a good one, because he cared so much about people.

As for all the stuff that happened a minute ago, nothing... but who needs to remember the little things? What you just ate, who was on the phone, what TV show you've just seen. The big things – his childhood, the family, his children and grandchildren, and most important of all, Mum – were all still there. Every day, he told Mum he loved her and that made her the happiest woman in the world.

Actually, recently I became convinced he didn't have Alzheimer's at all, but had been misdiagnosed and was just a very old man who'd had a long and remarkable life.

He was extremely lucky to have had the extraordinary love, loyalty and devotion of my mother, Sally. They had been on one long honeymoon ever since that day she had dragged him along to Gamblers Anonymous and he stopped gambling, on 13th August 1964.

My father was the love of my mother's life and had been since the night they met in the Cafe Royal Long Bar in May 1942, on a blind date when he was home on leave from the army.

She never stopped loving him. Through all the 17 years of gambling, alcoholism, two heart attacks, the clinical depression he had for five years in his seventies... and for the final years during this last illness, she had loved and looked after him 24 hours a day.

She is simply the most amazing and strongest woman I have ever known. And they have had one of the world's great love affairs, lasting 70 years.

"Grandpa, wake up! Happy birthday!" Lily said.

He opened his eyes and beamed; "Lily!" She gave him a big hug.

"Happy birthday, Dad!" I said.

I opened the champagne and Mum handed him his favourite drink, a St Clements – orange and bitter lemon. It had been 30 years since he'd had a drop of alcohol.

We raised our glasses and sang 'Happy birthday'.

Dad then sang for us, as always, 'I belong to Glasgow'!

I had recently started telling everybody I met – clients, waiters, people at bus stops – that my father was 97 and my mother would be 90 in June.

I loved telling people about how old my parents were, not because I thought they would be interested, but because it inspired me. It reminds me that at 66, clearly I'm just starting off! That with their genes, and a bit of luck, I am only halfway through this incredible journey, this adventure we call life.

It was only when I started telling people this that I discovered how lucky I am, as hardly anyone I ever meet in their fifties upwards have both their parents. How incredibly fortunate I have been to have had them both for so long.

Often, I'd tell people how, when I rung my father, he'd asked me to call him back, as he was on the other line.

"Who are you talking to, Dad?" I asked.

"My older brother," he said. Louis was 98 when he died.

Dad died peacefully at home. My mother and I were at his bedside. My father, at the time of his death, hadn't gambled for over 48 years (the longest of anyone in the GA programme, anywhere in the world). He was a remarkable man who against all the odds had turned his life around, and in beating his own addiction went on to rebuild not only his own and my mother's and our family's lives, but then helped thousands of others and their families to find happiness. He had never wanted acclaim or recognition, he had the gift of true humility; but as he'd said at so many GA meetings over the years, by sprinkling the perfume of happiness over others, some of it had inevitably landed on him.

The story of 'When Jack Met Sally' had finally come to a close. I am pretty sure he's already started a Gamblers Anonymous group in heaven, and I can see him in the 'chair', red carnation in his lapel, mesmerising them all with his stories, with that twinkle still in his eye and a smile on his lips. The *Times* of 26th October 2012 carried Dad's half-page obituary.

Over one hundred and fifty people packed the chapel at the funeral, but it could just as easily have been fifteen hundred as each one of them represented at least ten others. "Most very old people who die have only a handful of mourners," the rabbi told me afterwards. "He must have been a very special man." He was. Many people, some of whom had never met him, wrote to me calling him a 'great man'.

He would never have regarded himself as one.

How to think about life

On 21st March 2013 it will be 42 years since I last had a bet and – like my father before me – I've never been so lucky as the day I stopped gambling. One thing is certain; if I hadn't stopped, you wouldn't be reading these words.

When I finally hit rock bottom with my gambling and went back to the Gamblers Anonymous meetings, I discovered their 'Just for Today' programme: that you can do something for 12 hours at a time that would appal you if you felt you had to keep it up for the rest of your life. And that's how I stopped my compulsion to gamble... one day at a time. It was like being born again; only this time, I put all the energy and enthusiasm I'd put into my gambling into my new life.

Every morning since I stopped gambling, I've asked myself the same question; "Do I want to be happy or unhappy today?" Every day I've chosen to be happy. And I have been happy! I also discovered many years ago that inside every job is a game, and that once you discover what that game is – what the rules are and how to win at it – then you never have to go to 'work' again.

In May 2013 when this book comes out, it will also be exactly 44 years since I set off on my adventures of a life insurance salesman – telling my story to people, talking to strangers, one day at a time. It's been a roller-coaster ride... a lot of excitement, a lot of laughter and fun and most importantly, a life of freedom.

People ask me all the time, "When are you going to retire?" and I always reply the same way; "Why would I want to stop doing something I love doing!?" I've booked my breakfast table at Claridge's until 12th December 2046. I'll be 100 years and one day old, and I might then think of slowing down... a little.

A lot of my early life was spent never knowing when I'd had enough: chasing losing bets, chasing the wrong girls... I could never stop until it hurt too much to continue. Now I think it's time to stop – as I'm sure that you too have had enough!

A couple of years ago Mark Strong, one of the UK's most successful film actors, was on the back of my scooter as we zoomed through the evening rush-hour West End traffic. "Peter, don't you ever have a normal day like other people?" he shouted.

"Certainly not!" I said. "Mark, if you wanted a life of glamour, excitement and adventure, you should have become a life insurance salesman!"

I love life! I love selling! I love selling life! And every day I say, "Thank God I'm not a dentist!"

INDEX

Index

Index

Index

Lightning Source UK Ltd.
Milton Keynes UK
UKOW05f0619050417
298388UK00006B/382/P